The Making of a Surgeon in the 21st Century

THE
MAKING
OF A
SURGEON
IN THE
21ST CENTURY

CRAIG A. MILLER, M.D.

Blue Dolphin Publishing

Published by Blue Dolphin Publishing, Inc.
P.O. Box 8, Nevada City, CA 95959
Orders: 1-800-643-0765
Web: www.bluedolphinpublishing.com

ISBN: 1-57733-115-X

First printing, January 2004

Library of Congress Cataloging-in-Publication Data

Miller, Craig A., 1965-
    The making of a surgeon in the 21st century / Craig A. Miller.
        p. ; cm.
    ISBN 157733115X (hdc. : alk. paper)
    1. Miller, Craig A., 1965- 2. Surgeons—Ohio—Biography. 3. Residents
(Medicine)—Ohio—Biography. 4. Ohio State University. College of
Medicine.
    [DNLM: 1. Surgery—education—Popular Works. 2. Internship and
Residency—Popular Works. WO 18 M647m 2003] I. Title.

RD27.35.M55A3 2003
617'.092—dc21

                                              2002154708

Printed in the United States of America

10   9   8   7   6   5   4   3   2   1

Contents

Preface

WHAT DOES IT TAKE TO MAKE A SURGEON?

In a strict (but simple) academic sense it takes a college degree, followed by a medical school education, followed by a residency. And it takes excellence at each of these levels.

In a broader sense, though, it takes an individual who is willing to subordinate his personal life—and sacrifice much of his youth—to acquiring the skills and knowledge which a surgeon must possess. This sacrifice takes its toll—on families, on mental health, on life-style. A surgical trainee may not get out on his own until well in his thirties—living, in the meantime, a meager existence at best. It's a hell of an extended adolescence.

Most people believe that a person who graduates from medical school is a doctor. Of course this is technically true, but that person is not yet a *physician*. And he (or she, of course) is a long, long way from being a surgeon. He has to go through residency first.

It has been said that if medical training is like military service, then surgical residency is Marine Corps boot camp. Post-graduate training in surgery is longer than that of any other medical specialty, five years at least and frequently longer. Tortuous on-call schedules often demand exceedingly long work hours almost unimaginable in any other profession, 100-hour work weeks being the *norm* for a surgery resident. Compounding the problem are the very high stress level intrinsic to the job, the burdens shouldered by the resident's family in his frequent absence, and the enormous educational debt under which the large majority of trainees labor.

One highly regarded university hospital boasts (off the record, of course) that none of its residents' marriages have survived the ordeal of its surgical training program.

Despite the startlingly unattractive qualities surrounding surgical residency, every year hundreds of fresh medical school graduates compete for the few available positions. They are consistently the very best of their classes.

This begs an obvious question: why would otherwise intelligent, highly motivated individuals actively seek such a miserable existence?

Part of the answer lies in historical perceptions. Surgeons have, of course, been glorified in the mass media as the swaggering, brilliant, fiercely independent cowboys of the medical profession (Hawkeye Pierce from *M*A*S*H* was a surgeon, as is Dr. Benton from *ER*). Traditionally, at least, their compensation has also been greater (no small incentive after a decade of expensive higher education). But beyond this, I think, the medical school graduates who opt for a surgical career do so mainly from a personal quality best defined as decisiveness. They want to make the difference, in no uncertain terms. In surgery, when the patient enters the operating room, he is suffering from disease. Thanks to the surgeon, he may be wheeled out cured. It doesn't happen every time, of course, but the possibility is there (in other disciplines of medicine "cure" is, unfortunately, an unusual event). Who wouldn't want to be such a healer, making a palpable, tangible difference? "I saw the problem and I fixed it...."

This quality of decisiveness must be deeply ingrained in the resident, along with tenacity and force of will, or else failure in the field of surgery is inevitable. Lacking these, that resident simply won't survive the training, not to mention the practice.

Before delving much further, some definitions are in order.

Surgery, like most of the disciplines of medicine, is divided into subspecialities. Speaking broadly (and thus somewhat inaccurately) these subspecialities are defined in reference to the system or anatomic region which constitutes the focus of their practice. Thoracic Surgery focuses on the heart, the lungs, the great blood vessels of the chest and the esophagus. Plastic Surgery is devoted to the cosmetic and anatomic correction of deformation, whether congenital or secondary to disease. Neurological Surgery is that of the brain, spinal cord and peripheral nerves. Orthopedists treat surgical disease of the bones, joints, ligaments and their associated tissues. Urology deals with derangements of the kidneys, bladder and male genitalia. Gynecology addresses problems associated with the reproductive system of women. The domain of General Surgery (which, in an earlier era, encompassed all of these divisions) has been whittled down over the years as these subspecialities and others have branched off. By tradition, but with some practical sense, too, the general surgeon-in-training is exposed for extended periods to all of these disciplines and expected to develop expertise in them.

My training—the topic of this book—was in General Surgery.

Surgical residency programs in the U.S. are broadly divided into two substantially different categories: "academic" and "community-based." Academic programs exist in university teaching hospitals, are overseen by faculty who are professors of surgery, and are generally perceived (at least by graduating medical students interested in surgery) as being more rigorous and demanding than their community-based counterparts. Community programs are found in metropolitan and larger suburban hospitals without official university affiliation. These are administered by surgeons with an interest in surgical education but no specific university position. As fiscal concerns have grown more prevalent around the turn of the century, community surgical training programs have withered. Many have disappeared. The training of surgeons turns out to be expensive, in dollars as well as other forms of currency less tangible.

Operative experience in the two types of residencies is probably about the same. Non-operative patient care is comparable, too. Actual resident work load and on-call schedules are typically more taxing in university hospitals—a clear disadvantage, it would seem. However, these institutions also tend to treat more of the unusual and complex problems, which renders the novice surgeon better prepared to face difficult situations after he graduates. Probably the main edge a university trainee has is that if his program has a favorable national reputation, he can land an attending job virtually anywhere one happens to be available (or a "fellowship"—even more subspecialized training). No one outside his own state may have even heard of the community hospital where the other resident trained.

This, then, is a highly personalized description of one individual's experiences during a five-year residency in general surgery at a major university hospital in the 1990s. In many ways these experiences are, no doubt, unique to the time and place in which they occurred. In other ways, they are probably universal. In 1968 Dr. William A. Nolen wrote a compelling memoir of surgical residency in the '50s entitled *The Making of a Surgeon*. At the outset he attempted to summarize his thoughts concerning this pivotal time of his life, from the confounding perspective of a decade later. He observed that residency was both the most difficult and the most exhilarating time of his life. He was challenged as never before or after, dealing with thrilling triumph and devastating tragedy, and he ultimately survived to tell the tale.

This book attempts to tread this same path in a different era, and to describe the experiences which comprise the making of a surgeon in our own time. It may come as a surprise to learn that the advent of spectacular new technology has not altered the process of learning to become a surgeon by much, at least in a human sense. The personal challenges and rewards, the drama of triumph and tragedy, the agony of indecision and the thrill of success all remain the same. Residency remains the most profoundly life-altering sequence of events in a surgeon's life.

As Dr. Nolen wrote: "The man that suffers through it will ever forget it. I never have...."

1

The Internship Year—
Batten the Hatches

MR. COLSON WAS IN TROUBLE.

Bathed in sweat, he was lurching about on his hospital bed, wracked with waves of nausea and intermittently vomiting up pints of partially-digested blood from what seemed to be an inexhaustible supply. The bloody vomit covered Mr. Colson, his bedclothes and most of the room—including his panicked nurse, whose page had summoned me to the scene. I stood transfixed, alternately trying to gather my wits and dodge the brick-red plumes which spewed from Mr. Colson. What should I do?

It was the evening of July 1, 1994, and my first day of surgical residency was drawing to a close. My first night on call was just beginning....

In the United States—and most industrialized nations—medical school graduates must complete a post-graduate training program in the specialty of their choice before they may practice medicine independently. This training program is called "residency," a term dating from the nineteenth century when the trainee would literally live within the hospital in which he was treating patients and being educated. In contrast to medical school, where the large majority of learning comes from lectures, books and (more recently) electronic media, in residency the journeyman physician learns his profession from actually performing the duties of a doctor on a day-to-day basis. Residency is on-the-job training, in a sense.

1

The principle concept is one of gradually increasing responsibility. That is, the first-year resident (also known as the "intern") is given essentially no meaningful responsibility while he learns the basics of patient care, while the fifth-year resident (the "Chief Resident") is supposed to be able to function in an entirely independent fashion, as if he were a practicing surgeon. In between, the responsibilities of residents in their intermediate years increase in proportion to their level of experience. Overseeing the process of teaching the residents are the Attending Surgeons, those who have completed their training and are already practicing surgery independently.

Following medical school, I had spent three years in research at the University of California in San Francisco. This was a position I had been recommended for by a Dr. Zollinger, who was a near-legendary surgeon at Ohio State. After these three years I had chosen to return to Columbus for surgical training.

It would be an understatement to say that the residency program at the Ohio State University Medical Center had a reputation for being demanding. In actuality it was perceived as being unremittingly harsh, with standards of training derived from the norms of a draconian surgical era that was decades in the past. I had been a medical student there a few years before. At that time I had experienced a two-month clinical clerkship in surgery at the main hospital, which was required of all med students. It had been a truly miserable experience. The sheer number of hours spent at the hospital was almost unimaginable. The residents seemed entirely devoid of spirit, wandering the wards in a sleep-deprived daze and looking for all the world like beaten animals. (One resident noted that a large blue beacon on the edifice of the main hospital—which was intended to guide LifeFlight helicopters to the appropriate building—had the shape of the letter H. While it seemed obvious that this stood for "hospital," he had become convinced that it really stood for "Hell"). The attending surgeons were surly and pompous. Even the scrub nurses were, almost without exception, insufferable bitches. In short, a less attractive setting in which to train could scarcely be imagined.

Yet this was the place I had chosen to do my residency. This was the place where I would spend five long years—after college, after medical school—learning to become a surgeon.

General surgical residency is meant to provide in-depth experience in most of the surgical specialties and, accordingly, the resident is required to spend some time learning the specific patient care provided by those specialties. As an intern, in the course of the coming year I would spend a total of nine weeks learning cardiothoracic surgery, six weeks learning transplant, three weeks learning urology, etc. These periods of time on specialty services were called "rotations." Most of these were spent at the main University Hospital, but some were at other, outlying institutions.

My first day of residency actually began the night before. I had opted to visit the wards a little early to learn about the patients on my service and acquaint myself with the nuts and bolts of the hospital. Knowing from the rotation schedule that my first tour of duty would be on a service called Surgery 2, I read through all the patient charts bearing that notation. Manila computer cards were ubiquitous on the inpatient units and I grabbed a handful, jotting down obscenely long and detailed notes to myself. In a way I still had the mentality of the interviewee, trying to outdo everyone, but I genuinely wanted to be the best resident I could possibly be—and I knew that meant being familiar with all aspects of the patient's care.

After an anxious, sleepless night I showed up on 10 East Doan, the floor where the majority of the Surgery 2 (or "Surg 2," for short) patients were residing. The intern who had been on call the night before (and who was this morning a freshly minted second-year resident) was nowhere to be found, although his beeper was waiting for me at the nursing station. A tiny yellow post-it note was attached which read "Quiet night. No trouble with Surg 2 patients."

I swiftly made some "pre-rounds," checking the patient's vital signs and so forth. Poking my head gingerly into the rooms, I silently cross-referenced the sleeping faces with the diagnoses I had compiled on my obsessive-compulsive manila cards. Surg 2 was a straightforward general surgery service, with a particular emphasis on colorectal problems.

Around 6:30 AM the rest of the team arrived.

The chief resident, Ramya Singh, was a diminutive Indian woman with a surprising, wry Kentucky cackle for a voice. She was accompanied by a third-year resident, Paul Striker. He was a red-haired, ruddy-faced Chicagoan in the plastic surgery residency who immediately expressed nothing but disdain and disinterest in anything related to general surgery. Bringing up the rear were two medical students who had begun their training in clinical medicine the day before. After the introductions were complete, we started to round. At the first patient's door I produced the appropriate card and began to spew forth information:

"This is Mrs. Jackson. She is post-op day three from a right hemicolectomy for adenocarcinoma. Her vital signs are stable, she's been afebrile overnight, and her I's and O's are 2.5 liters over 2.3. She's currently on a clear liquid diet...."

I droned on for several minutes. The chief listened patiently while I delivered my soliloquy, then glanced at Striker.

"He's one of *them*," she said with a bemused grimace, slipping by me into Jackson's room.

Dr. Singh was remarkably low-key, not nearly as frenetic and nerveworn as the Ohio State residents I had remembered from my med school days. By "one of *them*," I understood her to mean that I was being lumped into the category of quasi-military, anal-retentive surgical hard asses that peppered the resident—and attending—ranks. Of course that wasn't my nature at all, but I imagined that there were worse first impressions to give, so I kept it up through the rest of rounds. Singh would listen to my spiel, then examine and question the patient. After a brief pause she would give me the orders pertaining to the care of the patient that day and we would move on.

We came to Frank Colson's room. Mr. Colson had undergone a stomach stapling and bypass procedure, called a *Roux–en-Y Gastric Bypass*, in an effort to reverse his morbid obesity. The severely overweight suffer from numerous significant medical conditions stemming from their size, far beyond the stigma that society places on their appearance. They develop diabetes, have joint degeneration, metabolic disturbances, sleep apnea—a whole host of problems directly attributable to their obesity. Dietary programs are almost universally unsuccessful as a long-term solution. One treatment for this disease of "clinically severe obesity" that has gained credence in recent years is a combined surgical procedure wherein a segment of the intestine is bypassed while the stomach is stapled. This will produce a sensation of satiety, "feeling full," after even small meals, and also avoid exposure of a long segment of the intestine—which does the absorbing—to the stream of food. This was the procedure that Mr. Colson had undergone two days earlier.

After my presentation we walked into Colson's room. Immediately Dr. Singh stopped in her tracks.

"What happened to your NG tube?" she asked the patient.

"Oh, did you miss Dr. Fleischman?"—Fleischman was the attending—"He was just here. He pulled it out."

Singh said nothing and examined Mr. Colson's vast expanse of an abdomen, listening with her stethoscope and then palpating gently. After proffering a few comforting words to the patient, she led us out of the room.

"That idiot Fleischman!"

She was furious.

"He forgot that Colson's only post-op day two. Craig, watch him like a hawk today. If he gets bloated or nauseous, let me know right away."

The problem was that the stomach and bowels do not function—do not push food along—for several days after an abdominal operation, a poorly-understood but well-documented phenomenon which goes by the name "ileus." For this reason, patients undergoing such abdominal procedures generally must endure a nasogastric suction tube—an "NG"—until their gut is functioning more normally, typically after three to five days. Compounding the concern in Colson's case was the fact that his stomach had been stapled across, creating a little pouch. The NG tube had been deliberately placed in this pouch in order to keep it from distending—due to gas or secretions—and blowing out the staple line. The pattern which had been established in this relatively new operation was to get an x-ray study of the pouch—to prove it and the other reconstructions were intact—before pulling the NG. This was almost always done on the third postoperative day. Fleischman had apparently forgotten what day it was and had taken the tube out before there was any suggestion that Colson's intestines were working. Because of the staple lines at the pouch, we couldn't even replace the NG safely. So the waiting game began. If Mr. Colson didn't get nauseous or distended, it meant that somehow the gas and secretions which form in the gut even in the absence of food—and we weren't about to let him even smell food—were passing through. If he did get sick, we'd have our hands full.

The rest of the patients were, mercifully, straightforward cases of postoperative management. Singh and Striker vanished after the last patient had been seen, taking with them the two students. This irritated me, because I had already been mentally assigning these med students various tasks of the sort that I had performed at their stage. Now they were all off to the operating rooms, and I was left alone on the floor to do the work.

As the day went on, I felt much more comfortable doing the various intern duties than I thought I would. Every hour or so I would check in on Mr. Colson, who was my main worry, my "star player" as we would say. He looked fine all day, never turned a hair. Singh appeared on the floor around noon to look in on him, and she was surprised and relieved both that he was okay and that I was staying on top of his condition.

After the day's surgery was over, the team reconvened for evening rounds. Again we traveled from room to room, this time with my relating the day's events for each patient and reporting the results of various tests and so forth which had been ordered. We spent the longest time in Colson's room. He said he was doing fine and, truthfully, he looked all right to all of our eyes. Fleischman never checked in on him the whole day.

When rounds were over, I checked the "post-ops"—the patients who had had surgery that day—then wandered down to the cafeteria to get some dinner. There had been so much work to do that I'd actually forgotten to eat lunch, so I was pretty hungry. After wolfing down a breaded fish sandwich and some fries (this is served in a hospital? I thought), I headed to my call room. Within a few minutes the other interns had "checked out" their services to me. This entailed providing me with a printed list of all their patients, with a military-style briefing as to the vital aspects of their cases. Three other services were covered at a time: Surg 1 (another General Surgery service), Surg 3 (Surgical Oncology) and Surg 6 (Trauma). The man or woman covering this call was said to be "in the box."

The origin of this term, "the box," is obscure, at least to me. Some said it referred to the tiny six feet by ten feet call room to which we were assigned. Others were sure that it referred to the fact that we were covering four services at a time, and that they had appeared on some ancient schedule in the shape of a box. There was no consensus. Whatever the origin of the phrase, I was in the box that night.

I called my girlfriend to let her know how things were going. She wished me luck and I told her I'd see her the next evening. It was about 9 PM.

The calls started at about 9:05.

When I say calls I really mean pages: the nurses may or may not have known where the call room was, and what the corresponding phone number was, but there's no question that it was far easier for them to page me than to dial a number and wait for an answer. Who knew, I might be on the other side of the hospital, putting out some figurative fire? Plus, by paging me they could go on about their work until I called back. Many times during residency I wondered how hospitals ever got along before the paging technology arose (one old-timer said that in years past, when nurses wanted to summon residents who had wandered over to the nearby stadium to watch the Ohio State Buckeyes play football, they hung bed sheets from the windows of the upper floors with the docs' names written on them).

Most of the questions the nurses had could be answered over the phone. Early on in my internship I didn't do this, though. I went to see every patient I was called about, since I was both scared to death of missing a problem and trying very hard to establish my bad-ass reputation. In time the nurses grew annoyed by my constantly appearing on their wards. I think they thought I didn't trust them (although I actually didn't trust myself—to make decisions about patients sight-unseen, that is). This misconception had the unexpected benefit of curtailing the number of pages I received: the nurses were happier taking care of small things themselves than involving that SOB who kept showing up every five minutes, asking questions and poking around!

I was happily playing my utterly-involved bad-ass role when I got the first really scary page of the night. It was from 10 East Doan, my home floor. Sure enough, it was Frank Colson's nurse. He was vomiting. A lot.

When I sprinted into Colson's room I nearly slipped and fell on the blood and puke. The nurse, a very experienced sort, had a look of disappointed resignation on her face, as if the horse she always lost money on had come up short again. A young student nurse standing alongside the bed had a more animated appearance: clutching a hope-lessly-overmatched vomit basin, her once-white uniform dripping with the bloody gastrointestinal secretions of the mammoth (and still-erupting) Mr. Colson, she had a look on her face as if a scene from *The Exorcist* had come to life before her eyes. In truth, nothing in that film came close to matching this tableau for pure stomach-turning gruesomeness. And you can't smell a movie, either. The overwhelming stench of partially digested blood really has to be experienced first-hand to be appreciated: descriptions just don't do it justice.

Mr. Colson himself was unquestionably, at that point in time, the most miserable human being I had ever seen. He was throwing up with such frequency and violence that he could barely catch his breath.

Ever since Dr. Singh's early-morning alert outside Colson's room I had been dreading the possibility of having to cope with the after-effects of the rash decision to pull the NG. Now here I was, and the problem was much worse than I could have anticipated.

There was a cardinal rule of internship at Ohio State: "The intern who has made a decision has made a mistake." I hadn't heard that rule yet, as it happened, yet I realized that the input of more experienced individuals was going to be of considerable importance here.

Before calling the junior resident for help, though, I reflected on my choices. Only two really came to mind right away.

The first option was to try powerful IV "anti-emetic" drugs to suppress the nausea and vomiting. But no, the nurse had done that before even calling me.

My second thought was to try to be the hero and blindly pass an NG tube, unsupervised. In that case, if I was successful, the patient would be happy, the nurse would be ecstatic, and the student nurse would get an opportunity to take a well-needed shower. However, if I perforated the staple line the patient might die from peritonitis—even if we did get him to the operating room in time to fix the damage I'd have caused. No, that brand of heroism seemed a little too close to stupidity for my comfort.

I paged the third-year resident in-house that night and described the problem. She arrived and we debated the possibilities. By now another consideration was arising: what were all this vigorous retching and general gastrointestinal upheaval doing to Colson's staple lines? It couldn't be good. We had to act fast.

We came up with a plan and phoned Singh to tell her about it. After she approved (with a few more choice words for Fleischman) we brought Mr. Colson down to the X-ray suite. There, we sat him upright on the fluoroscopy table ("fluoro" is a kind of real-time live-action x-ray). Then we inserted the NG tube in the patient's nostril and guided it down his esophagus into his stomach. This was dangerous work for us, too, because we were still intermittently dodging the copious projections which Colson was continuing to spew. When we got the tip of the NG close to the stomach we shot some contrast material—which would show up dramatically on the fluoro screen—through the tube. Perfect! The little gastric pouch was still intact, and it was clearly delineated by the contrast material. We gently slid the tip of the NG into the pouch and secured the tube to Mr. Colson's nose with about six rolls of adhesive tape.

When we hooked the end of the NG to suction, literally gallons of secretions poured out and into the affixed canister. Mr. Colson looked utterly exhausted, but he actually managed to coax some humor out of the horrid experience, drawing in enough breath to say, gratefully, "Who should I kiss first?"

Given his less-than-appealing appearance and highly pungent scent, we opted to forego any physical expressions of affection.

After a few days I began to settle into a comfortable rhythm on the Surg 2 service. Before long I could get things done quickly and efficiently, and I began to pay attention to the reasoning behind the things we were doing. This is exactly the point of residency, of course—this is its method. Although there is some exposure to actual real-world patient care in medical school, it is minor in comparison to the intensive experience of residency. Medical students spend most of their time learning the basic science which underlies clinical decision-making: the subjects of anatomy, pathology, pharmacology, biochemistry and the rest. Residency is the time for the application of that science to practical use. There is a famous aphorism in medicine, attributed to the legendary 19th-century physician, Osler: "To study the phenomena of disease without books is to sail an uncharted sea; while to study books without patients is not to go to sea at all."

It was good to get back in the water again.

The internship rotations usually lasted three weeks, although a few stretched to six. This was good for keeping us from becoming intellectually stagnant, but it was bad for continuity. The poor patients couldn't keep track of who their doctors even were half the time. The nurses were always contacting the wrong residents. For the interns the frequent changes could be frustrating, too, because we would only just be getting the hang of a service—figuring out its eccentricities, how to really make it hum—when we were moved to another. As my short time on Surg 2 drew to a close, I also noticed a disturbing trend every time I was on call: the Surg 1 intern always checked out her service the latest, as late as 11:30 at night (remember, these were nights when she was *not on call*). The ominous aspect was that Surg 1 was the next service I was scheduled to join. Surg 1 was also Dr. Atcheson's service.

Dr. Atcheson was the Chief of General Surgery and the Director of the Residency Program. As such, to the residents he was a kind of god-king in the ancient sense: wearing the crowns of both Upper and Lower Surgical Egypt. He was our boss on two levels: as the head of the Division of General Surgery, in charge of all the hospital's general surgeons—resident or attending; and as Program Director, the final authority over all the residents. His extraordinarily busy clinical practice was also the centerpiece of the Surg 1 service. As interns we had little interaction with him: he only operated with the chief residents and we were so busy that we never made it to his clinic to see outpatients. Occasionally he would round with us, but more frequently he would see his patients accompanied only by his nurse and the chief resident.

This last fact was okay by me because, although Dr. Atcheson was personally very likable, I always hated when he showed up on the wards alone and wanted to round with me. He tended to do this unannounced, so I would not be prepared for the barrage of questions that would suddenly come at me like Hamlet's slings and arrows; I had been occupied with other tasks. Being unprepared, there were times when I didn't have the answers and looked bad, and this played hell with the bad-ass image I was trying to cultivate. (In retrospect Atcheson may have had a purpose in putting the interns at a disadvantage like that, though. Later I experienced his unique wrath while he was master of ceremonies at the Morbidity and Mortality Conference; then there was no question that he had a system of catching you off-guard, verbally probing for soft spots. There was a point to that effort: the goals were both to toughen the resident and to shore up any weaknesses Atcheson may have found. It's possible that he started toward these goals during the first year.)

Thankfully he didn't round on his patients with me very frequently. But Dr. Atcheson cast a very long shadow over the Surg 1 service even in his own personal absence. He typically had around fifteen patients in the hospital at any one time, and frequently had twenty-five or more. This was consistently more than were in-house on the whole Surg 2 service (which encompassed three attendings' practices). The work load was correspondingly greater, which explained—partially—why the previous intern had been checking out so late every night.

Another reason for the long days was the chief resident, Ron Rausch.

Dr. Rausch had been in the Army before (and actually, throughout) residency, and certainly looked the part of the cadet. Short, muscular and prematurely balding, he exuded an aura of energy and intensity, if not a great deal of self-confidence. Partly this last quality stemmed from his military training, but most of Rausch's nervous activity was by this time, I believe, a function of his having been a surgery resident for nearly five years. He was usually active and ebullient, with a quick grin, just as quick a temper, and the odd habit of sticking his tongue out between his teeth when he smiled. Rausch also, however, had the unfortunate characteristic of slowing down perceptibly when he grew fatigued. I mean everything he did just slowed to a crawl: he thought slower, responded slower, moved slower—like an old LP phonograph record on 16 rpm. So just when everyone was ready to get out of the hospital and go home, Rausch was entering molasses-mode. Evening rounds, which usually started anywhere from 8:00 PM to 10:00 PM, would last literally hours. The negative effect this had on the morale of the Surg 1 team was palpable.

Occasionally compounding this already frustrating situation was Rausch's unusual capacity of being able to fall asleep anytime, anywhere. He could fall asleep standing, like a horse. And I don't mean dozing, as anyone can if sufficiently fatigued. Rausch could be standing ramrod straight in a deep sleep. One evening on late rounds, close to midnight, he was leaning over a patient—a Mrs. Devers, listening carefully to her lungs with his stethoscope. Mrs. Devers, an elderly lady with pneumonia, was looking up at him intently, waiting for the verdict. Rausch's eyes were closed as he concentrated on his examination, and the entire team of bone-weary residents and medical students stood gathered around the bed as he continued to listen for what began to seem like rather a long time. I broke the silence after two minutes or so:

"Dr. Rausch?"

He did not reply.

"Dr. Rausch?"

This time a low groan: "Unnnhhhhh."

He was out like a light.

This was going to be tricky. How do I wake up Rausch without alerting the patient to the fact that her doctor, the individual making daily life-and-death decisions about her care, is standing above her, stethoscope in hand, sleeping like a baby? I decided to try the easy way once more.

"Dr. Rausch?"

Finally he woke up on this third address, mercifully not snoring (or worse) in the process. If Mrs. Devers realized what had happened, she was tactful enough not to let on. Rausch continued on rounds as if nothing out of the ordinary had occurred.

After the nighttime rounds were over, I finished up my paperwork and headed to the call room to find the intern who was "in the box" that night. As I passed a bank of elevators I noted that the cluster of short white coats waiting there comprised the medical students on my team. Because of Dr. Atcheson's presence on the service, and the strength a letter of recommendation from him might have in any residency application, only students with a serious interest in surgery ended up on the Surg 1 rotation. For this reason, despite its well-deserved reputation for being the most difficult student rotation in the entire curriculum, the wait list for Surg 1 was long.

None of these supposedly surgically-oriented medical students were looking my way as I proceeded to the call room, and since they seemed spent, I continued past wordlessly. As I turned the corner, though, I heard one of the students mutter, "I don't see how staying here until midnight every night furthers my education...."

With various terms of disgust, the others mumbled their agreement.

"Pussies," I thought, "no way these guys are surgeons."

Even then my visceral response to these overheard remarks seemed funny; both odd and humorous. Although as an intern I was getting my ass kicked on a daily basis, and hating nearly every moment of my time in the hospital, I still managed to draw a line between what I considered to be acceptable and unacceptable effort and attitude—certainly in the case of these medical students. In the past I had wondered why the surgery attendings and residents had been so intolerant of the slightest errors and the merest deviations from complete, undiluted devotion to duty. The best interests of the patient had seemed the clear answer, then. Now I began to see how another force was at work, a force that moved the inner mechanism of surgeons and made them drive themselves harder than any others could possibly see or appreciate. For better or worse, I could see that this unnamed and unseen force was beginning to drive me.

In the meantime, internship continued....

2

The Internship Year—
See the Man Run

A TYPICAL DAY. Does it exist? Even in a job that's reduced to mind-numbing routine, where each day seems superficially identical, events are different enough from day to day to give the lie to the idea of a "typical" one. From the distance of a few years, though, it's relatively easy for me to construct a day that's at least representative of my life as an intern.

Let's say we're on a general surgery service.

I've got to be at the hospital by 5:30 AM, and since I'll try to squeeze every last second of sleep out of my time off, I'll set the alarm for 4:45. That'll give me enough time to shower, grab a bite to eat (for the road, that is) and make it to the ward for pre-rounding. (I used to have a small picture of Dr. Zollinger—the world-famous Ohio State surgeon—displayed in the apartment in such a way as to be unobtrusive during the day, but prominent in the eerie pre-dawn light mingling from the hated alarm clock and the pink-orange filtered rays of the street lights. I used that picture as a springboard to consciousness every morning; not so much a source of inspiration as one of challenge: "You bastard, you won't beat me," I thought.) In the winter, if the weather is particularly bad, I'll add some time for scraping the windshield, negotiating the icy streets, etc. I know the chief resident will be there between 6:00 and 6:15, and s/he will want to have all the details on the status of the patients: vital signs, urine output, nutritional intake, and so forth. This is the basis for the concept of "pre-rounding." Actual rounds take place with the whole resident team,

14

but the interns (and medical students, if they were unfortunate enough to be assigned to the service) are expected to gather such information before rounds as will be essential to planning the care of the patient for that day. Then on morning rounds with the chief and other residents, he will "present" the patient and that information, the patient will be examined and interviewed, and those plans drawn up.

I use the 10-minute drive to the medical center to wake up, almost invariably with the considerable aid of a Coke and a Spartan breakfast consisting of some crackers or a fruit-sugary Pop-Tart. (I was living with my future wife at this time. She never offered to make a more substantial meal for me in the morning but, considering the hour, I never had the heart to ask her, either. She *did* get to sleep in for two more hours each day than I did, though. Those are the kinds of discrepancies that ultimately lead to trouble, of course.)

By the time I make it to the hospital, I am awake, to all appearances. The first thing to do is locate the intern who has been on call that night and find out if anything has happened to my patients. After that, I'll go from patient room to patient room, collecting the data I know the chief will want. If the patient is particularly sick or some aspect of their physical examination is of special interest (like the pulses in a vascular patient who has undergone an arterial bypass in the leg), I will wake them up and talk to them or examine them, but the routine cases I let sleep. After all, I certainly know what it is like to be awakened unnecessarily. This collection of information will usually be complete by the time the chief resident shows up.

Then the process is repeated, moving from room to room, but this time with the whole team (minus the attending, of course). These are morning "Work Rounds." I'll present the patient to the team in the time-honored manner of academic medicine: "This is Mrs. Stinchcomb, who underwent left colectomy for adenocarcinoma three days ago; currently she is afebrile (has a normal temperature) and has stable vital signs. She took in three liters of IV fluids yesterday...."

I developed a mnemonic device—a memory aid—to help me cover all the important stuff. Medical training is full of these tricks; the one I invented was "VIDMAP": Vital signs (temperature, blood pressure, respiratory rate, heart rate), Ins and outs (total amount of fluid or nutrition administered vs. urinary and bowel output), Diet (the current status of the patient's nutrition: were they being given intravenous fluids only? on a clear liquid diet? on a regular diet?), Medications currently being given, Activity level (were they permitted to walk on their own or at bed rest, for example) and Pulmonary status (were they breathing room air or on supplemental oxygen? Many of our patients were smokers and/or asthmatics who had plenty of problems with lung function after major operations). With the VIDMAP device I could rapidly cover all the significant aspects of the patients' care without worrying about missing anything.

As the team moves from room to room the chief resident makes decisions regarding the treatment of the patient that day. I carry with me the order book—a spiral-bound notebook containing blank spaces for physician's orders which the nurses, pharmacists, physical therapists, etc. consult to learn what the docs want done—and write down the things that only require a request and a physician's signature. Things such as medication orders, dressing changes and the like can be taken care of with a few scribbles in the order book. A number of other interventions will require the personal attention of the intern. When the chief requests these, I put them on my "scut list."

"Scut" is a term which is universally known among physicians. Although it has no real definition and its origins as a word are obscure, its meaning is clear to all who have been residents. Scut is the work which must be done to keep a service running well: the phone calls to reluctant radiology residents to prise time-consuming imaging studies from them, the placement of IV lines that floor nurses have "whiffed" on, the collecting of ultrasound lab reports, the contacting of medical consultation offices to obtain in-patient referrals: the list is endless. But it's all scut. And the primary function of the surgical intern is to perform scut.

As work rounds progress, my scut list begins to grow. Since it represents my task list for the day, I have an unhealthy dislike of it and, as the scut list enlarges, it sometimes appears to me to take on a life of its own, branching out and intertwining with itself like some grotesque flowering vine.

After my presentation we enter the room of our first patient, Mrs. Bostwick. She had a gastric bypass operation for severe obesity two days before. I have taken down her surgical dressing and we examine the wound as the chief resident banters with the patient. After listening to her chest with a stethoscope, the chief then turns to me:

"Change her IV fluids to D5 half-normal with 20 of K. Decrease the rate to 150. Make sure she gets up and moves around today—get a PT consult. She'll need an upper GI today, too. Don't take out her NG until that's done, and you've cleared it with me or Fleischman. Her lungs sound junky—better get respiratory to see her, too. Is dietary involved yet? Better call them and arrange gastric bypass post-op teaching."

He turns back to Mrs. Bostwick.

"You're doing great; sorry for the shop talk. We'll see you this afternoon. Can we get you anything else?" As the corpulent Mrs. B shakes her head, we file out of her room.

The translation?

"Change her IV fluids to D5 half-normal with 20 of K. Decrease the rate to 150." This means that whatever intravenous fluid Mrs. B has been getting needs to be changed to one with 5% Dextrose, with electrolyte concentrations in a standardized recipe known as "half normal"— sodium and chloride about one-half as concentrated as in blood—with a concentration of potassium (which has the chemical symbol "K") of 20 milliequivalents per liter of water. The rate at which fluids are given is communicated in milliliters per hour, so "150" means 150ml/h. No problem with this; a few lines in the order book will suffice and the nurses will take care of everything.

"Make sure she gets up and moves around today—get a PT consult." A little more effort here—I'll need to fill out a request form for "PT"— physical therapy. If the clerk at the ward's front desk likes me, she might make the phone calls necessary to get the therapists by to help Mrs. Bostwick put her considerable mass into motion.

"She'll need an upper GI today, too." Uggh. This requires a call to the radiology resident. If the test were needed the next day, I could simply schedule it with the radiology front desk, but since the chief thinks it has to be done today, I have to convince the radiologists that they should rearrange their schedule to accommodate us. Not easy. I'll have to get tricky here, maybe disingenuous, just to get the test done. Even worse, I usually end up having to go to the Radiology Department and do the lying face-to-face to get the study approved. This is a piece of scut which will take a half-hour to dispose of, easy.

Arranging Respiratory Therapy and Nutrition consultations requires jumping through hoops similar to those which needed traversing to get the physical therapists to visit: a few calls if the ward clerk was being difficult, maybe only a few "Please"s and "Thank You"s if he or she wasn't.

After leaving Bostwick's room, we move on to the next, accumulate another sub-list of scut, and continue in this fashion until all the patients on the service are seen. By now it's around 7:30 AM, and time for the chief resident to head for the operating room to help out with the day's surgery. As he disappears down the stairwell, I settle down at the nurse's station at the front of the ward and begin dissecting the scutlist. The key to survival as an intern is successful time management, which requires a careful assessment of the tasks summarized in the list. While it would be nice to accomplish in one trip all those tasks which require travelling to a certain, different part of the hospital—obviously a consideration in the quest for efficiency—an overriding concern has to be the urgency with which things need to get done. For example, I always tried to submit consultations and x-ray requisitions as early as possible. The reason for this was my knowledge that such requests were entertained on a first-come, first-served basis. If my x-ray requisitions arrived in that department before those of my fellow interns on other services, the studies would get done on my patients first and, consequently, I had a better chance of having all the results ready by the time the chief resident was done with surgery and ready to start evening rounds. Other scut, like Physical Therapy consultations or placement of routine IVs that the nurses couldn't get, could be taken care of later in the morning or in the afternoon, and the impact on the care of the patients or the smooth running of the service was minimal.

By the late morning I usually have a handle on things. The phone calls have been made, the forms filled out, the orders written. By about 10:30 AM, most of the results from the morning blood draws have been recorded by the laboratory, and I look these up on the computer. Those which require minor adjustments, like supplementation of electrolytes, I take care of with the trusty order book and my black-ink Papermate. Those which are more concerning, or x-rays or other studies which reveal important changes or unexpected findings, usually prompt a visit to the chief in the operating room.

In that case I head to the fourth floor. There I try to feign nonchalance as I pass through the great swinging automatic doors which cry out in bold red letters, "OPERATING ROOMS: NO ADMITTANCE." Who can be nonchalant in such a setting? After all, it is to learn surgery, to learn what it takes to be in command in one of these rooms that has driven me to this endless exercise in endurance, this series of thankless tasks. Outside the room itself I slip on the surgical mask and hat. After easing into the OR as unobtrusively as possible, I seek out the circulating nurse, to make sure the case is going smoothly and that an appropriate time is at hand to interrupt the procedure and ask a question. Thus assured, I sidle up to the chief resident and discharge my information. If the operation is going well, most attendings will offer up some small talk. After being given my instructions I tacitly am exiled from this inner sanctum and return to the ward.

Of course the big problem with scut is that it never disappears. There's always something else which needs to be done.

In the afternoon the admissions start to arrive. They'll be sent over from the clinic, where attendings have outpatient office hours, or come up from the emergency room, or appear as a preamble to their scheduled surgery the next day, or simply materialize from thin air. In any case their appearance requires at least an hour's worth of work apiece—taking and writing up a history, performing a physical examination, writing orders—and renders any hoped-for studying or down-time scotched.

Nevertheless by the early evening I'm usually caught up: all the consults have been ordered and their preliminary reports have been charted, all the x-rays have been performed and the results interpreted, all the abnormal lab values have been corrected and all the admissions have been tucked in (if there's been time for lunch, that's a plus). As the chief resident emerges from the operating suite, I'm ready to round. Once more, we physically make the rounds of all the patients on the service and I report the results of the scut which the chief requested twelve or so hours earlier. Tentative plans for the next day are made. The chief resident disappears, to attend to whatever further duties are required of him (I'll find these out in due time).

As a General Surgery intern, I'm on call either every third or every fourth night. If this is a call night, I'll head to the cafeteria and try to grab something to eat. Soon the other Gen Surg interns will be calling me so that they can check their services out to me. They'll be leaving their patients in my care overnight and the more details I have about them the better off we'll all be. Of course if I'm not on call, I'll be one of those doing the "checking out." With luck, I'll be home by 9:00 PM. After dinner and a little mental decompression courtesy of the TV, it's time to hit the sack. As I know full well, the damn alarm will go off as soon as my head hits the pillow.

And tomorrow will be more of the same.

3

The Internship Year—
A Little Knowledge...

THE INTERNSHIP YEAR SLOWLY DRAGGED ON, like some sort of malevolent glacier. Month-long rotations on transplant and cardiac surgery came and went. As fall descended, I moved on to the vascular surgery service.

Outside the hospital, in the real world, the tropic-like central Ohio summer gave way to a crisp, brilliantly-sunlit autumn. Countless leaves crunched merrily underfoot. The green trees I had only seen on fleeting weekends off-duty turned stunning shades of auburn and gold (I still only saw them on weekends, though).

At home my life was perhaps more peaceful than it had ever been. Evenings at the apartment were bliss: just my girlfriend and I sharing the day's events over a home-cooked meal, then, after taking care of the dishes and other chores, watching a movie or TV show until I inevitably fell asleep (the only show I refused to watch was *ER*—but does any cop go home and watch *Cops*?). Although my time away was taxing for both of us, my girlfriend certainly had enough to occupy her mind; at least I thought so. She was working a day job and singing with a band on weekend nights. When my schedule permitted it, I would sit in with her band at these gigs and unwind by playing some blues or rock guitar. The big news that fall, though, was that her younger sister (by seven years) was getting married.

In November I switched to the Vascular Surgery service. This group focused on the care of patients with severe disease of the blood vessels:

atherosclerotic narrowing or aneurysmal dilation of the arteries, for the most part. Over the years the successive waves of interns had consistently judged this service to be the most difficult of the entire internship experience. Not only was the number of in-house patients high, but the withering complexity of their medical problems was staggering. It seemed like they were all at death's door: heart disease, kidney problems, strokes—they ran the gamut. This made some sense, though; after all, if the arteries in one part of the body are diseased, they're probably all abnormal to some extent.

As on all other services, if there were patients already admitted to the hospital who were going to undergo surgical procedures the next day, it was the duty of the intern on the vascular surgery service to find all of them and "do the preops."

This simply meant seeing to it that all the appropriate paperwork and preoperative testing on a given patient had been completed. (The anesthesiologists confirmed some of the testing, such as chest x-rays and electrocardiograms, for their own purposes). The paperwork could be considerable: a written history and physical exam, preoperative orders including antibiotics and other drugs, and, most importantly, a signed consent form giving the surgeon the legal go-ahead to perform the operation, at the request of the patient. Given the tremendous demands on his time, the intern often would be forced to complete this paperwork very late in the evening, after rounds.

One night after the Vascular Surgery team had finished seeing patients, I started on the preops. One of these was a prisoner with terrible atherosclerotic arterial disease involving both legs. He couldn't walk more than a few yards at a time due to the pain from his inadequate circulation. His circulation was so bad, in fact, that he was sometimes having pain in his feet even without moving them. In addition, the atherosclerosis had affected his heart so that he had recurring chest pain. This was a fairly typical history for these vascular patients, so I didn't think too much about it. The cardiologists had seen him and said he was all right to undergo the surgery and, since I was a mere intern, that was good enough for me.

I went to the patient's bedside and took his history, then examined him. Finally I asked him to sign the consent form. We were going to perform an arterial bypass procedure on his left leg, in which a graft of the patient's own vein is used to bypass the area of blockage and restore blood flow to the oxygen-starved tissues. Both of his legs were diseased, and would likely need an operation. Typically in such instances only one leg at a time is operated on, though. It's too difficult for the patients to get around postoperatively if both legs have extensive incisions, and recovery times are greatly lengthened.

This prisoner was only reluctantly cooperative with me to begin with, but when the question of consent arose he was downright confrontational:

"Which leg are you gonna cut?" he asked, which was a reasonable question (unfortunately, just a few days earlier a major national news story reported the scandal surrounding a surgeon's amputation of the wrong leg in a Florida hospital, so this was undoubtedly on his mind).

"The left one," I replied.

He was incredulous.

"The left one botherin' me, don't be cuttin' on the right one now."

I quickly double-checked the operative schedule.

"Nope," I said. "We're just doing the left one."

He still looked doubtful, for reasons which eluded me, but he signed anyway.

The next morning, after a sleepless night on call, I was summoned to the OR by the vascular surgery fellow, an Indian with incongruous green eyes. He was livid, and this morning the green eyes were offset by tinges of crimson.

"Which leg did you consent that prisoner for?" he shouted.

"The left, why?"

"Weren't you there at conference? The right leg's worse on the angios; that's the one we're going to do!"

I *had* been at the conference where we looked at the angiograms— the x-ray studies in which contrast is injected into the arteries to define the sites of blockage—but I didn't recall any discussion about doing the right leg. Hadn't it said "left" on the OR schedule? Hadn't the patient insisted it was the left? Post-call and exhausted, I even doubted myself. I hesitated.

"Don't you have anything to say?" he asked.

"I don't know what happened—how that could happen—the right leg?" I stammered.

"Get over to room 20 and apologize to Dr. Wright."

I half-stumbled out the door and over to the adjoining OR, where the prisoner was undergoing his procedure. I was dumbfounded. Had I really gotten the leg wrong? What had gone wrong? I rehearsed how I would apologize to the attending.

Then I looked in the window of OR 20 and forgot all about the leg. The chief resident had broken scrub and was performing chest compressions on the prisoner, while the anesthesiologists frantically poured in the IV drugs. Oh my god, I thought, he's had a cardiac arrest!

In fact he had suffered a massive heart attack. The operation, which hadn't gotten much beyond the incision, was aborted. The patient was taken to the cardiac care unit where, amazingly, he briefly recovered. He even regained consciousness. But the damage to his heart had been too great: he went into profound cardiac failure and died in a couple of days.

I slipped into a deep depression.

How could I have made such a mistake? The vascular fellow—never one to let a lesson learned suffice—tortured me about it, too. It seemed as if everyone agreed that the right leg was the one we had planned on fixing.

I seriously questioned whether I should continue in surgery. Intellectually, I knew that my error had had no impact on the outcome of the patient's case and that he would have had the heart attack if the other side had been operated on anyway, but that did little to ease my feelings of inadequacy.

About a day later I ran into an acquaintance in the hallway, a medical resident named Greg Meier. By coincidence, he was the resident on the cardiology service who had taken care of the prisoner after the heart attack.

"Hey, Miller," he called out, "nice job you guys did boxing that prisoner." To "box" meant to kill, to put in a box (a pine box, that is).

"Aw, bite me, Meier," I answered.

"Yeah, yeah," he said. "By the way, do you guys always operate on the wrong leg?"

My ears perked up. "What are you talking about?" I asked.

"Don't you know what that guy said when he woke up? It was the only thing he said, actually. He looked down at his dressing and yelled 'Those motherfuckers cut the wrong goddamn leg.' You were supposed to do the left, Miller. It even says so on the OR schedule."

Meier must have thought I was insane when he saw me grinning back at him like the Cheshire cat.

Although by this time I had had some very minor exposure to the operating room (mostly as an over-educated courier), the vascular service provided my first opportunity to perform any real surgery. The major procedures in vascular surgery are frequently complex and technically demanding, and at this stage of the game there was no place for a neophyte such as myself in these cases, but there were some procedures that didn't require such exacting skill—where an intern could learn a little cutting and sewing. Amputations, for example.

The first time I performed an amputation was rather memorable for a number of reasons. First, the vascular surgeon, Dr. Chet Tovar, was the attending, and he seemed to have a deep-seated hatred of me for which I could find no logical reason (one time he actually yelled at me for using a word he didn't know—the word was "nonplussed"). Second, since I was a mere intern, I had essentially no operative skills to speak of (a fact which did not bode well for Tovar's volatile mood). Third, I was accompanied to the OR by a freshly minted Andy Hardy-type third-year medical student, who had never yet witnessed any surgery at all.

The patient's toes were gangrenous; irretrievably infected from diabetes. We "prepped" them—basically slathering them with an antiseptic solution of povidone and iodine called Betadine—and draped the surgical field with sterile towels. After scrubbing our hands and donning the sterile gown and gloves, we got set to begin. Tovar glared at me.

"What atlas did you read from to prepare for this operation?" he snapped, his voice a model of drill-order precision.

"Mastery of Surgery," I lied.

"Then show me where you'd place your incision."

(Panting, I reflected that one piece of information was clear: Tovar wasn't familiar with the book I'd cited. Even *I* knew there was no discussion of toe amputations in it!)

I passed my finger over where I thought we should cut in order to take the dead toes off. Apparently it was close enough. Tovar silently handed the knife to me and leaned in close to speak. The patient was awake—under a regional anesthetic only—and Tovar wanted to communicate something privately.

"To the bone," he whispered in my ear.

Grasping the handle of the scalpel like a pencil, I brought it down toward the ravaged foot. Tovar intercepted me and pried my fingers from the instrument. With a guttural sound for emphasis he demonstrated what was apparently the correct way to hold the knife: between just the forefinger and the thumb, the other digits steadying the handle. I mimicked his grip as if it were Nicklaus'. Encountering no further interference, I proceeded. The knife blade slid into the yielding, friable tissue. It slipped easily through the infected skin, muscle and tendons to the bones. I passed the scalpel around the foot, through the path I had outlined with my finger. Blood and ghastly, creamy pus gushed out in torrents.

Out of the corner of my eye, I saw the poor medical student begin wavering. His eyes were watering and he was ashen; quiet gasps were emanating from beneath his mask. I was sure he was going to faint. Tovar noticed, too.

"Go outside and get some air," he said firmly.

The student escaped wordlessly and we continued. I began to gain confidence and cut more aggressively. Too aggressively. I cut past my line and into healthy tissue. Tovar grabbed my hand and once more pried the scalpel from it.

"This is a lethal weapon," he seethed. "Treat it with respect, god damn it."

I nodded silently.

A drop of sweat fell from my brow to the corner of my eye. I blinked the sting away.

Next we used the bone-cutter to pinch through the metacarpals, the bones between the ankle and the toes. Finally we pulled the soft tissue together to form the new stump. After stitching it up we were done. None of these steps did I perform in a remotely capable fashion, according to Tovar.

He left and I dressed the wound, then took off my bloody gown and gloves and filled out some paperwork.

Outside the OR door I found the medical student, who had regained his composure for the most part. At least now he didn't look like a slight breeze would take him down.

"Well, what did you think of your first time in the operating room?" I asked, smart-ass as always.

"It was pretty cool," he replied, to my amazement. "I think I could do that for a living."

I thought he was full of it but, sure enough, two years later he matched in surgery at a program in Florida.

By winter of the internship year I had come to realize that the only thing that had kept me sane during the long hours and constant humiliation had been the steady, calming support of my girlfriend. We'd been together for five years by this point, and it was a comfortable relationship, so the time seemed right to formalize things. I surprised her on Christmas morning with a marriage proposal, and she accepted. I did have some concerns, because I knew that the loneliness of a surgery resident's spouse is a matter of legend, and I wasn't sure how she would respond over the long haul.

There is a classic, bittersweet joke among medical people:

"Q: How do you hide a $100 bill from a General Surgeon?"

"A: Give it to his family."

4

The Second Year—
Perchance to Sleep

GENERAL SURGERY RESIDENTS are required to spend a certain period of time learning the basics of the major surgical subspecialities. One of these branches is Orthopedics. Not enough time is set aside to enable the Gen Surg resident to be competent in any but the most straightforward of Orthopedic interventions; of course, that's not the point. The real goal is to be able to do the easy stuff and, more importantly, to be able to say to an examining board at some point: "I studied Orthopedics on the wards and in the operating room. Pass me."

During my second year in residency I spent six weeks on the Orthopedic Surgery service at a local private hospital. This was, it turned out, an almost-planned reprieve from the otherwise dreadful ostinato of life at "The U." I say "almost-planned" because the faculty constructed the schedule and it's difficult to envision them actually concerning themselves with whether we residents should have any form of reprieve. But, whether planned or not, that's the way it played out.

My time in Ortho was assigned to be at the private Riverside Methodist Hospital, a scant three miles from the University. By coincidence I had actually been born at this hospital, now 28 years before.

The differences between private and university hospitals are enormous. The evolution of the health care system in the U.S. is narrowing the gaps, but contrasts are and always will be present, because the two types of institutions are so profoundly different. University hospitals, in addition to caring for patients, are dedicated to teaching medical students and residents, and traditionally they have been willing (in the literal sense) to pay the price for that mission. That is to say, they haven't been very profitable. This is largely because they haven't been very efficient. Government-subsidized and thus not dependent on market pressures, they grew bloated and cumbersome over the decades. In addition, many diagnostic and therapeutic decisions continue to be made by inexperienced young physicians, who functioned in the past with a blissful ignorance of cost/benefit ratios. Only in the last few years has the shifting socioeconomic climate made it necessary for the university hospitals to streamline their operations, curtailing unnecessary tests and slashing hitherto sacred and unassailable budgets. At the same time, society has tolerated the excesses of the teaching hospitals because of the role they play in the education of future physicians. The indications are clear that that tolerance is at an end. The challenge for these institutions now and in the future is to continue the vital role of medical education in a manner that is fiscally competitive with private hospitals.

All of that is fascinating stuff, but (as far as I was concerned) it had nothing to do with me as I made the short drive along the Olentangy River road from my apartment to my first private-sector surgical experience. The differences between Ohio State University Hospital and Riverside Methodist were greater to me than the question of free market competition, or even the future of medical education in North America. The difference was that I would finally be getting some freaking sleep. Everyone knew that the Ortho rotation at Riverside was a breeze. It was part of the reason that that hospital had earned the nickname, "The Slide."

I've already described a "typical" day in the life of a surgery intern. The especially taxing part of the job which I haven't gone into revolves around the fact that you're on call every third night. That means that—on a call day—you work the long hours, from 6 AM the first day until 6 PM or so the *following night*. You then return the next morning for one "normal" work day of twelve to fourteen hours. The next day you return for another long day—another call day. The cycle would thus be 36 hours on, 12 off, 12 on, 12 off, then beginning over again with 36 on, etc. A few turns of this in a row essentially obliterated any kind of normal sleep/wake routine.

We went on like this for the whole internship year, with three weeks of vacation (only one week at a time, though). Occasionally the call schedule would be every fourth night, but it was just as likely to be every other night. Some simply could not tolerate this pattern and eventually quit, although complicating personal issues were probably at play, too. A minority truly suffered miserably but persevered. Most adapted to little or no rest and plowed ahead by force of will.

My own response to sleep deprivation was probably similar to most. Rather than becoming overwhelmingly drowsy, by the time I had been awake for more than twenty-four hours at a stretch—constantly working—I was primarily forgetful of details. I was also embarrassingly inefficient. I can still vividly recall being on Surg I as an intern, at the end of a "post-call" day, wandering over to the surgery floor in the cancer hospital to write an order which I hadn't gotten around to writing earlier. Numbly I leafed through the order book under the flickering fluorescent lights at the nurse's station, then stared down in disbelief at the completed handwritten order, with my signature attached. I had already written the order hours before, but now had no recollection of having done so at all.

One point in which I took considerable personal pride was my being able to stay awake, "post-call," through the most dizzyingly boring conferences. There were several weekly scheduled conferences in the Department of Surgery, including Morbidity and Mortality Conference (an examination of the bad outcomes which we had perpetrated on unsuspecting patients), Schwartz Club (a well-intentioned but poorly-attended gathering of the residents to discuss a chapter of the prevailing surgery textbook) and Grand Rounds (a lecture delivered by one of the faculty or a prestigious visiting professor). These conferences each were taxing to the muscles of the eyelids in their own way, but Grand Rounds were particularly tiresome.

Grand Rounds were held at 7:30 on Thursday mornings in a large, darkened and overly-heated auditorium. The room was filled with bone-weary residents, dapper (if scarce) attendings and befuddled medical students, all bolstered (and twitching) with massive doses of the ghastly, fetid brew proffered to us as coffee. Any but the most stimulating of topics and/or speakers would be hopelessly out-muscled by the arms of Morpheus in such an environment, and, indeed, (without exaggeration) some speakers would be assailed by clearly audible snores within minutes of beginning their presentations. This was usually met by a subcurrent of embarrassed giggling, which wafted through the room like so much hysterical mustard gas.

I determined early on that I would do my best to avoid being the source of this laughter. In fact, I needn't have worried. There was a particular resident on the Plastic Surgery tract, Peter Moats, who diverted the attention which any other dozing audience member might otherwise have drawn. He not only fell asleep at essentially every conference he attended, but he also always seemed to make a point of doing so in the most disruptive manner conceivable. Drooling, snoring, loud unintelligible gasps and grunts; these and more constituted the tools of somnolent disruption which he had at his fleshy fingertips. One time the concentration of a hopelessly sincere speaker was dashed by a loud thud which emanated from the very back of the room. We all turned to see a blinking Moats mumbling to himself and vigorously rubbing the burgeoning egg-sized bump he had received when his forehead struck the desktop as he lost consciousness.

While one could stay awake through these conferences, although only the hardiest, there were other places in the hospital where slumber was even more of an affront to decorum. Like the OR.

During my residency several interns—invariably "post-call"—passed out from exhaustion while holding retraction during operations. I wouldn't say this was exactly a common sight, but it did occur. In one of these instances the intern had been holding the heart during a coronary bypass procedure (some cardiac surgeons like the heart manually held in place while they do their sewing). He, too, had been up all night on call and was drained, fighting a pitched battle with his weary eyelids. As he lost the fight and drifted out of consciousness, the intern had slowly released his grasp on the patient's heart and—rather gracefully to some accounts—slipped silently to the floor. Without missing a beat, the cardiac surgeon had the circulating nurse page another intern. One can imagine the thoughts crossing this second fellow's mind as he entered the OR and saw his comrade, still unconscious and propped up against a wall with oxygen tubing in his nostrils.

"Scrub in," the surgeon had bellowed, "you're next."

Dr. Ron Rausch, my old Surg 1 chief who could sleep in any bodily position, took another eventful nap which was even more out of the ordinary. This occurred while he was performing (with Dr. Atcheson, of all people) a Whipple operation, one of the most difficult and technically challenging procedures in all of the surgical repertoire. In mid-operation, during the "heat of battle," Rausch simply drifted off, once again standing straight up—the way he had been taught as a West Point plebe. No instruments were dropped, no retractors slipped; Rausch just quit moving. After what must have been a few puzzling moments, Dr. Atcheson looked up at the suddenly paralyzed chief resident and imme- diately grasped the situation. He might have been expected to blow a fuse at this point, but instead (to his credit) he gently awakened his dozing assistant and casually sent him off to rest. Of course in true military fashion Rausch protested that he was perfectly capable of continuing (in another era I suppose a duel may have been in order), but Dr. Atcheson insisted that he find some place to lie down and sleep for half an hour.

Thirty minutes later, Rausch was back in the operating room.

While there were seriocomic events like these related to exhaustion from lack of sleep, there were other, less amusing moments as well.

I was always deathly afraid of missing a page by sleeping through it. In truth, there were few opportunities at behavior which could lead to a surgery resident's being fired, but unquestionably one of these few would be his sleeping soundly through a page while a patient crashed and burned without a physician by the bedside. Fear of this occurring was a great stimulus to me, and I only slept through one page (to my knowl- edge) of the thousands I received during my many hundreds of call nights as a resident. Luckily nothing dreadful transpired as a result. I guarded against falling asleep too soundly by always leaving the call room lights on, and lying on top of the bed rather than under the sheets. I also frequently placed the pager directly by the side of my head so as to hear the beep more easily. Others, who may or may not have tried these measures, sometimes had tremendous problems.

As an example, when I was a third-year resident on Surg 1, I had the misfortune of being on call with the intern on my service, who had the unlikely name of Tim Hurt, every third night.

Hurt was a quiet, fairly grim fellow who evidenced no real personal- ity during the daylight hours—at least none that I could elicit. By night, he proved to be the soundest of sleepers, able to withstand the onslaught of literally dozens of pages without being disturbed from his peaceful slumber. This, of course, meant that these floor call pages then began to come to me, the next highest-ranking surgery resident in the hospital. Since I was seeing all the surgery consultations on the wards and in the emergency room and taking care of the very sick ICU patients to boot, I had plenty to do myself already. One night things came to a head.

"Dr. Miller?" an annoyed voice on the other end of the phone whined, "This is the nursing supervisor,"—this meant the situation was serious: you almost never heard from this particular hospital officer unless something truly nasty was going down and heads were about to roll—"your intern, Dr. Hurt, is not answering his pages and we have some patient care issues that need addressed."

I put on my best calming air, assuaged her, and promised that I would take care of things.

Except I couldn't wake Hurt up, either. I paged him and paged him on his beeper, then had the hospital operator page him overhead—through the hospital loudspeakers—all to no avail. I had no idea where in the medical center he might be, so I couldn't even burst into his call room in dramatic anger. This, of course, pissed me off even further.

I fielded the calls from the floor (in addition to my own, from the ER and the ICU) for the rest of the night, in a mood of quietly gathering fury.

The next morning Hurt appeared on rounds, looking well-rested but perhaps a bit concerned.

"What's the matter, Hurt?" I asked innocently. "Tough call-night?"

"No, not really, it was pretty quiet. But I think I might have missed some pages last night."

"Oh really?" I was playing him like a Stradivarius, if I do say so myself. "What makes you think that?"

"Well, all these numbers on my beeper are blinking."

Together we glanced at his pager. Nodding thoughtfully, I sprung the trap: "Hey, what do you know? Those are all the same numbers I got paged to last night after they couldn't wake your ass up...."

I proceeded to point out to Hurt the manifest dangers of being unavailable for emergencies and how he was letting down the patients as well as his fellow residents. He apologized profusely, and—being something of a soft touch in those days—I let it go at that.

As you might guess, two nights later the same scenario took place. Being rehearsed in this role now, however, I could stretch out and expand on the part. I searched the call rooms methodically and found the sleeping Hurt, then took him by the arm to the main surgery nursing station and set him down there. I placed a cup of nursing station Folgers beside him.

"You are staying here all night, where the nurses can find you," I said. "No call room, no sleeping, no TV. If you don't screw up, I may let you get up to take a piss."

Despite my rebukes, I couldn't help but feel a little sorry for this intern, being as tired as he obviously was. Still, we all were chronically sleep-deprived, and there could be no tolerance for placing one's own welfare above that of the patients. He could go into Internal Medicine if he wanted to work normal hours and get a good night's sleep on a regular basis. Or better yet, become a lawyer. (In fact, within a year he transferred out of General Surgery and into Urology).

And so, although this particular experience with Tim Hurt was still in the future at the time, my knowledge of the rarity and value of the experience of sleep was much on my mind as I began my six-week sojourn in private Orthopedics at Riverside. A glance at the call schedule would invite the feeling of much rest to come—I was set up to take in-hospital overnight call only every six nights! It was true that I had to take at-home backup call every third night, in case I was needed for emergencies, but this was still like Club Med compared to the hardships of the intern experience. Call from home?!? Where do I sign?!

And for once the other shoe didn't drop, at least not very hard. The call nights were busier than I expected, but the daytime schedule was, for me, remarkably light. There was a full contingent of Ortho residents, and they took all the operative cases. My role was primarily just to be available in case anything came in through the emergency room that needed Orthopedic assessment or treatment.

In this regard the elderly were, by far, my largest contingent of customers.

Working on an Ortho service one would begin to think that geriatric patients are the most egregious risk-takers this side of motocross racers. They certainly must be more active than the popular press would have us believe, because while I was there every senior citizen in Columbus, Ohio must have come through the Riverside ER at some point with one sort of fracture or another, all incurred during outdoor activity. The worse the weather, the more anxious they were to sample it. One 86-year-old lady who had broken her wrist as she fell on her icy outdoor stairway attempted to explain why she had stepped outside to begin with: "I heard there was a blizzard coming and I wanted to get to the grocery store to stock up...." Crazy.

But who could help but adore these folks. They had lived around the bad winter weather their whole lives and couldn't recognize that it was a genuine peril to them now that they were old. My personal record was 13 consultations for broken bones from the ER in a twenty-four hour period (the overall record was supposedly 19). Of these, the overwhelming majority were fractures of the distal radius (the forearm bone on the same side as the thumb). This is the so-called Colles fracture, the break you get by trying to absorb a fall with your hands. They were all old people who had fallen.

If that was the most common thing I saw, the most unusual Ortho case which showed up in the ER was that of a certain middle-aged man with a fractured collarbone, or clavicle, among other minor traumatic injuries. When the nighttime page came from the emergency department, the clerk gave me no more information than that. Arriving in the main bay, I was startled to see television crews with brilliant klieg lights and smartly-dressed "on-air personalities" milling about. At first I thought that some visiting celebrity had gotten appendicitis but no, the focus of attention was *my* patient. It turned out that he had sustained his relatively minor injuries in a private airplane crash. As it happened, he was being lionized by the local media that evening for having touched down (if that's the appropriate term) on an unoccupied interstate highway rather than into the adjacent subdivisions. As I examined him, far from the glare of the TV cameras, he seemed to be both surprisingly blasé about his injuries and oddly concerned about the status of his airplane. The next day I found out why.

When I came to see the man in the trauma inpatient ward the following morning, I was surprised to find my way blocked by two armed policemen. Although they let me in to examine the patient, they were tight-lipped as to the reason for their presence. The nurse, though, gave me the story (but not before remarking snottily, "Don't you watch the news?"): apparently, the guy had been smuggling cocaine into the country. He had performed an emergency landing on the highway after a mechanical failure, in hopes of somehow being able to stash the drugs (what was he going to do, jump out of a plane he'd crash-landed on the interstate and run with a bale of cocaine into the woods?). Unfortunately for him, the landing wasn't so smooth and he had injured both the plane and himself, the latter badly enough that he hadn't been able to get out of his seat, let alone get rid of the coke before the authorities arrived.

(Although I wouldn't expect anyone to believe this, I actually took care of another airplane crash survivor during my brief sojourn on the Orthopedics service at Riverside. Once again, the patient was a private pilot who had had mechanical problems and crashed, breaking several bones. I only saw him in the clinic, though, long after the actual injuries. I'm happy to report that there were no drugs found in the wreckage of *his* plane.)

Part of the requirement of the rotation at Riverside was attendance at the morning Orthopedics conference, in a secluded room off the main cafeteria. The Ortho residents would collect the x-rays they had accumulated from the consultations of the previous twenty-four hours and then, while everyone ate breakfast, present them to the gathered attendings, who would argue over the proper therapy.

This conference was a riot.

The attendings must have been under some mandate to appear, because several took no active part in the proceedings other than making sure that their signature made its way to the attendance sheet. One fellow took absolutely no notice of the cases being presented and simply eyeballed his copy of the *Wall Street Journal* throughout the hour-long gathering. Most of the others at least feigned interest.

The residents, though, were far more entertaining. Now it must be said that, within the community of medical professionals, residents in Orthopedic Surgery have a certain reputation. It is a reputation which most of them cultivate, although a few find it demeaning. This reputation would have it that Ortho residents are weight-lifting, womanizing anti-intellectuals who are only in medicine for the money, sort of like surgical post-graduate frat boys. While this may not describe all of the nation's trainees in this particular specialty, it would definitely be an accurate precis of the group at Riverside during the time I spent there.

They all ate the same breakfast: two milks, three hard-boiled eggs (the whites only), wheat toast, cereal. This was disturbing to watch, by the way: about seven guys, all with the same high-and-tight haircut, the same clogs, the same scrubs, eating exactly the same breakfast. I felt like I had missed the memo to become a Tom Cruise clone.

It was also impossible for any of these guys to finish a sentence without putting the word "dude" on the end.

"I think we're going to have to pin his femur, dude."

"How many reps can you do at 220, dude?"

"Did you check out that sweet little honey on the seventh floor, dude?"

Well-versed in surfer talk from some time spent in California, I was not intimidated by such lingo, and (after adding some novel variations to their vocabulary such as "Shee-ahh, dudical") I was quickly accepted. After a couple of weeks, though, I realized that the morning conference attendance sheet was not finding its way back to Ohio State. No one in the residency office had any way of knowing whether I was actually present at the morning hard-boiled egg/*Wall Street Journal* conference or not. I perceived that the hour or two of extra shut-eye I could get from skipping this otherwise-amusing conference was definitely more to my advantage than suffering through it for the tiny morsels of bone-setting info that might filter down my way. I stopped going.

The only real surgery I did while on this rotation, and even that wasn't much, was as a result of my shadowing a certain private-practice Orthopod named Ron Hendricks. Although he was not affiliated with the medical school in any way, he took on general surgery second-year residents during their Riverside rotation and spent about three out of every four weeks in nearly daily contact with them, both in his office and in the operating room. He didn't need to do this—I'm positive he wasn't getting compensated, and the presence of the resident was not especially helpful, I can assure you. For these reasons we residents were especially grateful. On top of everything else, he was a good teacher and—from years of experience—had reams of practical information filed away in his mind. It was fun to sample some of this information and pick up some practical pearls of wisdom.

Dr. Hendricks was old school in everything, including appearance. Approaching sixty, he was tall and lanky, with a warm grin and shaded, aviator-style spectacles. But he had one peculiar habit that, once you noticed it, you couldn't ignore. He would always stare at his own reflection in the glass of the framed prints which decorated his examining rooms—while he was interviewing the patients. He would sometimes adjust his tie or run a finger through his thinning hair but he usually just stood there, admiring himself while he talked. New patients sometimes caught on to this and I would try to distract them if I saw them start to look at Hendricks strangely—open a window, tie my shoe, anything. The old, established patients were used to it. As it happens, Dr. Hendricks was not an especially physically attractive man, which just added to the harmless weirdness of the whole thing. What the hell was he looking at? It became a kind of game with the residents to see whether the new guy rotating with Hendricks had picked up on his idiosyncrasy yet. That meant those who had already done the rotation had to keep the secret, which wasn't easy.

In any case, Dr. Hendricks spent much more time and expended much more effort on teaching the general surgery residents than any other Orthopedics attending (private or university-affiliated) by far, plus he was a very likable guy. Naturally he was popular.

Years later I referred a good friend of mine to Dr. Hendricks for a back problem. After his first office visit I asked my buddy:

"What do you think of old Hendricks? He's a pretty good guy, eh?"

My friend agreed, then thought for a minute.

"I've got to ask you something. Does it seem to you like he's always checking himself out?"

The whole private experience at Riverside was over after six short weeks. Although I didn't learn enough during that time to be able to competently treat complex Orthopedic problems, I did pick up enough to treat simple fractures—which was the only realistic goal anyway. I also learned another very valuable bit of information: I had no interest in being an Orthopod.

Although I enjoyed the opportunity to catch up on some much-needed sleep, I found myself—to my own surprise—anxious to get back to work at the big hospital. Six weeks of relative vacation were more than enough; it was time to get back to the task at hand.

Soon enough, of course, I would be longing for the quiet days and nights at Riverside.

5

The Second Year— Don't Do Nothin' Dumb

AFTER MY PERIOD OF COMPARATIVE RESPITE in the private practice setting at Riverside, it would not be my lot to return directly to the University Medical Center. Instead I was headed to yet another hospital, albeit one I already had some familiarity with. Next I spent six miserable weeks on the pediatric cardiothoracic surgery service at Children's Hospital.

Now the work of congenital heart surgery is surely some of the most noble in the medical profession. What could be more admirable than devoting one's life to repairing otherwise fatal lesions in the hearts of infants and children? It's tough work and it requires tough individuals. Of course the sanctity of the effort doesn't mean that the field attracts the most noble characters.

There were two pediatric cardiothoracic surgeons at Children's. The chief, Dr. Dennis, was universally loved and admired. He had chosen his career after his first child died in early infancy from a congenital cardiac defect. I suppose the psychology of this is best left to the experts, but in any event Dr. Dennis was far from the morose individual one might have expected him to be, constantly challenged as he was by rare surgical diseases similar to that which felled his first-born. He was always smiling a toothy grin—a wealth of warmth and personability and full of an endless supply of witticisms. In short, he was a genuine pleasure to be around. Everyone loved to scrub with him: nurses, residents and technicians alike. He was, of course, a highly skilled surgeon, and his patients generally did very well postoperatively.

One day Dr. Dennis and I were surveying a small child's ribcage to decide the most appropriate place to make an incision. He looked at me with sincerity in his eyes and asked, "Do you know how to remember the names of the twelve ribs?"

I was puzzled; while mnemonic devices are a mainstay of medical education and I certainly had committed dozens to memory (most are ribald rhymes, and the first letters of each word correspond to the first letters of the terms to be remembered), the ribs had no names to remember, so what was he talking about?

Without hesitating to allow me to ruin the joke, Dr. Dennis announced that the mnemonic device in question was, "Frank Sinatra takes four fifths of Seagram's Seven each night to ease tension."

"Huh?" I said.

"Sure," he replied. "That way you can remember first, second, third, fourth...."

During another case Dr. Dennis was taking great care to avoid producing air embolisms while placing his tiny patient on the cardiopulmonary bypass machine which allows operations to be performed on the heart. These embolisms can travel to the brain and produce devastating strokes, so of course much effort is expended in avoiding them. There can't be a more horrendous outcome than fixing a child's heart only to render him hopelessly retarded in the process.

"Don't make no people for the *short bus*," Dr. Dennis muttered.

Curiously, like many surgeons he did not particularly enjoy the vagaries of ICU postoperative management. For the most part he preferred to leave his patients in the care of the pediatric cardiologists, typically observing that he was "just getting in the way" as he wandered out the ICU door.

The counterpart of Dr. Dennis was Dr. Klein. While Klein may not have been as universally reviled as Dennis was loved, the antithesis was close. Diminutive, always nattily dressed and possessed of a musical South African accent, at first glance the graying, fiftyish Klein seemed affable and educated. In the operating room, however, he was a tyrant. In a sense he was really an anachronism, a throwback to the bygone age of the surgical ogres, when attendings could get away with abusive, frequently misogynistic behavior. I think he was under such constant pressure from the magnitude of the operations he performed and the enormity of their implications (failure might cheat the infant patient of seventy years of life instead of perhaps five in the seventy-year-old grandmother with coronary artery disease) that his only means of survival was to lash out periodically to release his tension. His temper was violent and unpredictable, and expressed itself only while he was performing surgery. As an example, on my first day on service, while scrubbed in the OR, Dr. Klein quietly inquired as to whether I had really been a rock guitarist in a previous incarnation. I answered that I had and the conversation continued pleasantly as the case proceeded without event. I was surprised that he had a fair knowledge of modern music. As the surgery became more difficult and luck turned against him, Klein's mood became dark and surly. He tortured the assisting cardiothoracic surgery fellow with scathing remarks as to his lack of technical skill, then turned on me. I was innocently holding a suction device and expending no more mental energy than it takes to create a shadow when suddenly he exploded at me, "Goddamn it, you've got to *help* me! Suck with that thing! Suck! Suck!"

Then, to assure me that not only were we not friends but his earlier interest in my musical sidelight was, in fact, based on contempt, he shouted, "Look, pal, this isn't fucking Woodstock!"

Klein was no hack, but it was clear that his operative skills did not match those of the highly-experienced Dr. Dennis. To top this off, he frequently performed the most technically demanding and hazardous of the pediatric cardiothoracic operations, sometimes appearing to seek them out. As a result his complication and mortality rates were quite high. This really was through no fault of his own, but his constant berating of the nurses and residents did not earn him much sympathy when things went poorly.

Things went particularly poorly one drizzly spring morning when young Kyle Bardeen came to the operating room. Kyle was a two-year-old who had previously undergone the first procedure in a three-stage sequence of operations designed to correct an otherwise-fatal congenital heart anomaly called tricuspid atresia. In tricuspid atresia the valve which normally exists between the atrium and ventricle of the right heart is of such a small caliber that virtually no blood can pass through it to the lungs to collect oxygen. Surgical correction is complex, and results are generally rather poor. In the first stage, among other manipulations a conduit is created from the right atrium to the aorta to allow blood to flow to the general circulation. This conduit is made of a synthetic polymer named polytetrafluoroethylene, or Goretex (when baked onto cookware, it's called Teflon). During the second stage procedure this Goretex graft is frequently found directly beneath the sternum, as everyone in the operating room was about to find out this morning.

Klein liked to cut the sternum with a vibrating saw. This has the advantage of being swift and relatively clean. The disadvantage is that the operator is blinded to what he may be cutting directly beneath the sternum (Dennis always used scissors on the tiny sternum of any patient who required reoperation). As his preferred classical music percolated in the background, Klein began to divide Kyle's sternum. Predictably, he cleanly transected both the sternum and the Goretex graft. This effectively opened Kyle's entire cardiac output into the operative field. Normally so verbose, Klein could only exclaim, "Oh, my!"

An oft-heard remark among surgeons defines bleeding as being visible, while hemorrhage is audible. If this is accurate, it was the first time I had witnessed hemorrhage. The chest was a geyser of blood, and all available suction couldn't keep the field clean enough to attempt a repair. In seconds Kyle's circulation was empty, and panicked efforts to place him on cardiopulmonary bypass, the "heart-lung machine," were futile: there was nothing to circulate.

Kyle was gone.

Klein was in a state of shock: a stunned, glazed look settled over his eyes as his glance traveled from face to face in the suddenly oppressively hot operating room.

"I couldn't do anything else, could I?" he pleaded to the room. "What else could I have done?"

Individually, he asked that question of every physician and nurse in the operating room.

By the door hung a plaque which Dr. Dennis had brought into the OR months before. It was a print of one of his favorite mottoes, and read simply: "Don't Do Nothin' Dumb."

6

The Second Year—
Plastic People

PROBABLY THE MOST ENTERTAINING ROTATION of my second year in
residency was the six-week stint on Plastic Surgery. The operations were
interesting and certainly very different from anything I'd seen in General
Surgery, and the patients were generally younger and not very sick,
meaning there was less of the constant worrying which I did on other
services. Plus the nighttime call—taken, by the way, from home (a
tremendous boon)—was typically quiet. So the rotation was relatively
laid-back, even restful.

The term "plastic surgery" is, I think, misunderstood by most of the
general public. Most people think of plastic surgery in the Hollywood
sense: the celebrity cosmetic procedures and "nips and tucks" that we
read about in the pages of *People* magazine. But, although these people
themselves may be plastic, that's not what the word refers to. The
"plastic" in plastic surgery specifically refers to reconstruction; it's a
word derived from ancient Greek. For example, when a cardiologist (a
species bearing no resemblance to a Plastic Surgeon except with regard
to bank account) expands a tiny balloon inside the arteries that feed the
heart, this is called an angio-*plasty*, a reconstruction of a blood vessel.

The point is that plastic surgery involves much more, at least in its
purest sense, than just cosmetic procedures like "nose jobs" and "tummy
tucks." For example, at most academic centers, at least, the plastic
surgeons are charged with the care of burn patients—from the mildly to
the severely injured.

43

The burn unit was a place I particularly hated. Taking care of the burns was the one part of the plastics rotation I despised. The odor of the unit was the worst. Even now, thinking back on it, it's as if I can still smell the sweet, sickly stench of the burn dressings. And when a fresh victim arrived, the whole unit smelled exactly like an Outback steakhouse. A few weeks on a ward like that would be just about enough to make a person a vegetarian. In fact, several of the burn nurses *were* vegetarians, although I never asked them if that was because their patients had a tendency to smell like a well-done Porterhouse. I had nothing but the highest regard for the burn nurses, who were a separate group distinct from the other floor nurses. They spent their whole time tending to these patients, and never seemed to let it get them down. Interestingly, they almost all were young and attractive—and engaged to surgery residents.

I wasn't on call the night Mike McConnell came in through the emergency department, so I didn't encounter him until he'd already been in the burn unit for a few hours. Still, I'll never forget the smell that positively assaulted my nostrils when I passed through the automatic doors and into the unit that next morning. Mingled odors of gasoline and seared flesh permeated the place. What had happened was McConnell had crashed his car while drunk. The car had rolled over into a ditch and caught fire. Strapped into his seat, he stayed unconscious either from smoke inhalation or the impact of the crash throughout the ensuing car fire. Responding rapidly, the emergency personnel had doused the flames and extricated the unconscious McConnell from the scorched wreck of his car. Realizing the severity of his burns they had immediately summoned a helicopter to transport him to our hospital, where he had arrived in the pre-dawn hours.

At this point, the patient was on a ventilator, completely unconscious from intravenous sedatives—and, judging by his appearance, this was a good thing, too. Both arms, both legs and his trunk were badly burned; his face somehow was spared. There is a term which those not in the medical profession rarely hear: "fourth-degree burn." First- and second-degree burns are called "partial-thickness burns;" some or all of the underlying basal tissue, the dermis, remains intact and viable. Skin can spontaneously regenerate at sites that have suffered partial-thickness burns. In third-degree or "full-thickness" burns, the dermis is also destroyed, and skin will not grow back over these areas—they normally require skin grafting. In so-called fourth-degree burns, the skin, fat and muscle have all been completely destroyed and the bone itself is charred.

McConnell had fourth degree burns of both his legs. The feet were literally gone—no sign of them at all—they must have either been vaporized or were still back in his car. His legs now began about mid-calf, but there was no soft tissue here, either. The muscle and fat had all been broiled away, and only blackened bone remained. His knees still had some tissue on them, but what was there looked like charcoal. The thighs were covered with full-thickness burns, but at least the muscle was still alive. There was no choice, though. The legs would have to be amputated in a surgical fashion, above the knee. And right away, too: if McConnell was to survive (which was not especially likely, based on his injuries) the dead tissue would need to be removed before it became infected. Infection in burn patients is frequently catastrophic. We took McConnell to the operating room that morning and performed above-the-knee amputations on both legs.

When we got back to the unit I noticed that the thick, dense burn scars on his arms were circumferential—they went all the way around the limb. Now one of the unique features of serious burn victims is that their capillaries (the tiny blood vessels which bridge the arterial and venous branches of the circulation) become tremendously leaky. This means that you have to pump literally gallons of fluid into their circulation just to maintain an adequate blood pressure, because much of this fluid leaks through the capillaries and into the surrounding tissues. If the tough, leathery burn scar (called "eschar") completely surrounds, say, an arm, the tissues cannot expand as they normally would with the extra fluid in them. The pressure within the tissues in that arm then can become so great as to block off the blood flow. At this point the arm which has survived the burn may die from the resultant "compartment syndrome"—strangled to death by the burn eschar.

This is what seemed to be happening to McConnell. He had lost the pulses in both his wrists.

The solution to the problem was "escharotomy," an operation in which the burn scar is split open in order to decrease the pressure in the expanding, underlying tissue and prevent the possibility of blood flow compromise.

Having just gotten the patient back from the OR, we got set up to do an escharotomy at the bedside.

Several trips back to the operating suite eventually netted me the necessary equipment: sterile drapes, gowns and gloves, lots of sponges, and a Bovie electrocautery device. Making sure that the patient was adequately anesthetized (he was on a constant sedative IV infusion, but, just to be sure, I had the anesthesiologists come by to help—if McConnell were awake, what I was about to do would be painful beyond comprehension), I prepared to start. One of the burn nurses, an impossibly perky (given her job) twenty-something, had volunteered to assist.

The Bovie device has two primary modes of operation, which depend on the characteristics of the high-frequency electrical energy which the system directs. In the "cut" mode the Bovie is supposed to simply divide tissue, provoking the same results as a knife. In the "coag" mode, on the other hand, the device is supposed to cauterize any tissue it comes into contact with. As the energy is dispersed, the tissue may be divided as well. Special controls allow the surgeon to mix the two modes.

Now a fair number of surgeons would have done this escharotomy with just a knife, which is defensible. But this procedure can be extremely bloody, given the inflamed nature of the tissue underlying the full-thickness burn. I was hoping to avoid some of this blood loss by using the Bovie on "coag."

The problem was that the eschar was too thick. The Bovie wouldn't penetrate it, at least on "coag." It just sat on the burned surface and kept cooking, raising slate-grey trails of foul smoke. Reluctantly, I set the device to "cut" and began dividing the thick, waxy eschar. I cut two long lines on either side of each arm, then similar ones on the chest, which looked like it was getting tight, too. The bleeding was profuse, and soaked through many gauze sponges. The nurse kept chatting away idly as we proceeded. It turned out she was engaged to one of the hard-boiled-egg-dude Ortho residents I'd known back at Riverside. I absentmindedly mentioned that he seemed like a good guy. You'd have thought we were exchanging pleasantries over paté at some God-forsaken country club.

I guess you can get used to anything.

Although within a few hours he had suffered a grievous injury, and had been subjected to two major procedures in an effort to salvage his life and some reasonable quality of that life, John McConnell had one tremendously important factor on his side. He had been a young, healthy person to start off with, only in his early 20s. This would prove to be of vital importance in both these early battles for survival and the many others down the road.

Over the next months, after I switched rotations, I continued to follow the case peripherally. McConnell eventually had to have both his hands amputated. He had what seemed like dozens of skin grafts performed. The plastic surgeons really only had a few places to harvest from: mainly the back. What they did was graft as many areas as they could with the limited supply of normal skin they had, then wait until the skin had grown back at the previous donor sites and harvest it again. Of course this took a long time. On several occasions John developed near-fatal system-wide infections, but he always recovered. He seemed to have nine lives.

After his condition had stabilized to the point where he could be taken off the ventilator, I sat down and talked with John. With his arms gone at mid-forearm and legs gone at mid-thigh, I expected him to be both morose and helpless. I was wrong on both accounts. The physical and occupational therapists—faced, I imagine, with the ultimate challenge in their profession: the salvaging of a functional daily existence for a young person traumatically and profoundly disabled—had persevered and ultimately worked wonders. It had taken months of the most frustrating, painful kind of effort imaginable, but now he could move around almost without assistance and, with the aid of some special prosthetic devices he had been given, perform many of the ordinary "activities of daily living." McConnell had no memory of the accident (I didn't ask him about it; he volunteered this) but mentioned that he wouldn't have been surprised if he'd been drunk. He said that he was sure he had been an alcoholic, and he was glad to be free from that now. He was surprisingly, even stunningly upbeat.

John's family was uncompromisingly supportive throughout the whole ordeal, and I'm sure that that played a large role in his recovery. From that first, horrific morning they had stood by him; never accepting defeat, never even acknowledging the tragedy. They had been dealt the cards, and they would play them. From the example of the McConnells and some other families I have dealt with, I can say without reservation that the people of the rural Midwest are the strongest I have ever encountered.

It's a delight for me to report that the next spring, approximately nine months after he was admitted with burn injuries that appeared almost certainly fatal, John McConnell left the Medical Center for a rehab hospital. As he was being wheeled out the front door, all of his family, every single one of the burn nurses (on- and off-duty) and nearly all of the surgery residents lined the last hallway. As John passed, we let out a tremendous cheer. Tears were streaming down his cheeks, but John was smiling.

Naturally, most of the major burn cases did not end so happily. During residency I heard a rule of thumb about serious burns which I quickly adopted and which has proven to be almost perfectly accurate. This rule states that the chance of a patient dying from a full-thickness burn is equal to the sum of their age and the percentage of body surface area that has been burned. Thus a 70 year-old with a 30% surface-area full-thickness burn is almost certain to die from the injury (30% of the total body surface area is about the same as the entire front of the trunk, plus one whole arm—in other words, a very substantial amount of personal real estate to be subjected to burn injury).

Thankfully, not all of the plastic surgery service was devoted to the burn patients. In reality, the bulk of the service was composed of much less dramatic patient care, and much more intriguing reconstructive procedures. As with the other surgery services, the patients who came to be treated by the Plastics people appeared either by inpatient consultation, or by referral to the outpatient clinic.

The plastic surgery clinic could be exceptionally entertaining. On the days when we knew that the cosmetic cases were coming in for preoperative evaluation, the number of residents—male residents, that is—that showed up for clinic was amazing. If it was a burn clinic, you might have trouble rustling up one or two residents—they always had something else to do, it seemed; but if there were going to be breast augmentation patients in the clinic, it was amazing how efficiently the floor work got done and how swiftly the boys made it to the office!

While most of the patients who came in for augmentation counseling and evaluation were just regular women—that is with nothing professional to gain from the operation—quite a few were strippers and "exotic dancers," whatever that means. These, of course, were the ones that the guys would get in line (and elbow each other out of the way) to interview. Some of these girls were rather well-endowed to begin with, but even those who weren't were usually pretty hot numbers, and they all dressed in the least amount that the weather would allow. So the guys jumped at the chance to examine them. After all, these girls basically took off their clothes as soon as you got them in the examining room! Unfortunately, the head of the Plastics Division picked up on our ogling and promulgated a rule forbidding male surgery residents from examining the breast augmentation patients. We argued that this was an important part of our surgical education but, of course, it was a losing battle. There's always somebody to come along and spoil the fun, isn't there?

A lot of the breast reconstruction patients had undergone mastectomies for cancer, of course, and their plight was very different from the augmentation patients. The disfigurement from mastectomy is obviously considerable, and given our society's bizarre focus on the female breast (exemplified perfectly by the lining up of male residents to examine the strippers), the anguish of the alteration in body image is no doubt profound. Most of the time, these women could opt either for immediate reconstruction at the time of their mastectomy or wait a few weeks or months. The plastic surgeons could construct breasts from either the patient's own abdominal muscles or from saline implants. Either way, the results were usually acceptable and sometimes fabulous. When she is clothed, there is usually no way to tell that a woman who has undergone mastectomy and reconstruction has ever had surgery at all.

There was a fairly steady stream of referrals to the Plastic Surgery Service from the general surgeons who performed surgery for obesity. The fact was that, much of the time, the results of the Roux-en-Y gastric bypass operation were rapid and significant—even spectacular. It was not unusual for a patient to lose one hundred pounds in a year (although there was a tendency for the weight to plateau at a level still above the ideal figure). One frequent consequence of this profound weight loss was a rather extreme excess of skin, usually around the abdomen. Obviously, if a person has grown over the course of many years to a weight of 350 pounds or so, if they lose one-third of that weight in one year, they are going to have some extra flesh which used to be covering the now-missing fat. On the belly this excess tissue is called a "pannus," and it can be tremendously annoying to the patient. The pannus hangs over belts, rubs against itself until it gets raw, and is generally in the way. The plastic surgeons performed an operation, called "panniculectomy," in which this tissue was removed and the flesh of the abdomen stitched together in a more contoured fashion.

One day in the Plastics Clinic, when we were evaluating general reconstruction cases (no strippers, unfortunately), a familiar-looking fellow walked in. As he took his seat in the waiting room, I tried to place his face. After a few moments I realized, with a start, that it was Frank Colson, the Roux-en-Y patient who had made my very first call night (now twenty months ago) so memorable. He had lost at least 125 pounds and was, in fact, barely recognizable. When I approached him in the examining room, he seemed incredibly blasé about the whole thing: he barely remembered his NG misadventure (good thing, that) and—a blow to my ego—he scarcely recalled me at all. In fact he appeared depressed, which was a great surprise to me. I assumed that he would be ecstatic about the success of the procedure, as I was. Later I did some reading and found out that depression is not an uncommon sequel to this type of surgery, for reasons that are unclear.

Olson was in the Plastics Clinic to be considered for a panniculectomy. When he took off his shirt, I could see why. Great folds of dimpled, rolling skin hung from his waist, stretching down to the middle of his thighs. They looked like flesh-colored sails swinging limply on a windless day. When Colson lifted them, the undersurface was red and raw, glistening and inflamed. (Briefly I was reminded of another tremendously obese patient—one who had never had the bypass operation—who had developed recurring infections in the moist regions under her skinfolds. A home health nurse had said that one day, smelling something like rotting meat, she—the nurse—had lifted the folds and found part of an uneaten sandwich, which had apparently been lost in the flesh-folds for days.)

It was clear that Colson would benefit from a panniculectomy; he was at risk for developing a serious soft-tissue infection. Besides, the damned thing looked like hell. So we scheduled him for the OR.

I wish I could gracefully relate the details of the elegant procedure we performed on Mr. Colson, but, in fact, it was one of the more nauseating things I've been involved with. With a sterile magic marker in hand, the attending drew a series of lines on the man's abdomen: some dashed, some complete. They criss-crossed and subdivided one another, and soon enough Colson's belly looked like a work of early twentieth century abstract art. Then the attending and I began cutting along the webwork of El Marko lines, gouging out the pannus in such a way as to fashion a new, better-fitting fatty waist-jacket for our corpulent but much-reduced friend. Fat is greasy, of course—whether it's attached to a rib-eye or an accountant—and within a few minutes it was hard to grip anything firmly. Colson's pannus slipped through our fingers and flopped around on the table, as if it were capable of independent movement. For a while I imagined myself a nineteenth-century Nantucket whaler in the South Pacific, balanced on the back of a slain sperm and slicing off slabs of blubber to feed the lamps of Europe, the scent of ambergris in the salt air. The attending brought me back to reality with a mind-numbingly lengthy verbal travelogue of his family's multiple trips to the living-history park at Colonial Williamsburg. While the small talk passed the minutes, strips of pannus accumulated on the back table.

After removing the majority of the pannus, we brought the edges of Colson's abdomen together and began stitching it in place with many, many nylon sutures. Among the Williamsburg anecdotes, the attending showed me a clever way of placing something called a vertical mattress suture, which helps the skin edges to come together better. I knew an awkward way to place this stitch, but his was definitely slicker and I extricated myself from my mental foray into antebellum whaling long enough to thank him.

A couple of weeks later I saw Colson back in the clinic. His mental outlook was decidedly better (he was on an anti-depressant medication). It took more than a half-hour to remove all the nylon sutures—and I'm absolutely sure that I missed some, too. Hopefully they'd work themselves to the surface over time. Colson was healing well and certainly was delighted to have shed his pannus—even if the incisions did make him look like he'd been worked over by a mail-order meat-packing company.

7

Strange Problems

WHEN I FINALLY CATALOGUED ALL MY OPERATIVE CASES at the end of residency, the total number was greater than 1,000. The number of patients whom I had taken care of obviously far exceeded that. So, with such large figures, it should come as no surprise that nestled in amongst all the straightforward hernias and gall bladders there might be one or two cases which drifted toward, shall we say, the bizarre side. After all, not every surgical patient was a seventy-five-year-old grandmother. Some got caught with their pants down, one way or another.

While in San Francisco, before starting residency myself, I had heard a story (or was it a legend?) that I thought couldn't be topped. Anyone with any sense would question whether it actually occurred, but several of my resident friends there assured me that it did, and they would ordinarily be considered (by me, at least) to be reliable sources. According to them, one night on the graveyard shift in the ER at the San Francisco General Hospital, an ordinary-looking man in his twenties appeared, with a history of several days of constipation. Otherwise his story was unremarkable, at least as he initially related it. His abdominal x-rays looked suspicious for large bowel obstruction, but were especially notable for multiple, small circular densities apparent throughout the belly. No one could remember having seen anything quite like them. They numbered perhaps a dozen and were distributed evenly throughout the abdomen. One appeared to be present at the apparent level of the colonic obstruction. Was it some unusual presentation of cancer? Obstruction of the colon is usually due to this, but the man was so young. On the other hand, this was San Francisco, and one notable sexually-transmitted viral disease can certainly present in odd ways.

The ER docs thought it must just be constipation and gave the man an enema. The patient didn't respond to this, and it became apparent that he would require colonoscopy, probably for decompression. The flexible, fiber-optic scope was passed "from below," and the resident grew apprehensive as he advanced it, nearing the position of whatever it was that was causing the obstruction. Gradually something flesh-colored began to take shape within the colon, and by the bright fiber-optic light the resident could make out something small and round and vaguely familiar. Suddenly the scope slipped forward an inch and he was face to face with ... *Barbie*!

Actually, it was the disembodied (and shorn) head of a Barbie doll.

Upon further questioning the patient confessed to a most unusual habit. This guy liked to ingest these doll heads, wait however many hours it took for them to traverse his gastrointestinal tract, then masturbate as they emerged from his rectum. Hideous as that is to contemplate, it was just the tip of the stomach-turning iceberg. As any parent knows, Barbie dolls are far from inexpensive, and this fellow began to realize that his unique habit was starting to put a strain on his finances—buying all these Barbie dolls just to rip the heads off. So he decided to (gasp) recycle them! He did this by shaving their heads, following his previous pattern of autoeroticism, then retrieving the heads after they had, as it were, emerged. He would wash them off and begin the cycle over. Finding that he could time their passage relatively accurately, he would eat one of the heads every few hours, thus having several afloat in his gastrointestinal tract at any given time, eagerly awaiting their resurfacing. This was why all the circular densities were present on his belly films: they were all Barbies at various points along the track!

This story, which all the surgery residents in San Francisco swore was true, was obviously going to be tough to top in the relatively mundane metropolis of Columbus, Ohio. To the rescue, though, came the drunks and, especially, the prisoners.

The Ohio State University Medical Center had long since acquired the contract to provide medical care for all the prisoners in the state penal system. Those sick enough to require inpatient hospitalization occupied a wing on one floor of the University Hospital, and since the attendings had essentially no incentive, financial or otherwise, to see them, these patients were taken care of almost entirely by the residents.

These prisoners were a patient population unlike any other. They were afflicted with a variety of ills associated with their backgrounds and institutionalization which even experienced, practicing physicians rarely encountered. This, I suppose, was a plus for the residents from an educational standpoint. However, they also had extremely high rates of the more fearsome communicable diseases like TB, hepatitis and AIDS, and this made us correspondingly reluctant to get too terribly close to them. Plus, they were prisoners, after all. While we tried to be idealistic and treat everyone alike, the fact always lurked in the back of our minds that these people were serious criminals: murderers, rapists and the like (one was said to have killed several people by stomping on their heads). Having said this, I should note that they were always on their best behavior with the doctors. They were astoundingly polite and deferential for the most part, probably because we had it within our power to send them back to the slammer whenever we wished (or at least they thought we had that power). No matter how bad off they were at the hospital, it was better than in the lockup.

One "frequent flyer" prisoner who gave most of the surgery residents fits at one time or another (and helped make the problems of patients in our humble Midwestern town seem not too far removed from those of the big, cosmopolitan City by the Bay) was Frank Reed. Frank was either nuts or, just as likely, trying to pass himself off as being so. The first time you got called to see him you tended to be a believer. Frank would appear in the prison unit of the ER every few weeks or so, shouting and flailing about, with some sort of foreign object shoved up his penis. This all began with small objects like toothpicks and paper clips. Eventually he graduated to pencils and even forks. Of course the sight of a large male prisoner dressed in a fluorescent orange jumpsuit with a gleaming faux-silver fork stuck up his penis was a memorable one, to say the least. The first time I laid eyes on him I was aghast (this time it was a pencil). I was the intern on the urology service and had never seen anything approaching this before. Certain that Reed would require complex urologic surgery—and probably extensive reconstruction—to repair his trauma-tized urethra, I telephoned the senior urology resident and informed him of my grisly ER discovery. At first the resident seemed appropriately concerned, questioning me in detail about the nature of the injury, but then his voice suddenly took on a skeptical monotone, "Hey, wait a second," he said. "Is this guy a prisoner?"

"Yeah, he is," I replied innocently, wondering how the resident knew this.

"Aw, shit, that's Frank Reed. That fucker's in here with something or other shoved up his dick at least once a month. Just pull it out and send him back to the slammer."

"Are you sure?" I answered. "It looks like he could have a urethral tear."

"Look, Miller, that guy's urethra is tougher than shoe leather. He's been sticking things in it since you were in diapers. If he ain't bleeding buckets, get him out of there."

It took a few minutes, but I eventually worked up the nerve to go in Reed's room and extract the pencil. I didn't even need to sedate him (I thought I might need to revive the guard, though). Although he didn't show up again while I was on service, his frequent trips to the emergency department kept the Urology residents busy during my entire period of training.

Although Reed with his penile-abuse preoccupation was unique in my experience, he did have many kindred spirits amongst a different group of prisoners, although their choice of orifice of insertion was different. This gang was collectively known (to the surgery residents, anyway) as "The Swallowers."

For some reason, there is a subpopulation in the prison system which believes that swallowing foreign objects is a good idea. These guys (I never encountered a woman who did this, and we treated the female prisoners, too) did not have the same ulterior motive that the San Francisco "doll collector" had, though. The motivation of these swallowers was much less clear. I should stress that these guys came from different prisons and, as far as I know, had never even heard of each other—though I acknowledge that the grapevine may extend beyond barbed-wire. In any case, the objects they swallowed were pretty consistent. Bed springs were a favorite, as were ball-point pens, paper clips and even the temple-pieces from eyeglasses.

The party line was that these prisoners enjoyed the treatment they got in the University Hospital, and so they were willing to endure both the pain of swallowing indigestible parts of their surroundings and that of abdominal surgery, just for a few weeks out of the hoosegow. I never bought into this, though. For one thing, we not only didn't operate on all of them (only the ones who developed bowel obstruction or perforation really needed surgery—the rest would usually pass the objects in time), we didn't even admit them all to the hospital. If we felt safe in the belief that the object or objects would pass along uneventfully, we just sent the prisoner to the Correctional Medical Facility a few miles down the road. No prisoner wanted to be there: at the Facility they had to sleep four in a room, with little activity time and one small black-and-white TV on the ceiling; far less appealing than the cell back at prison. Back at the big house they could at least watch Jerry Springer if they wanted (the guards at the Medical Facility knew the prisoners loved that show and, having the controllers, would occasionally put *I Love Lucy* reruns on instead).

No; I thought the swallowers were crazy, like Reed. They weren't looking for some easy time in the infirmary (it wasn't counted toward their sentence, anyway). Their only plan was to chow down on the nearest mouth-watering Papermate or make a quick evening snack out of a twist of bedspring. Those guys were nuts, plain and simple.

One of the repeat-offender swallowers was Marty Willets, a skinny, 40ish felon with an alarmingly low "teeth-to-tattoo ratio" (this was one of our of seat-of-the-pants ways of measuring patients' IQs: if the number of tattoos exceeded the number of intact teeth, the likelihood of much native intelligence was decidedly low). I'm not sure Willets ever actually spent time at his assigned prison: he was always either in the Correctional Medical Facility, an inpatient at the University Hospital, or in our ER. Like most of his peers, he started small: paper clips, ballpoint pen caps and the like. He was pulling this sort of crap when I was an intern. By the time I was the senior (fourth-year) resident on the prison service he had definitely elevated his game. Late one evening I was called to see Willets in the Emergency Department. He was writhing on the gurney in apparent pain, clutching at his belly and doubled up, knees-to-chest. Although he seemed to have no recollection of me, I was acutely aware of who he was (and was especially pissed off that this self-abusing lunatic was now cutting into my valuable sack time).

Without bothering to talk to Willets (he was barely coherent on his best days), I found the ER resident, who showed me the abdominal x-rays which had been taken. There didn't seem to be any perforation, which was encouraging. There were, however, the expected silhouettes of a number of household and not-so-household items on the films. Sure enough, there were the usual suspects: chunks of bedsprings, a folded-up ball-point pen, a piece of a pair of glasses, lots of coins. One unusual finding was a razor-blade, which looked to be caught up in the stomach. The only other difference between this presentation and the many other swallower soirees was that the number of objects was considerably greater than normal—this time there were literally dozens of things. Many of them had begun their slithery passage through Willet's intestines, but a large number were stuck, like the razor-blade, in the stomach. It was my immediate thought that he couldn't have swallowed all this stuff in a short period of time; he had to have been accumulating all these objects over days or weeks, until he'd finally exceeded the ability of his stomach to simply pass these metal pieces through. Although the outlet of his stomach was not blocked by all the hardware, in this case it didn't seem likely that any of the foreign objects would themselves ever slip out.

After examining Willets and proving to myself that he didn't have any cause for immediate, emergency surgery I telephoned the attending.

"Dr. Burns? Hey, it's Craig. I'm seeing one of the swallowers down in the ER."

"Does he need to be admitted?"

"Yeah. Actually, I think we need to do him. He's got a ton of garbage in his stomach and I'm sure it's been sitting there for a while. No way it all gets past his pylorus (the muscular sphincter between the stomach and intestines)."

"All right then, let's pop the hood." (Burns was young—my age, in fact—and eager to do as many cases as possible. At first I was afraid that he'd want to sit on Willets and follow him with physical examinations and follow-up x-rays, but he was an easy sell on a good stomach case like this one.)

I called the OR front desk and scheduled the case. It took a few hours to get everything arranged, but soon we were in the operating room. While Burns scrubbed, I opened Willets' abdomen through a relatively small, upper-midline incision, then explored his belly. Burns poked his head in the door.

"Watch out, Miller. It's easy to stick yourself on one of those bedsprings or that goddamn razor-blade, right through the gut wall. God knows what this idiot may have."

This was an excellent point, and I slowed my exploration to a crawl. We weren't planning on opening any intestine anyway: anything that had made it that far would most likely make it the rest of the way. I absentmindedly wondered what it would be like to shit out a broken bedspring.

Burns joined in and we completed our exploration. We found the pieces in the small bowel—from the outside—just where the x-rays had shown them to be. As per our plan, we ignored them. Instead we addressed the stomach. I put two stitches through the thick muscular wall about an inch apart, not cutting the suture material but leaving the long threads intact. These would serve as handles when we opened the stomach itself. With the cautery device I made an incision in the wall of the stomach, which bled vigorously (the blood supply to the stomach is considerable, and derives from several different arteries). In a few seconds I had stopped the bleeding with the cautery and was through the wall completely. Thick yellow bile bubbled up out of the hole in the stomach wall. Using the suture-handles, I opened up the stomach while Burns inserted a long, ring-tipped forceps inside, trying to find the stuff Willets had swallowed. On the first pass he pulled up the temple-piece from a pair of eyeglasses. Amazingly, it had been ingested whole, although I noticed that it had been pried loose from its armature rather than detached by the tiny screw. I guess Willets hadn't had access to any tools which might have aided him in his efforts to break down the metallic components of his environment into more easily edible fragments. If he had had such access, of course, it would be easy to picture him detaching the temple-piece from his cellmate's glasses with a tiny jeweler's screwdriver, then swallowing the instrument itself.

Burns kept diving with his forceps into the stomach, which was flabby and elongated and extended so deep that it seemed to be attached to Willets' backbone. After the first few successful forays, which yielded a few pennies, some bedspring fragments and the folded-over ball-point pen I had seen on the ER X-rays, the pickings got slim. Multiple blind stomach-spelunkings brought forth no further gulped pay-dirt. But the amount of gastric alloy we had mined was still far less than that which had appeared on the abdominal films. Where the hell was the stuff hiding? We debated passing a fiber-optic scope down Willets' throat to visualize the parts of his stomach which we were blindly exploring with our too-crude instruments. This wasn't a bad idea—the stomach was spectacularly distended and patulous, and, having made the skin incision too short, we were now handcuffed—yet the only reason we abandoned it was the realization that word would quickly get out that Burns and Miller couldn't find something that was stuck in the stomach by simply opening the organ up and looking inside: they needed to add the high-tech endoscopic suspenders to the good old-fashioned surgery belt. We'd look like a couple of dolts (truthfully, Burns—the attending—would look worse than I did, but I'd be the one on the hot seat at Morbidity and Mortality Conference the next week).

The only solution was to reach down with a hand and probe the inside of the stomach manually.

Now this guy Willets was a prisoner, a convicted felon, and an apparent lunatic. The likelihood that he harbored some undiagnosed blood-borne disease was fairly high. And he had swallowed sharp metal objects—including the "goddamn razor-blade"—which we were con-templating removing by extending our barely-protected arms up to the elbows in his belly.

Looking back on it now, I realize it was stupid, but at the time I was still trying to impress people. Taking a deep breath, I thrust the index and ring fingers of my right hand into the hole in the stomach wall and started to feel around. Nothing. I pushed my whole arm down into the skin incision and probed with the right-hand fingers. I just couldn't reach the back of the stomach. With a muttered curse I grabbed the cautery device and extended the cut on the stomach wall (it needed to be repaired anyway, I reasoned, who gave a crap about a couple of extra stitches?) Soon I had my whole hand inside Willets' stomach. Sure enough, at about mid-forearm depth I found the mother lode of swallowing relics: everything we'd seen on the films came up from the depths of the prisoner's expanded stomach, including the razor-blade. I learned some-thing here, too; Willets may have been crazy, but he wasn't suicidal: the blade had been bent on itself so that it's silhouette on the X-ray was unmistakable (think "Wilkinson Sword") but no actual sharp edges projected out. Very clever.

In a few minutes we were closing.

We kept Willets in the hospital for five days after his exploratory surgery and hardware retrieval. The psychiatrists came by and recommended some medications, but their interest in swallowers was surprisingly limited.

I'm sure that Willets was insane, but after his discharge to the home penitentiary, I never saw him again, although I would return to the prison service for three more months as a Chief Resident the next year. I like to think that the experience of major gastric surgery soured him on the idea of swallowing indigestible objects, but it's just as likely that he took a well-placed shiv from another inmate and quietly bought the farm.

8

The O.R. Team

DR. MATT ARTHUR WAS A COLON AND RECTAL SURGEON on the University Hospital staff. He had a wickedly dry sense of humor which was sometimes difficult—challenging, that is—to appreciate, but he made one remark which has stuck with me over the years, an observation which requires very little mental digestion in order to comprehend it.

"Surgery is a ballet."

Although Dr. Arthur mainly used this aphorism to point out how un-Baryshnikov-like a given resident was in his operative skills, the analogy has other merit.

In essence, if an operation is performed by a coherent, effective team, it is usually performed well. If the chain that is the O.R. team has any weak links, they are exposed immediately, and the procedure becomes a tedious, frequently dangerous exercise. Many surgeons take for granted the presence of an efficient supporting cast and suffer tremendously when, for whatever reason, it is absent. Who makes up this important team?

In the operating room the surgeon is in command, the "captain of the ship" as a lot of the old-timers still say. It is the surgeon's legal and ethical responsibility to care for the patient, and his orders are ordinarily (and appropriately) followed without question. The surgeon may have assistants—usually residents or students—with him. The residents may exercise the surgeon's authority by proxy when he isn't physically present, but this is shaky ground and some nurses either ignore or pay little attention to what a resident says in the operating room.

In many cases the most important member of the surgical team isn't even a surgeon, however. He's a "gas-passer."

Anesthesiologists function like multi-skilled internists in the O.R. They protect the patient's airway, monitor heart rate, blood pressure and the other vital signs, and are responsible for essentially every aspect of the patient's care that doesn't directly relate to the operative procedure during surgery. If the surgeon is the captain, the anesthesiologist is the first mate, and his opinion is every bit as valuable in the heat of battle. At a university hospital the anesthesiologists have residents, too, and they require about as much clinical supervision (and freedom, too) as surgery residents, I imagine. It's probably worthwhile to point out that different types of professionals provide anesthesia. All the descriptive words sound the same, but their meaning is different. In a broad sense, an "anesthetist" is anyone who provides anesthesia—a doctor, a nurse or a technician, while an "anesthesiologist" is a medical doctor who is providing the service. Most anesthesiologists will bristle if called anesthetists—sort of like calling an electrical engineer an electrician, I suppose. Some people get upset by the implications of words.

The actual job of anesthesiology strikes me as being similar to front-line military service during wartime: long periods of tedious inactivity punctuated by moments of sheer terror. Most of the time, surgery proceeds uneventfully: the patient is put to sleep, the operation is performed smoothly, the patient awakens. Things can get so routine that a lot of anesthesiologists bring newspapers into the O.R. to read. Some even have been known to fall asleep themselves during the case. When the operation goes well and the patient is otherwise healthy, almost anyone can do the anesthesia. It's when things go bad that a good anesthesiologist can make the difference.

Dr. Tim O'Rourke was my personal favorite among the attending anesthesiologists. He had a commanding presence that even few of the attending surgeons possessed; you got the comforting sense when he was around that no matter what might happen, he had seen it before and would know what to do. O'Rourke was in his fifties, of average height and weight, and had a vigorous, ruddy complexion. He sported a salt-and-pepper beard and moustache to go with his full head of hair, but in the classic Greek configuration that you rarely see outside of a museum these days. O'Rourke had a reputation as a stout drinker—which got him into trouble—and I have no reason to doubt it, but he was both an enormously entertaining and extremely effective educator in the fields of anesthesia and critical care. When he said something, you tended to pay attention. If you didn't, chances are you'd find cause to regret the decision soon enough.

Since I wasn't an anesthesiology resident (saints be praised), I didn't get a chance to get the full O'Rourke gas-passing tutorial experience, except during the times when he happened to be holding forth at the head of the table when I was operating. At those times, of course, I was spending so much time focusing on what I was doing that I didn't really pay much attention to the anesthesiologists (unless they were screwing up). But I got a very solid dose of O'Rourke while I was on the ICU rotation, because he did double duty as a critical care specialist (as it happens, he was actually doing fiscal triple-duty at the time, because he had somehow [allegedly] attained the private ownership—and then made a cottage industry of leasing—all the mechanical ventilators in the hospital!). As an intensive care attending, O'Rourke always seemed to be hitting on all cylinders.

We would begin rounds with O'Rourke after he had begun his morning cases and left his anesthesia residents to their own devices (of course, we had made residents-only rounds hours before). O'Rourke always showed up with a styrofoam cup of coffee in his hand, dressed in blue scrubs. He would begin by asking which patients were the sickest, then insisting that he be taken to their bedside first. This, of course, is sound and sensible practice—looking at the most ill first—but it turned out that Dr. O'Rourke had another motivation. About halfway through our first rounds (which were on a Saturday morning) O'Rourke stopped, looked at his watch, and announced, "All right, that's been an hour. Rounds are over. That's my limit. I've got some yard work to do...."

Then he simply walked away. He was done. Mouths agape, we residents stood staring at each other. Quickly we learned to be concise in our rounding, at least if we wanted O'Rourke's input!

While he was still there, O'Rourke was an invaluable source of practical knowledge. He taught me so many pearls of surgical critical care that I have a hard time now identifying which bits of my current ICU knowledge were not his originally. But he also had some hilarious faults....

O'Rourke had a weakness, as many academic physicians do, for quoting—or at least citing—the medical literature at almost any opportunity. Granted, this is sometimes appropriate, as when an ill-informed internist recommends against surgery when the published data proves it to be the best option. But more often citation of the literature is used in a chest-thumping fashion, not to broaden anyone's horizon, but to broadcast the citer's self-perceived superiority. I'm honestly not sure what Tim O'Rourke's motivation was, but he was an incessant citer.

O'Rourke would refer to at least one published paper, and frequently several, for each patient we rounded on. He seemed to have an inexhaustible command of the critical care literature at his fingertips, and it was most impressive. After a few weeks on his service, though, I began to notice something a little odd about O'Rourke's references to the medical literature. They started to sound a little "samey."

It seemed like an awful lot of the papers he cited had come from one particular medical center in Colorado. Now I knew that there were some fine hospitals and critical care centers in the Rockies, but O'Rourke made it sound as if every third paper of significance in the rarefied world of intensive care medicine had come from there.

The other suspicious thing was O'Rourke's ability to recall the exact issue of the journal which the article he was citing had appeared in. As we discussed a patient, he'd remark, "In the January, 1977 issue of the *Journal of Critical Care*, Bill Johnson's group from Colorado Tech talked about just this problem. Their findings were...."

Now only a few, really epoch-making papers make that sort of impact on one's memory—like Watson and Crick's discovery of the structure of DNA. There are just so many articles in so many issues of so many journals that eventually they become smeared in one's memory—but not, apparently, in O'Rourke's. I was getting suspicious enough that I decided to enlist an unwitting accomplice in my effort to unearth the truth and, in so doing, unseat the king. I asked one of the medical students on the service to write down every reference to a paper that O'Rourke made during rounds. I couldn't do this myself without drawing attention to the effort, but the med student possessed the proper combination of proximity (he could hear what was being said) and anonymity (O'Rourke definitely had no idea who he was and couldn't have cared less what he was doing).

So on the next attending rounds my stooge began taking notes. He had no idea what I was up to—as far as he knew, he was collecting references to look up, for the whole team then to review. O'Rourke performed up to his usual standards, and the citations began to fly.

"Blah blah blah, *American Journal of Surgery*, August, 1987. Blah blah blah, *Trauma and Critical Care*, January, 1991. Blah blah blah, *New England Journal*, April, 1976...."

The stooge was jotting down rapidly, like some untrained court stenographer. At the end of rounds he handed me a list of about twenty citations. He asked me if I wanted him to go to the library to get copies of the articles. Knowing what the results of such an effort would be, I declined. Even though I only wanted to prove something to myself (and maybe a few others), there was no need to leave a trail.

Later that day I crossed the street to the medical library and looked up the references. It was what the baseball fans would call an "O-fer." Not a single citation was correct. Wanting to be generous, I even gave a considerable benefit of the doubt and looked in other journals, other months, under other author's names. It was just all total bullshit. Actually, everything he said was correct—he knew the proper things to do, as supported by the medical literature—but he had absolutely no accurate recollection of where the information had originally come from.

I never did broadcast my findings about Dr. O'Rourke's references (beyond some oblique depictions to a few close friends) because I really did like and respect him. More importantly, he was clinically very good, and both cared for patients and taught the residents how to care for patients so well that I couldn't hold it against him when he got a little carried away and began misquoting. In a way, though, the whole remainder of that rotation was a challenge. The temptation was very strong to interrupt a O'Rourke soliloquy with a remark like: "Didn't Bill Johnson's group in Colorado Springs demonstrate that back in the May, 1882 issue of *Frontier Critical Care*?"

The Scrub Nurse is the individual who passes the instruments to the surgeon. As the name implies, this member of the team wears the sterile garb and is part of the actual operative group, although he or she is usually not permitted to actually perform any aspect of the operation which could be defined as surgery. Although the duties I've described sound simple enough, there are literally hundreds of different surgical instruments and they all have their own names. A lot have been named for their surgeon-creators: "Kelly clamp," "Metzenbaum scissors" and so forth. The scrub has to know them all, be prepared as to when they might be needed, and deliver them to the surgeon in precisely the right way at exactly the time that they are needed (which, by the way, may not be the time that they are asked for). A good scrub nurse can be the key to a successful surgery with rapid, efficient provision of instruments—the best ones know the sequence of an operation as well as the attending and anticipate the surgeon's needs. Conversely, a lousy scrub can hamstring the most gifted operator.

At Ohio State we were training nurses as well as doctors, so many operations were performed with scrub nurses who were inexperienced novices. Sometimes they would be supervised by a scrubbed preceptor who shadowed and guided them through the case.

A few of the surgeons had their own personal scrub nurses. How this was arranged involved politics far above my head, but the dividends could be substantial. Obviously, a scrub and a surgeon who've been doing the same operations together for years could develop a highly efficient interaction. Dr. Atcheson had his own, at least for most cases. So did Dr. Treves, the head of vascular surgery. Student nurses rarely, if ever, scrubbed on these guys' operations. There were plenty of other opportunities for them to learn what to do and Treves and Atcheson tended to do mainly big cases anyway, where a rookie scrub nurse might even put the patient's life at risk.

The most memorable scrub nurse I ever encountered, though, was Maile Ota. She was the vascular surgery head nurse at the Medical Center of the University of California in San Francisco, where I did my fellowship immediately after finishing residency. Maile had held her position for something close to forty years, and had been the personal scrub nurse of one of the really towering figures in twentieth century surgery, Dr. Jack Wylie. Dr. Wylie had been one of the pioneers of vascular surgery in the 1950s and 60s, and Maile had been right there with him, literally helping to develop the instruments and techniques that were needed for the new field, and even many of the procedures themselves. After Wylie's death in the early 1980s most had expected her to retire, but she had continued in her role as vascular scrub nurse while his successors, prominent surgeons in their own right, carried on the work. I suppose Maile must have been close to seventy at the time I knew her, but she was still going strong. Although she enjoyed a good laugh, Maile was tough as nails; when she walked through that hospital door, she became completely focused on one thing: the efficient running of the vascular operating room.

Because of her tremendous experience, Maile was a great resource. One fellow surgeon told me, "If Maile hands you an instrument you didn't ask for, try to figure out what you're supposed to do with it, because she's right...." At the time I thought he must be kidding to make a point, but a few weeks later that actual scenario transpired: there I was, staring at an instrument I not only hadn't asked for but had never seen before. Maile must have seen my look of confusion, because she leaned over and whispered into my ear what I was supposed to do. (I was awfully lucky that Maile seemed to like me; the Division Chief never noticed my hesitation).

Beyond this, though, Maile could provide even more really useful information; in forty years of scrubbing on the most complex and involved vascular surgery operations there were, she had seen essentially everything. Since we continued to have cases of this sort referred to us in San Francisco, hers could be a very valuable opinion. Although Maile was tactful enough never to offer advice (some of those vascular surgeon types are headstrong and confident), many's the time when even that Division Chief—an extremely self-reliant individual, to say the least— would ask her advice in the O.R.

The last member of the intrinsic O.R. team is the Circulating Nurse. Unlike the scrub, who may be a trained technician, the "circ" is nearly always an R.N. The duties of the job—which include measuring drug dosages and checking the ABO type of blood products to be given— pretty much demand this. The circulator's function is to provide the surgical team with whatever they need—whatever is not already available to them on the sterile field, that is—in order to proceed with the operation. This may be suture material, medications, instruments, etc. Circulators also spend a lot of time on the telephone, sometimes for legitimate reasons. Perhaps their greatest power and importance comes from the fact that they have the final say over what sort of music gets played in the O.R.

Some surgeons don't like to have any music playing; they feel that it's a distraction and they want to concentrate (as well as have others concentrate) on the work at hand. Others bring their own tapes or CDs to the O.R., and these can range from Mozart to Metallica. Most surgeons just have the circulator dial in a radio station with a format that fits their tastes. Early in my training I disliked hearing music during surgery: since I was a former guitarist, it was nearly impossible for me to have music playing without *listening* to it. I would be continually, consciously analyzing the harmonies, chord progressions, meter and so forth, as I had for years. It was only later in residency that I became fully acclimated to the idea of music-as-wallpaper. Of course in my early years of training I was at the mercy of others with regard to the presence or choice of music in the operating rooms; if the attending wanted to listen to some top-forty drek, there wasn't much I could do to avoid it. It was from this experience that I learned to drown out or, really, just ignore the ambient radio garbage during surgery. Nowadays I find that I'm able to appreciate the music and focus on the operation at the same time. It's just another form of walking and chewing gum at the same time, I suppose.

In any event, it's the circulator who ultimately decides what music will play in the operating room. After all, everyone else (except the anesthetist) is scrubbed and sterile. I have never seen a circ nurse overrule an attending's choice and play his or her own musical selection instead, but the potential for such a tuneful coup d'état always exists!

Another important role of the circulator, and one they generally despise, is to answer the pages that the members of the operative team may receive while they are scrubbed. Most circs hate to do this because they start to feel like secretaries after answering more than a couple beeps. Since the general surgery residents were *constantly* getting paged, the circulators often spent much of the case answering calls from the floor, the ER, the radiology department, etc. This was one reason why they were on the phone all the time. Still, although the task was odious, it was vital. In amongst ten or fifteen silly pages for minor questions, a genuinely life-threatening issue might appear that needed immediate attention. Thankfully this only happened rarely, but it was another good reason to have a qualified nurse as the circulator: she could sometimes sift through the piles of information coming from the other end of the phone well enough to identify if a situation was serious and needed the personal attention of the resident or attending.

Of course, as a general rule it's a good idea to stay on the good side of everyone you meet if you happen to be a surgery resident: there's no telling who might turn out to have some power or authority over you, and absolutely anyone can write a letter to your boss that gets you in hot water. It's especially wise to avoid infuriating any nurses, anywhere. They have a near-infinite memory capacity, which may be exceeded only by their tendency toward vindictiveness. A resident with the somewhat odd name of Bubo Shih forgot this rule, and paid the price.

Shih was a corpulent, grinning plastic surgery intern with tiny, rat-like eyes hidden behind thick spectacles. These wire-rimmed eyeglasses were perched precariously atop a tremendous, hooked nose that seemed to be making a sincere effort to touch the topmost of Shih's several chins. Although he laughed a lot and could tell an amusing story, he had a dark streak that extended to personal betrayal when it served his immediate needs. He was a mediocre physician at best and achieved the lowest score on the surgery in-training exam that had ever been recorded at Ohio State. Dr. Atcheson would have fired him, but he was on the Plastic Surgery track and he considered Shih pretty much their problem. I always hated having to sign patients out to him, because you never knew what kind of foolish decisions he'd make. One particularly poor choice he made—not in the field of patient care—was to raise the ire of a certain cardiothoracic OR nurse. He managed to do this, while still a lowly intern, by falling prey to the temptation to lord his (questionably) superior education and intelligence over her while closing the leg incision during a coronary bypass graft operation (some of these grafts are fashioned from leg veins). He must have succumbed to a moment of anger, because he normally was sufficiently motivated toward self-advancement (at least if it didn't involve actual study) to avoid situations that might come back to haunt him. In this case, however, he insulted the nurse and she remembered.

A few weeks later—with all seemingly forgotten—this same nurse was performing the circulator role in a chest case involving Dr. Pat Ronson. Ronson was a decent enough guy if you were a senior resident or a fellow, but he seemed to have developed a vicious, near-obsessive hatred of interns. At the time I thought this must be because he had trained at another "tough" program where strict discipline and brow-beating had ruled the day, but I really don't know why Ronson hated the first-years so much. In any case, once you were on his bad side you were there to stay, and he could make life hell for you. Everyone, including the OR nurses, knew this.

The operation was a tough one, a lung resection for cancer. The tumor had turned out to be more extensive than what had been thought, although it still could be removed with a chance for cure. The problem was in getting enough exposure, and Ronson and his assistant were not enough personnel to do the job adequately. Ronson called the circulator over and asked her to page the intern. With what must have been a wicked smile, she looked on the call sheet and found that Bubo Shih was the one to page. She did so, and a few moments later the OR phone rang. She answered it.

"Dr. Shih?" she asked, sweetly.

"Yeah, what is it? Somebody paged me." He was probably finishing off another Wendy's double. And a large "Frosty."

"Dr. Ronson would like you to come down to the operating room."

Shih sighed audibly. He clearly didn't recognize the nurse's voice or else forgot his insults to her capabilities and intelligence, or he never would have given her the opportunity that he now placed for her on a silver tray:

"Great. Look, does that asshole want me to help out or does he just want to yell at me, goddammit?"

The nurse didn't bat an eyelash, and turned to Ronson without hesitating. She left the receiver uncovered, too, so Shih could hear what she was going to say.

"Dr. Ronson, before he comes down, Dr. Shih would like to know whether you want him to help out or you just want to yell at him, goddammit."

Ronson stopped operating, laid down his instruments and looked up. He was stunned.

"What did you say?" Ronson asked, as if he literally had not believed his ears.

I wonder what was going through what passed for Shih's mind, as he listened to the exchange. The circ continued in her coquettish voice: "I *think* he was referring to you, Dr. Ronson. Do you think Dr. Shih could have meant someone else when he said "that asshole?"

Ronson broke scrub—an astonishing thing in the middle of a major lung resection—and stalked over to the telephone. Snatching it from the nurse's hand, he began to verbally pound Shih into quivering submission.

"Listen, you stupid fuck, when I ask you to come to the OR, you get your fat fucking ass in gear and MOVE, do you hear me?!'"

It was like a boot camp scene from *Full Metal Jacket*. Shih stammered a reply. Ronson, so angry that he was literally shaking but—strangely enough—in his derisive element, went on: "I'll get your fat ass fired from this program so goddamned fast it'll make your head spin, understand? If you're not in this room in thirty seconds, you'd better start memorizing a new phrase, because you'll be saying it a lot. Do you know what that phrase is, numb-nuts? 'Would you like fries with that?'"

Shih was a big enough (in more ways than one) screw-up that the Ronson incident didn't really sway things for him in any significant way. If he had been in General Surgery, he would have been toast long before, but the Plastics attendings at the time were inclined to accept some pretty shoddy performance from their residents, and he survived.

But the belittled cardiothoracic OR nurse had gotten her sweet revenge. The scrub and circ nurses told the story of Shih's comeuppance for years afterward.

Most surgical procedures take a couple of hours to perform. An inguinal hernia repair usually takes less than an hour, while a laparoscopic cholecystectomy typically lasts an hour to an hour-and-a-half. Bigger cases, like major bowel resections, can take two to three hours. The biggest general surgery operations, like the Whipple procedure, may drag on for up to six hours.

The really complex specialty procedures often go on much longer. When the vascular surgeons removed infected aortic grafts or repaired the difficult thoracoabdominal aortic aneurysms (where the whole aorta from the chest to the pelvis is dilated and liable to rupture), the surgery might take eight or ten hours, or even more. Whenever I mention the amount of time that surgeons spend in the operating room on complicated cases, laymen look incredulous: well, you take breaks, don't you? Generally, no. Don't you get hungry or thirsty? Rarely. Wait a second; how can you operate for ten straight hours without going to the bathroom?

The answer is, I don't know. But we do it all the time. Throughout residency (and beyond, in fact) I cannot recall a single instance when I had to scrub out to answer the call of nature. (One time I had the stomach flu and had to excuse myself to vomit—that was during a kidney transplant in the middle of the night: the attending said that we would have set a record for the fastest transplant done at Ohio State if I hadn't scrubbed out to puke. As it was, it was the second-fastest; the attending said that it didn't count, though, because—like at a track meet where high winds can alter timed events—our transplant was "hurl-aided.")

It's not clear to me why the ordinary voiding urges are suppressed during surgery. I suppose that the urinary bladder must not get distended much, but the question is, why? The bladder is certainly capable of reabsorbing the water from urine, which would keep that organ relatively deflated—this happens all the time in dehydration (although obviously the kidneys do most of the important work when this situation arises). How the efforts of surgery—which are certainly physical as well as mental—affect the kidneys and bladder in such a way that one doesn't feel (or even consider) the need to void is something of a mystery, at least to me. Maybe somebody knows the answer, but I don't. Some of the older attendings would be careful to hit the john right before starting a big case, but other than that it simply never came up.

Same thing with food. This is more understandable, I think, because people rarely get hungry when they're concentrating on an important task. Some people, though, can't seem to accept the idea of going ten hours without food, yet not getting hungry. One research scientist acquaintance of mine, an erudite if somewhat entrepreneurial Russian émigré, briefly focused his energies on developing a system for delivering food to the scrubbed-and-sterile surgeon during a long operation. He never got much past a name for the product, which was actually pretty clever: Clean Break. He had visions of trade journal ads featuring distinguished-looking surgeons glancing up from open wounds to hungrily state "It's time for a Clean Break."

At the end of a long operation, after the patient had been delivered to the recovery room or the ICU, I usually *would* feel a sudden sensation of considerable, if not tremendous thirst. That was the only physiologic effect of protracted cases which appeared consistently. Maybe it all ties together. I suppose it makes sense that the dehydration of eight or ten hours of strict fasting leads to the concentration of urine by the kidneys and bladder, which keeps the surgeon from feeling the urge to go to the restroom, but I do think there's a little more to it than that. In any event, after a long operation it sure was nice to take a load off the feet, kick back and savor one of the ice-cold fruit-juice cups (concord grape or apple) that the nurses always kept in a nearby refrigerator. (The drinks were for the patients; the nurses couldn't have cared less about the docs!)

Ultimately, the success or failure of an operation is dependent on the seamless interaction of a coordinated team, not the petty concerns of physiologic urges. The surgeon must have the dedicated support of an assistant, competent and attentive anesthetists, and experienced or at least focused scrub and circulating nurses. These five individuals, working together, are the nucleus that creates an environment where surgical success is possible. Like any group, a surgery team is only as strong as its weakest link. It was a disturbing fact that, for most of the early period of training, as the resident I was that weak link.

9

Hands and Hans

"How did you learn how to operate?"

That's a question I've been asked dozens of times, as I think most surgeons have.

This is different from asking how one becomes a surgeon. Becoming a surgeon is the lengthy, exhaustive process which this whole book attempts to describe. Learning how to operate is only one aspect of learning surgery. But, since the ability to perform surgery is defining for the profession, this is a topic which merits some attention.

Most medical students spend some time learning how to do simple manual tasks which are described as surgical: suturing and tying knots, for example. These are not as easy as you might think—for instance, there are many different ways of tying surgical knots and each is appropriate for its own set of circumstances. Nevertheless, I think it's safe to say that, while practice in these rudimentary skills may be useful for those who are headed for careers in emergency medicine or family practice, virtually nothing of value to the surgical resident is taught—in the way of surgical technique—in medical school. It's more common to initiate bad habits, which then may require great effort to break.

Armed with his inadequate or flat-out bad basic skills, the intern begins his period of learning how to be a surgeon in the way we have already seen: by never going anywhere near the operating room! As I've mentioned, the goal of the internship year is to become skillful at the pre- and postoperative management of patients, not to learn how to operate. The few opportunities which may pass his way are usually limited to suturing lacerations or surgical incisions (we used to get to "close the leg" on coronary bypass cases—sew up the incision which had been made to harvest a leg vein for use as the bypass conduit). Occasionally, as at Children's Hospital, the intern was permitted to assist on groin hernia repairs, but this consisted mainly of holding retractors for the attendings and cutting suture after they had tied their knots. In short, the actual surgery performed by the intern was minimal and, when he did make it to the operating room, the contribution he made was hardly greater than that of a med student.

Of course this could get disheartening. While one might have the insight to realize the importance of learning patient care, and even to recognize his growing competence and even expertise in it, it just wasn't the same as doing an operation. After all, we had gone into surgery, not internal medicine, and make no mistake—there is very little difference between surgery and medicine internships (of course, internal medicine residency, and then practice, stay the same throughout—uggh). Still, I personally tried to keep my "eyes on the prize." Like a backup quarterback, I tried to keep myself prepared: you never knew when some unforeseen situation would arise and you might have to go in the game. Knowing my basic skills were inadequate, I tried to practice them during my rare down-time (when things were quiet on call, for example). I practiced knot-tying incessantly, and soon every call-room bedpost had multiple knotted sutures hanging from it. I tied surgical knots on pieces of suture material looped around my shoelaces, the belt of my scrub-pants, desk-drawer handles. At one point the tiny screw holding the temple of my glasses in place vanished: rather than replace it (who could leave the hospital to go to a hardware store?), I put some suture through the minuscule screw hole and surgically knotted it in place.

Sure enough, one evening in the fall of the year my opportunity came.

A young man, about my age in fact, appeared in the ER with nausea and abdominal pain of several hour's duration. The pain had gradually drifted down to the lower right side of his belly over this time. He had a slight fever and a mildly elevated white blood cell count. Pushing his abdomen in the lower right side caused intense pain. The third-year resident and the chief had evaluated him at the behest of the ER docs and everyone agreed that he had appendicitis. After explaining the operation to the patient and his family and obtaining their consent, the residents wheeled the man (on a gurney) into the elevator and up to the Operating Suite. I was up on the Gen Surg floor, going about my intern scutwork, completely unaware that there was a patient being taken to the OR for an appendectomy.

I did hear when the hospital operator called a Level 1 Trauma alert overhead, though. As an intern on Gen Surg, to me this was only of passing interest. I wasn't on the trauma service and thus had no responsibilities when such an alert was called.

Within a few minutes a second Trauma alert was called, also a Level 1. A few minutes later, still a third sounded.

"Man, those guys are getting their asses kicked," I thought. "Maybe I'll swing down to the ER and see if I can help."

I hadn't made it to the elevator when my pager went off. To my surprise, though, the number on my pager wasn't the ER, it was one of the operating room numbers (I had memorized these from the cardiac surgery leg-closing days). They needed me to come down and help with the appendectomy; all the other residents had gone to the trauma blitz.

"Is the patient asleep yet?" I asked.

"No," the circulator replied. "They're getting ready to induce him." That meant they were about to start the general anesthetic.

"OK, I'll be right there."

I made a mad dash to the third-year call room, where I knew they kept a copy of Zollinger's *Atlas of Surgical Operations*. I threw it open (briefly catching a glimpse of the book's frontispiece—a dedication to the residents at Ohio State!) and shuffled through the pages to the short section on appendectomy. Over the past months, in anticipation that this would be the first procedure I would perform, I had very nearly memorized the chapter. Now I quickly reviewed the steps involved in the operation. Then I sprinted off to the OR, repeating the steps in my head as if I were chanting a mantra.

In most operating rooms there is a small antechamber where the personnel scrub at a large sink. As I entered this scrub room I saw that the attending, Dr. Marvin, was already washing up. Damn, I thought, better hurry up or he'll have the whole thing finished by the time you're ready to get started. I poked my head in the OR and shouted my glove size in the general direction of the circ nurse. Then I started to scrub.

"What the hell took you so long to get down here?" Marvin grumbled.

He was quite young—in his mid-thirties—and had a healthy component of smart-ass to him, so I didn't know if he was pulling my chain or being serious. Safer to assume the latter, I thought.

"I just had to finish some scut on the floor," I said, scrubbing frantically. Telling him I had gone to the call room to review the procedure wouldn't score me any points, I decided. But then I saw the grin under his surgical mask: he was just screwing with me.

Surgical scrubs are supposed to last five minutes. They're usually done with either a povidone/iodine solution (Betadine) or a chlorhexidine mixture. Both are highly antiseptic, but need some time to work. Studies have shown that scrubbing for any time significantly less than five minutes will not kill all microorganisms, while doing so for longer periods doesn't add any appreciable benefit. If I had to guess, I'd say that most surgeons scrub for three to five minutes. (Dr. Arthur, the colorectal surgeon, would sometimes scrub for—no exaggeration—five seconds! He used to say that in his line of work he mainly needed to scrub *after* the operation!)

After scrubbing, Marvin and I backed our way into the OR (you have to back in because you can't let your now nearly-sterile hands touch anything—like a door).

The scrub nurse handed us sterile towels, and we dried our hands as we watched the circulator prep the patient's abdomen with Betadine. Then the scrub put our gloves and gowns on and we draped the patient with sterile sheets.

After some other, minor preparations, we stood wordlessly in front of the operative field. I was on the patient's right side: the side of the operating surgeon. Marvin took the scalpel from the nurse and handed it to me.

"Make a McBurney," he said.

A McBurney, which sounds like an overdone sandwich from the Golden Arches, is in fact an oblique incision in the right lower quadrant of the abdomen. It was originally described by the surgeon whose name it bears, back in the 1890s, and is intended to bring the operator directly down on the appendix with the least amount of trauma to the patient.

Sifting through my recently-updated Zollinger *Atlas* memory files, I recalled the proper landmarks and began the incision. Marvin didn't say anything so I continued.

This, by the way, is an important tool in surgical education; one that is nearly universally employed: the resident keeps doing what he's doing until some message (verbal or otherwise) from the attending makes him stop. It has always reminded me of the story of Kluge (Clever) Hans, a horse in the German village of Elberfeld around the turn of the last century. Clever Hans supposedly had the ability to solve complex mathematical problems, and even express himself verbally, through the use of a code which translated his hoof taps into letters and numbers. The scientific community, being naturally skeptical, had reservations about the veracity of Hans' apparently considerable abilities. They considered Hans to be a hoax. But no one could figure out how the trick was done. The horse's owner appeared guiltless. Eventually it became clear that the ruse of the brilliant animal was perfect, because it wasn't a ruse. Clever Hans was indeed, highly intelligent—but not enough to know German and do cube roots by arithmetic. He was extremely observant, as it turned out, and sensed the subtle body language of the spectators in the room (especially his owner, in whose absence he was not nearly as impressive). The observers all knew the answers to the questions he was asked, and Hans would continue tapping until their slight, completely unconscious changes of expression, stance, etc. let him know to quit tapping. Then he would get his reward (an apple, or whatever)—which was all he was really after in the first place.

Surgery residents learning to operate behave just like Clever Hans, continuing to do whatever it is that they're doing until some signal is given to stop.

In true, early twentieth-century, German genius-horse fashion I continued my incision until I heard Marvin grunt something that sounded vaguely like "Okay." I had only cut through the most superficial aspect of the skin—the epidermis. Marvin then handed me the Bovie, a yellow plastic electrical cautery device that bore a vague resemblance to a pencil. I used this to cut through the rest of the skin. Now we were in the subcutaneous fat. This yellow, lobular translucent tissue melted to fluid under the Bovie. I then incised the fascia—the tough fibrous tissue which encases the muscles of the abdominal wall.

Marvin took over at this point and used the hand-held retractors to separate the muscle fibers along their courses, without dividing them. At the time, this seemed like a near-miraculous feat. In a moment, a gleaming silvery surface presented itself—the peritoneum.

The peritoneum is a single cell layer sheet which envelops the abdominal organs, like a blanket lying over a cluster of children. Penetrate this, and you are within the abdominal cavity.

There is a classic method of entering the peritoneum, and we utilized it. Marvin took a hemostat (a small clamp) and grasped the peritoneum. I took another one and did likewise, a few millimeters away. He then released his clamp, and replaced it again. The idea behind this is to avoid cutting through the bowel or some other organ—which might be very adherent to the undersurface of the peritoneum—as you are entering the abdomen. Grasping, releasing, and re-grasping is supposed to cause any adherent viscera to fall away from the peritoneum. Then the peritoneum can be cut with impunity, which I now did, with another scalpel.

At this point we were in the abdomen, although via a window through which I could only fit two fingers. A small amount of clear fluid came forth. The next step in the operation was to grasp the appendix and draw it out of the wound. I put my index and middle fingers into the patient's belly. The cavity was warm. Through my gloves, everything felt the same: it seemed as if the man's abdomen was filled with rubbery, yielding balloons. I realized that I must be feeling the small bowel. The appendix lies at the junction of the small and large bowel, typically fixed in the right lower segment of the abdomen—just under the McBurney incision. It looked so easy to find in the line drawings of the surgical atlases. Now here I was in the middle of an appendectomy and the tips of my fingers, covered in hypo-allergenic latex, couldn't distinguish a section of small intestine from colon. In my controlled panic, I forgot the anatomy I knew very well. If it wasn't the appendix, what else could I be feeling? The bladder? The ureter? I decided to take a chance and pulled on the first structure that fit comfortably between my two fingers. A loop of small bowel emerged from the incision with my hand. I stuffed it back into the wound and tried the same tack again. Same result. I felt completely incompetent. Defeated, I removed my fingers from the wound.

"Dr. Marvin, I can't seem to find the appendix. Maybe it's retroce-cal."

I was trying to hide my inexperience behind the remote chance that this man's appendix was in an abnormal anatomic location—*behind the colon*. Marvin wasn't having any of it.

"No such thing as a retrocecal appendix. It's in the books so shitty surgeons can feel better when they can't find it. Try again."

Obviously, after a remark by the attending such as this, the pressure was on me: if I didn't find the appendix, I was a lousy surgeon. Never mind "green," I would have graduated straight to "shitty."

I plunged my fingers back into the wound, thinking about how much happier I would be if the incision had been two inches longer. For a moment I considered how much happier I would have been if I had gone into investment banking. I grabbed what had to be another piece of small intestine and began to pull it out. If I went down, by God I'd go down fighting....

As my fingers emerged from the incision, from between them the appendix sprung into view, bouncing around on its little stalk like an impudent child at the playground. A bead of sweat took that opportunity to roll down my forehead, directly into my right eye. Blinking away the sting, I looked up at Marvin.

"Nice work, Miller," he said. "Does it look hot to you?"

"Hot" meant inflamed; in this case, infected. I didn't know for sure what to look for, but the whole appendix seemed an angry red to me. Of course, this could have been due to my less-than-expert efforts to find it. Maybe it had been a healthy pink before I fooled with it; who knew? But then, right at the tip, I saw something—the very nubbin at the end was black: dead, gangrenous. There was no question that the diagnosis had been right. I displayed this to Marvin without a word.

"Right," he said. "Let's get it out."

We found the blood supply to the appendix—the tiny appendiceal artery—and, through the adjacent fatty tissue, passed clamps around it. Taking the Metzenbaum scissors (which are made for cutting and dissecting tissue) I divided the artery between the clamps, then tied sutures around the clamps' tips to ligate the ends of the blood vessel. Following the *Atlas'* cookbook directions, I next placed a purse-string suture around the base of the appendix. This entailed taking a needle driver in my hand and pushing a tapered-tip suture needle, with "chromic" catgut attached, through the outermost two of the three layers of the bowel wall, in and out repeatedly in such a way as to form a circular pattern which could then be cinched up like an old-style handbag. Suturing bowel, as it turns out, is an art which must be experienced and practiced before one can attain any expertise. It's not at all like sewing up skin. Although it's easy enough to describe in words, the actual sensation of piercing the bowel with the needle is what guides the surgeon as to how deep to go and how far apart to place the stitches. As I attempted to place the purse-string, Marvin repeatedly grabbed my hand and drove the needle through the bowel wall with me, trying to show me how to get the feel.

After the purse-string was done, I took a clamp and crushed the base of the appendix, a centimeter or so away from the purse-string. Then I placed the clamp firmly across the base of the appendix and cut it off with a knife. In time-honored fashion, I passed the organ off the field along with the knife—they were both contaminated (the inside of the colon, which I'd exposed as a normal part of the operation, is like a sewer). Beneath the clamp I placed a catgut suture-ligature (a tie which is buttressed in the tissue by having been placed in with a stitch) in order to close the hole in the bowel wall which we had created. As I tied this suture, Marvin dunked the stump of the appendix into the cecum with a forceps and pulled up on the purse-string, our safety valve. He then tied the purse string up—effectively sealing the appendiceal stump within the colon—and we let the bowel drop back into the belly. We closed the incision uneventfully and the case was finished. My first appendectomy was over.

During the second year, we residents were given an opportunity to learn some of the newer surgical techniques which were arising out of the proliferation of electronic technology. Advances and refinements in the medical imaging industry, in particular, were having profound effects on patient care at this point in time. The primary goal of these advancements was a move toward the "minimally invasive" treatment of patients who required surgical intervention.

For example, improvements in fiber-optic technology and microprocessors allowed for the development of "laparoscopic" procedures. In these, a miniature television camera mounted on the end of a metal stick (the "laparoscope") is used to visualize the inside of the abdomen, and similarly-mounted surgical instruments are employed to manipulate the organs—cutting, tying, suturing, etc., just like in traditional, "open" surgery. The operation is carried out through tiny incisions, just big enough to admit the sticks, and the patient accordingly suffers much less trauma. Recovery times are minimized, hospital stays greatly reduced. Intriguingly, these changes have not greatly altered the costs—one can make of that what one wishes.

At the time I was training, these new procedures were all the rage. Over the ensuing years, some have demonstrated staying power (the laparoscopic cholecystectomy—gall bladder removal, for one) while others have fizzled (for a while some hearty souls were trying to do laparoscopic Whipples). At that time, it seemed like the future of surgery was tied to the ends of these fiber optic sticks, and residency training programs were jumping over one another to get in on the action: if they couldn't train their residents in laparoscopic techniques, they would get buried. Soon no one would even apply to a residency which offered no laparoscopic training.

The problem, of course, was that the techniques were so new that no one really knew what they were doing. It was the blind leading the blind. The older attendings mostly ignored the new technology; they were going to tread water until retirement. But even the young guys had only done a handful of these operations, so they had a hard time communicating techniques that they themselves were unsure of.

In order to further the application of the new technology—and, in so doing, sell their products—many of the laparoscopic equipment manufacturers had set up training programs and tutorials. Initially, these were at national meetings and at the companies' factories, but as the popularity increased, they could afford to take their show on the road, so to speak. Training seminars began to pop up at university and community hospitals. Eager and earnest company representatives, untrained in surgery, of course, demonstrated what passed for proper laparscopic surgical technique, all the while hawking their wares.

Several times a year one of these dog-and-pony shows would appear at Ohio State, and the residents would line up for the opportunity to get some experience with the new technology. As it happened, these seminars were less Rin-tin-tin and Mr. Ed, and more Arnold Ziffle.

We practiced on pigs.

Picture, if you can, a darkened room filled with half a dozen upturned, anesthetized pigs, the same number of flickering TV monitors, and twenty-five surgery residents huddled around the sleeping beasts. It looked like a scene from some space-age *Macbeth*; all that was missing was the bubbling cauldron.

The factory rep moved from group to group, passing out what limited assistance and minimally helpful suggestions he could render. We residents took turns doing simple dissections: getting out the gall bladder, isolating the esophagus, running the bowel. It was disconcerting at first, because one had to look at a TV screen that was off to the piggy-patient's side while trying to coordinate the movement of the sticks. The hand motions are not reflected in a one-on-one fashion by the motions of the instruments, so you have to mentally compensate. Some people have said that performing laparoscopic surgery is like playing a video game, but in my view that's inaccurate. The artificial intelligence of video games is designed to mimic reality as closely as possible, but in these laparoscopic procedures one has to *translate* his motions to a TV monitor and mentally adjust his minute-to-minute actions based on what sort of effect these translations have on the movements initiated by the hands. It is a counterintuitive thing, overcoming the accumulated experience that if your hands move this much, the thing you're holding moves that much, but it can be learned. It is nothing like a Play Station, though.

So we worked on pigs. We practiced taking out their gall bladders and doing Nissen procedures, an operation wherein the stomach is sutured as a wrap around the esophagus to prevent acid reflux. If the animals died during our efforts, as a few did, we practiced bowel surgery, including stapling. I don't know where the animals came from—the company probably bought them from the same vendor who sold them to the nearby veterinary school. Wherever they came from, they certainly were pungent. As soon as you walked into the building, you could tell if there was a laparoscopic pig class. When they died, the smell of decay came on with astonishing speed. Within half an hour the unmistakable odor of rotting meat began to waft through the room. I have no idea why this smell comes on so quickly, but it does make me wonder how pork can be prepared safely.

The experience was unquestionably of value, though. Although no one walked out of the pig lab with utter confidence in his ability to do laparoscopic surgery on humans, once we actually did get down to doing these cases with human subjects, things certainly went much more smoothly than they would have if we had never touched the specialized instruments before.

I don't know what happened to the pigs that survived our practice session. When we left the lab they were still asleep, the veterinarians monitoring them (they were using this opportunity to learn a little large-animal anesthesia). We didn't do anything to them in the class that would ordinarily be fatal (at least intentionally), but I suppose that they were given an overdose of anesthetic by the vet students and shuffled off their porky mortal coil in that not-unpleasant fashion.

After the laparoscopic skills lab it was tough to grab a ham sandwich in the cafeteria.

So the process of learning how to operate is a multi-dimensional one. While simple manual tasks can be practiced at home or in a quiet call room, the more advanced maneuvers of dexterity can only be mastered in the operative suite. The actual conduct of an operation goes far beyond the straightforward technical aspects, though. Laymen are exposed to situational television dramas where sincere young surgery trainees diligently memorize the sequence of a procedure. I think that elements of rote memory—step 1, followed by step 2, etc.—are far less important than an ability to improvise, though, because every patient and every operation is different. Just like a jazz pianist, a skillful surgeon must have a mastery of technique in order to be able to improvise in a seamless fashion. There are a few prodigies, but most of the great ones have worked very hard to make it look effortless.

10

Mistakes

ALTHOUGH IT'S UNFORTUNATE that a book dealing with the training of surgeons should be so full of mistakes, the fact remains that we are all human. All doctors make mistakes. Not some, not most; all. The trick, of course, is to minimize their occurrence. Another important aspect of dealing with mistakes is damage control: one must be able to recognize and correct a serious error before its consequences become catastrophic. In addition, it's vital to learn from the experience, so the mistake will not be repeated in the future. We can't ever hope to eliminate mistakes, but we should strive not to duplicate them.

An easy mistake to make is to approach a minor operation with insufficient respect. Even the most run-of-the-mill surgical procedures can take truly ghastly turns and become life-threatening crises. Thankfully, this is a rare event, but such was the case with the Groshong catheter of Mrs. McLaughlin.

A Groshong catheter is a special intravenous line which is surgically placed in one of the large central veins of the body. It is made of soft silicon and is meant to provide venous access for an extended time, months or even years. Most commonly this is for long-term antibiotics or chemotherapy. We placed them routinely, and even junior residents did so in the OR without supervision. Mrs. McLaughlin, who had metastatic breast cancer, already had a Groshong catheter in place for chemotherapy. It had been there for two uneventful years, in fact. But she wanted a new one because the nurses had trouble drawing blood from it and she hated needlesticks, as everyone does. She was about to get the needlestick to end all needlesticks.

We took her to the operating room one morning to place a new Groshong. Her old catheter was in her left subclavian vein, just below the clavicle on her left chest. We opted for a right subclavian approach for the new line. After numbing the right clavicular area with some local anesthetic, I inserted a two-inch long large-bore needle below her clavicle and directly into the subclavian vein. It was a chip shot, which should have been my first warning. I passed a guide wire through the needle without event. Next, as I'd done a hundred times before, I threaded a stiff plastic "dilator" over the wire. This well-intentioned weapon is meant to open a pathway by blunt force for the flexible Groshong catheter to pass through the surrounding fibrous tissues and on into the vein. The dilator passed, but with difficulty. Mrs. McLaughlin, who was sedated but awake, expressed considerable discomfort with this maneuver. That wasn't unexpected. What was unexpected was the gush of pulsatile, bright red blood which occurred after I removed the dilator. The hard plastic had taken its own path, independent of the guide wire, and pierced the innominate artery (which courses directly behind the vein), one of the largest arterial vessels in the body.

From this point, things went rapidly downhill. Mrs. McLaughlin quickly became short of breath and her blood pressure plummeted. It was obvious that she had developed a rapidly expanding hemothorax, blood pouring into her chest from the gash in the artery which I had made with my plastic javelin. Her lung was being crushed by all the blood. We had to put a chest tube in immediately to have any hope of saving her. In essence, she had the same injury as if she had been shot or stabbed in the upper chest. With determined, shaking fingers I made an incision in her chest wall and slipped the tube in between her ribs as the panicked anesthesiology resident fought to place an endotracheal tube into her windpipe to breathe for her. By now word had gotten out and the operating room was filled to capacity with the curious. Nearly a liter of blood dashed out onto my feet as the chest tube went in. Her breathing instantly improved. Miraculously, the bleeding also stopped. In minutes she was stable again.

Instead of at home, Mrs. McLaughlin spent the night in the SICU, on a ventilator and with a chest tube suction device bubbling merrily by her bedside.

I tried to comfort myself with the knowledge that what I had experienced was a known complication of the procedure, one which had occurred several times at OSU in the two years I had been a resident. But it had never happened to me, and I was tortured by the thought that I had come very close indeed to killing a patient. I was reminded of an observation made by the cardiothoracic fellow when I was an intern: "General surgery residency is five years...one of these days you're going to be the one holding the smoking gun...." At the time I had nervously dismissed the remark: all I had to do was be careful. Now I thought I *had* been careful, and there was no one holding the gun but me.

The next week at Morbidity and Mortality Conference was profound torture. I had to sit silently and listen to the chief resident explain my complication in lurid detail (he even—unknowingly—exaggerated some of the painful facts), then I had to endure the criticisms of the faultless attendings, by proxy. I thought about ducking out before the conference started, but decided that that would be particularly gutless. I had to take my medicine, a bitter dose of public humiliation. From now on, I would be that much more careful and meticulous. No more smoking guns, I vowed.

Mrs. McLaughlin left the hospital a week later.

One of my fellow residents had the distinct misfortune of being the assistant on a case of Dr. Atcheson's in which a sponge—a piece of sterile gauze—was left inside a patient. Dr. Atcheson said that it was the first time in his career that such a thing had happened, which was pretty remarkable since he had been practicing for fifteen years or so. Knowing how the typically-good-natured Chief of General Surgery could "go postal" when a clinical oversight resulted in patient harm, I was particularly glad to be completely uninvolved. But I knew what had happened just like everyone else in the Department: gossip like that sweeps over a hospital like a well-kindled brush fire.

The operation had been a straightforward colectomy: a removal of part of the large intestine, in this case for cancer. After the key elements in the case were completed, Dr. Atcheson "broke scrub"—took off his sterile gown and gloves—and left the O.R., leaving the resident, Scott Guy, to close the patient.

During the closure, the scrub nurse and circulator together count all the needles and sponges which have been used. If the number they come up with is different from the number that have been delivered to the sterile field during the course of the operation, the surgeon will stop his closure and re-explore the operative site. In the unusual event that the stray sponge or needle still escapes detection, an x-ray of the field is performed (surgical sponges are impregnated with strips of a metallic material which shows up clearly on x-rays). Together, these efforts almost always locate the wayward object.

In this particular case, though, human error interfered. The nurses got the count wrong. Now I wasn't there so I don't know how it happened, but unquestionably at some point two nurses looked at each other and said, "The count's okay," when they knew (or should have known) that it wasn't. No X-ray was done, and the patient was taken to the recovery room like any other. She awakened from the anesthetic, was taken to her room on the ward, and was beginning her convalescence from apparently successful cancer surgery. Then she made the mistake of briefly running a mild postoperative fever. An overly-aggressive cross-cover intern ordered an x-ray to rule out the possibility of pneumonia. The chest x-ray definitely excluded pneumonia as a possibility, but it also demonstrated the clear outline of a sponge in the patient's upper abdomen.

I can only imagine the thoughts which must have been going through poor Guy's head as he contemplated having to tell Dr. Atcheson that he had left a sponge in the patient. Somehow he made it through the ordeal and Dr. Atcheson, characteristically, stated that he would tell the patient what had happened himself. I actually happened to be on the ward when this took place, and got a chance to eavesdrop on the conversation. Otherwise there were no others around except Dr. Atcheson and the patient, a 72-year-old blue-haired lady named Mabel Gardner.

"Good evening, Mrs. Gardner," he began, "how are you feeling?"

Mrs. Gardner lit up when she realized it was Dr. Atcheson. I think it's easy for docs to forget how important the few moments we spend with a post-op patient are to that person—it's really the highlight of their day.

"Oh, I'm doing just fine, doctor. I had a little fever this morning, but it's gone away. Everyone has been so nice to me."

"I'm very glad to hear that; listen, Mrs. Gardner, I have a bit of bad news to tell you."

"Oh," the patient replied, pausing a moment. "Is it about the cancer? Didn't you get it all?"

"No, Mrs. Gardner, it's not about the cancer. I think I got it all, but we won't be certain until the pathology report comes back in a few days. But it's not about that."

Dr. Atcheson let out an audible sigh. I'm sure he was envisioning various ways of torturing Guy to death.

"I'm afraid I accidentally left a sponge inside you. We saw it on the x-ray we took this afternoon. I can't explain how we missed it—this has never happened to me before. But we did. And we have to go back to the operating room and take it out. I'm sorry."

There was a long silence as Mrs. Gardner's blue head absorbed the information. She seemed sweet, but who knew for sure? Maybe the pause was spent trying to remember her lawyer's phone number....

"When do you want to take it out?" was all she asked.

"Tomorrow, Mrs. Gardner, first thing. It'll be a very short operation."

"Well, you know best, doctor. I appreciate what you and your people have all done for me. I think you're trying to save my life."

So that was that. Mrs. Gardner had decided that her doctor was doing his best and that human beings make mistakes. It was a great lesson for me, too, of course. Dr. Atcheson had treated the situation with straightforward, uncompromising honesty and—most importantly, I think—he had kept in close communication with the patient. Mrs. Gardner had responded with a renewal of her trust and a re-establishment of their doctor-patient relationship.

Before and since, when I've seen a surgeon get involved in legal issues with patients and their families, it has almost invariably been because of (if you'll excuse the *Cool Hand Luke* reference) a "failure to communicate." Patients realize that bad things can happen; they accept that. They will not accept being kept in the dark, and they shouldn't.

When I was still an intern, there was a chief resident who seemed— quite against his will—to gather bad luck and poor outcomes around himself like an old shawl. Howard Baum was highly intelligent; he'd had nothing but outstanding grades and test scores throughout his life, and he'd done meaningful research during both medical school and residency, in some of the most prestigious medical laboratories in America. In addition, his brother was a prominent neurosurgeon at a top-flight academic medical center. He was personally charming in a Jerry Lewis-"Nutty Professor" sort of way. In short, all the tools of a successful university surgeon seemed to have devolved on Dr. Baum, and he himself was entirely focused on putting them to their utmost use. But there was a problem.

Howard was a menace. Both in and out of the operating room, he was simply dangerous in his role as a resident physician with responsibility for patient care. Although he could maintain a sensible and even erudite conversation about issues in the surgical literature or clinical controversies, he seemed to jettison this knowledge when actually dealing with patients. This could both cause the patients to suffer and put them in danger.

One day early in my internship I was rounding with Dr. Arthur, the colorectal specialist, on his patients. The first one we saw was a Mr. Cochran, who had had a bowel resection, in which Dr. Arthur had left a drain. As we walked into the room, the patient looked as if he might jump off the bed and attack us.

"What the hell's the matter with Baum!?" he shouted.

Dr. Arthur, who was very cool and collected at all times, looked extremely tense as he asked the necessary question: "Why, Mr. Cochran, is there something wrong?"

"Yeah, your goddamn right there's something wrong! That son-of-a-bitch was just in here. He pulled my drain out without cutting the stitch that held it in!"

Cochran pulled up his hospital gown to show us the area of torn skin where the advertised event had taken place. I winced. A first-year medical student should have known better.

Dr. Arthur looked at me and, very gravely and in the full presence of the patient, said, "Dr. Baum is not to see any of my patients from now on, do you understand?"

I had to suppress a laugh. I, the intern, was somehow supposed to keep the chief resident from even seeing the patients on his service. How the hell was I going to do that?

As it happened, of course, Dr. Arthur was just trying to make a point (and look good in front of the patient; in the way a cat tries to look good by bringing dead birds to its owner's doorstep, I suppose).

A big part of the danger of Howard was that not only did he do absurd things himself, he ordered *me* and the other subordinate residents to do things which made absolutely no sense.

When a patient is unable to utilize their own gastrointestinal tract to obtain nutrition for some reason, they may benefit from a period of dietary support or replacement provided by the administration of an intravenous solution of protein, carbohydrates and fat called "TPN." This is prescribed in a fairly complex fashion involving the calculation of nutritional requirements based on age, weight, sex, nature and severity of illness and several other factors. A formula with the appropriate recipe of the various nutrients as well as vitamins, minerals and even some medications is arrived at, and a rate of intravenous infusion is also calculated. The pharmacists and dieticians were in charge of this, and they took the task of arriving at a recipe and rate of administration very seriously indeed. But they did not have the authority to actually issue TPN orders. These had to be signed by a physician.

Somewhere along the line Howard had developed the delusional concept that he was a master of TPN (a concept that was most assuredly not shared by the pharmacists and nutritionists). He behaved as if he had developed a kind of extrasensory perception about what formula and rate of TPN any given patient needed. For example, on rounds he might ask, "What's the amino acid content of Mr. Huston's TPN?"

I'd tell him (we gave patients protein in the form of amino acids).

Howard would nod meaningfully. "What's the rate?"

I'd tell him how fast we were giving Mr. Huston his TPN, expressed in cc's per second: "He's at 65, Dr. Baum."

Howard would think, or pretend to think, for only a second or two and then, dashing into the patient's room, say to me, "Go down to 63 per hour; and increase the amino acids by one-fifth."

At first I thought he must be a genius. How could someone, standing at the bedside, calculate that a patient was receiving two milliliters of TPN an hour too much and, moreover, that he was getting 20% too little protein, too? Howard was obviously some kind of extreme surgeon-mathematician super-genius.

In a few days, though, I realized that there was an alternative explanation: Howard was out to lunch. Admittedly, I was helped along in coming to this conclusion by the pharmacists: they were at the mercy of whatever he wrote (or had me write) in the order book regarding the TPN, and they were consistently appalled. Orders were written late in the day which altered highly expensive TPN formulas (it can cost up to $1,000 a day in the hospital) by ridiculously minuscule amounts, resulting in the dumping of dozens of already-mixed bags, for no substantial reason. Even now I cringe when I think of the thousands of dollars wasted.

Baum had another bizarre habit. If a postoperative patient had a fever, or developed redness around his wound, or really just failed to thrive, Howard would have the intern take a needle and syringe and insert it into the wound. The idea was to draw back on the plunger and see if there was pus in the wound. Now, infected surgical wounds will turn red, then begin to drain, usually about a week after surgery—but there's no mistaking the diagnosis. Inserting a needle into a fresh post-op incision was as likely to cause an abscess as to detect one. I wrestled with what to do. The other chief residents whom I canvassed said the idea was loony, just ignore Baum. But I couldn't: on evening rounds he was bound to ask me what had happened when I tapped the wound. I could just lie and say I'd gotten no pus back, but he might very well ask me in front of the patient, who might then say, "Hey, he never put a needle into my wound; that Miller's lying!" Although I was still acting the bad-ass, just intentionally disregarding a Chief Resident's order was not something I felt I could do with impunity—I didn't give a damn about what Baum thought of me (although we actually got along pretty well, in fact), but if word of my deliberate insubordination reached Dr. Atcheson, the consequences could be disastrous. I came up with a solution.

Gathering up the necessary supplies, I headed to the patient's room, ignoring the responsible nurse whom I otherwise would have made a point of involving. The patient knew what was coming from what he'd heard on morning rounds, so I just calmed him with some reassurance that the procedure would be painless (sometimes you say this even if you know it's going to hurt like hell, but this time I had complete confidence that there'd be no discomfort!). I wiped the wound down with some antiseptic Betadine, then carefully slid a monstrous 13-gauge needle onto the end of a mammoth 60cc syringe—directly in front of the patient. The idea was to unnerve him to the point that he would not want to watch what I was about to do. It worked to perfection: the patient swallowed hard and turned his gaze abruptly toward the window. Then, I leaned over him and gently, barely touched the skin next to the incision with the needle. No penetration. I waited about twenty seconds, humming to myself, then stepped away.

"All done," I announced.

The patient was amazed.

"My gosh," he said, "you're really something else, Doctor. I hardly felt a thing."

"Oh, it just comes with the territory."

If deliberate subterfuge comes with the territory, I laughed to myself. Still, the solution was a good one. As far as the patient was concerned, the measure ordered by the Chief Resident had been carried out. Howard wouldn't be any the wiser for my having faked his ridiculous, possibly dangerous intervention, either. Mainly, though, the interests of the patient were served best. I surreptitiously communicated this trick to the other interns, and I don't believe that another postoperative incision was violated by Baum's odd orders.

One of the interns simply couldn't cope with Howard's absurdities and, one morning on work rounds, the two of them got into a heated argument. The 'tern literally threw the order book at Howard—they almost came to blows—and stalked off, refusing to continue his work (and this was Surg 1!). Cooler heads prevailed after a time and the team regrouped, but the intern had made a fatal error. Incompetent as Howard may have been, he was still a superior and, more to the point, that intern had placed himself above the patients by walking off his job, an inexcusable conceit. He was fired from the program at the end of the year (it also didn't help that he had used some of his down-time to impregnate the Surg 1 clinical nurse—she got canned, too).

During his junior years in residency, Howard had raised enough concern about his abilities among the faculty that he was asked to spend time in the research lab. Now many of the very best residents spend a year or more in the lab; it helps to strengthen their resume when the time comes to find a job. In fact, most university medical centers won't even consider an applicant for a faculty position who hasn't spent at least two years completely dedicated to surgical research. For this last reason, Howard actually wanted to do the research, so I think he rather missed the point: he would have been required to do it whether he wished to or not. The faculty's idea (hope, really) was that during the lab time he might attain more maturity as an individual and, given the much lighter workload, he might have more time to read and learn about patient care. Howard spent a staggering total of five years in the lab (this was above and beyond the five clinical years of surgery residency), but none of the faculty's goals were met. Paradoxically, on paper Howard came out of the experience looking tremendous: because he had spent so much time in research, he had written a number of papers and presented at several national meetings.

Amongst all the articles and presentations, the one thing that didn't make its way onto Howard's resume was what the staff considered to be his defining characteristic. Although there was constant cringing (and real fear for patient safety) about his poor clinical judgment, and serious concerns about his inability to get along with any of his co-workers, the thing that really swung the pendulum against Howard in his particular choice of career was that he was a HODAD.

That's right, Howard was a HODAD; in fact the most extreme example of one that many could recall—years after he left, the O.R. teams still talked about it with awe.

HODAD is an acronym, and it stands for "Hands Of Death And Destruction."

You see, on top of his other problems, Howard was breathtakingly clumsy and uncoordinated. He dropped instruments, tied his own gloves into the patient's wounds, stuck fellow surgeons with needles, the whole shooting match. And, while you can teach any moderately intelligent person how to take care of patients, the same cannot be said about the manual dexterity that is simply indispensable to surgery. Learning the nuts and bolts of how to operate is usually the easy part, but not in Howard's case. You can't fake it if the hands just can't do the job. Such an individual is a HODAD, and Howard was the epitome.

Howard had spent the bulk of his research time in a lab investigating the surgical diseases of children. He wanted to do a fellowship in Pediatric Surgery. Because he was known there, he had no hope of securing the one associated with Ohio State, over at Children's Hospital. Others across the country did not have the benefit of this insider knowledge. I'm sure that Dr. Atcheson wrote a letter of recommendation on Howard's behalf, and knowing Atcheson's rare combination of scrupulous honesty and formidable language skills, I'd love to know what it said. In any case, Howard scored a fellowship position on the East Coast. There was considerable anxiety among the faculty about this, concerns about the reputation of the Surgery Department being sullied and so forth. A motion simply not to graduate him from the residency program was considered, but since he had spent *ten years* in training, no one had the heart to follow through. The majority opinion was that a two-year fellowship, such as the one he was embarking on, would be the best thing for Howard: the extra time in still more training might be enough to get him over the hump that had proven to be so large.

There were, however, dissenting opinions.

Dr. Arthur and I were discussing Howard's prospects as a Pediatric Surgeon one day near the end of the academic year. As we walked along a corridor, I mused that he was entering a new environment and might flourish.

"You know, Dr. Arthur, the folks at his new place might tolerate Howard's eccentricities a little better than we did here."

Arthur stopped and looked at me over the top of his wire-rim glasses. He had a deep frown.

"Craig," he replied, "no one will ever tolerate dead babies."

Late the next year word filtered through the hospital that Howard had been fired from his fellowship. I have no idea whatever became of him.

11

Publish or Perish

IN AN ACADEMIC SURGICAL TRAINING ENVIRONMENT there arise certain pressures—playing on both attendings and residents—which don't exist in the ordinary circumstances of private practice. The education of medical students and residents is, of course, a major factor which helps to define the difference between the two genres, and this duty can be both a tremendously rewarding and a supremely frustrating experience (I can certainly think of more examples of my causing a sense of frustration than one of reward among the attending surgeons I worked with!). One of the other major defining differences is the need and desire to perform meaningful research.

The academic medical centers are situated in major universities (for the most part), and the attending surgeons who operate there are faculty of the university. In addition to performing their roles as surgeons and educators, these docs are expected to contribute to the advancement of their field of knowledge, to "do research."

There is a saying amongst those who work in university settings, whether they be professors or graduate students. "Publish or perish" is the credo, referring to the fact that anyone who hopes to have a successful career in academia must produce apparently meaningful written examples of their research or opinion in the literature (the books and journals) of their profession. It's a dreadful reality, and it has led to the untimely demise of many innocent trees (through countless worthless publications) and not a few promising teaching careers. Academic surgeons are as haunted by this unfortunate fact of life as any other professors on campus, except that, unlike the other faculty, they are also expected to work as full-time physicians. They must give lectures and seminars like history professors, do good research, and also run full-time clinics and (in the case of surgeons) perform operations. Even more incredibly, they are expected to perform their clinical duties (all the academic considerations aside) in such a way as to be fiscally competitive with the docs in private practice! It's a nearly impossible equation, and it will go by the wayside in a few years, I'm sure.

But in the late twentieth century, the academic "publish or perish" philosophy was in full swing in the university surgery centers.

Most of the residents who came to Ohio State did so with the full knowledge that they would very likely be required to spend at least a year "in the lab," doing research. Few residents snuck through without any lab time. It was, at least, a self-consistent theme: there are, after all, many "community" surgery training programs which are geared to generate private-practice surgeons. University programs—at the least—ought to produce enough academic surgeons, focused on research and education as well as clinical excellence, to sustain themselves; why crank out private practitioners who would likely stay in the geographical vicinity and add to the burden of economic competitiveness which was steadily growing and steadily strangling the university hospitals? Many academic surgery programs are exclusively structured to produce academic surgeons only.

Of course, the only way to continue to produce surgeon-scientists was to train the residents in both surgery and scientific research.

While most of the residents performed research for a year or two in the middle of residency, usually after completing their third year, I already had three years' worth of surgical research under my belt by the time I started internship. For this reason I was allowed to forego any further research time and plow straight through the five-year program. In some ways, this was definitely a blessing; I'm not sure I'd have been able to endure the whole process if it had extended to seven or eight years. On the other hand, those who did take research time in the middle of residency remarked that it was nice to have a hiatus from the terrible schedule, stress and abuse for a while (most even made decent money by moonlighting at local hospitals and in emergency rooms, usually for about $50 an hour).

Although my research years came before starting residency, they were, I think, reasonably representative of the typical experience.

As I mentioned earlier, my letter of recommendation from the iconic Dr. Zollinger had garnered me a position in a surgical laboratory at the University of California Medical Center in San Francisco. This lab was focused on investigating the physiology of the gastrointestinal system, and was under the direction of three individuals: two professors of surgery and a full-time research scientist. The surgeons were very busy with clinical and administrative duties—one of them was Dr. Haile Addis, the Chairman of the Surgery Department, who soon became Dean of the Medical School—so my interactions with them turned out to be somewhat intermittent. I ended up working more closely with the physiologist, a sandy-haired Englishman named Ian Bennett, with a somewhat prim outward appearance but a mischievous, schoolboy sense of humor.

After settling in to my new surroundings in the lab, I got to work on the task which had been assigned me by Ian and Dr. Addis. This was the investigation of the effects of a certain protein, called CGRP, which had been identified in the nerves of the stomach and intestines. The hypothesis was that this substance was somehow involved in the regulation of gastric acid secretion. A fair amount of work already had been done on CGRP in the San Francisco lab and elsewhere, and there were strong indications that the hypothesis was correct. It was my job to prove that the protein had some influence on acid secretion, and then figure out how it worked.

The first part—seeing if CGRP actually had some effect on the production of stomach acid—would be conceptually easy; there would be a certain amount of grunt work involved, though. Actually, there would be more squeaking than grunting—I would be performing my experiments on rats.

I should say a word here about the whole can of worms that is animal research. It seems to me that—with regard to this very divisive topic— there are a few well-defined categories of people. On the far left are the militant animal rights activists, who have a sort of mystical belief in the unassailable rights of animals. They use the Gothic term "vivisection" a lot. These extremists believe that no consumer-product testing or medical research should ever be permitted on animals, who in their minds have at least as much right to life, liberty and the pursuit of happiness as any humans. Some of the more sociopathic of these individuals have styled themselves shock troops in a kind of guerilla warfare against those whom they perceive as purveyors of animal cruelty and even genocide. While I was there, one professor of genetics at the University of California, San Francisco campus became the unlucky target of such a deranged personality and opened a pipe-bomb in his daily mail: he lost a hand. I guess the radicals thought that'd show him. Most sincere animal rights activists don't advocate violence against scientists, but you sometimes get the feeling that they don't get all that choked up when it happens, either.

There's a certain subset of the radical-types that I call "fuzzy animalians." These are the mostly-female vegetarian-types (by the way, what about the rights of lettuce? That head was alive before it ended up doused in vinaigrette in a wooden bowl!) who complain loudly about the mistreatment of anything that's cute and/or furry—hamsters, baby seals, etc.—but always scream for someone to step on whatever spider crosses their path. Then they say (and actually believe) that they are defenders of animal rights! I guess to them only a critter with fur or feathers has rights; spiders and cockroaches only have the right to meet the bottom of a Birkenstock!

Less extreme folks acknowledge that some worthwhile medical research absolutely requires the use of animals, and they only rail against testing consumer products on them. I suspect that most people, if cornered, would place themselves in this category. Since they aren't cornered by the issue very often, you'd have to say that most people don't really give a damn either way. For what it's worth, media hype aside, cosmetics testing makes up less than 0.1% of all animal experimentation.

There's another group of people who have special insight, although you don't hear their stories very often. These are the patients and their family members who have had their own or their loved ones' lives extended or immeasurably improved from medical interventions which were developed from laboratory work done on animals, work which could have been accomplished in no other way. This diverse community includes the children who have survived congenital heart defects due to tour de force surgical procedures first attempted on dogs (sorry, there's no computer model that can simulate an open-heart procedure), the millions who have survived bacterial infections like pneumonia in recent decades due to the development of antibiotics (ironically Flemming, the discoverer of penicillin, missed the boat on its epoch-making potential by *not* performing the proper animal tests!) and the countless beneficiaries of animal-tested (and generated) vaccinations, which have nearly eliminated so many ancient scourges of mankind like polio. The list is practically endless.

If the radical animal rights groups had had their way all along, the world would be a much darker and more dangerous place than it is today. The thousands of women who succumbed after childbirth to puerperal fever in the pre-antibiotic era would be joined by an enormous contingent from our own time. The children that survived birth would be ravaged by the childhood exanthems which twentieth-century vaccination technology have rendered a minor nuisance. Any bacterial infection would harbor the potential for death (the first, transiently successful use of penicillin was in an English policeman who'd cut himself shaving— the cut became infected and finally killed him when the docs ran out of the drug). Anesthetic techniques like epidural analgesia would not be available. Diabetes, until recently only treatable with animal-derived insulin, would have killed and debilitated millions more. It's a bleak picture, but one worth considering for a moment.

What I was considering, as I pondered my assigned task, was the surgical anatomy of the Sprague-Dawley breed of laboratory rat. The plan was to place tubes in the stomachs of the rats, then measure the amount of acid which dripped out. I would simultaneously give them intravenous injections of either placebo solutions or the substance in question, CGRP, then see if there was any difference.

Getting the tube into the rat was going to be a challenge. It had to be done surgically—a sort of tiny NG tube wouldn't work because the little buggers had sharp teeth and would chew such a contrivance in half. For the same reason, whatever tube I came up with had to be metal. After worrying about this issue for a few days, I had the machine shop construct a hollow, stainless-steel cylinder with a perforated flange on one end. Then, after putting the rats to sleep and sterilizing their bellies with Betadine, I opened their abdomens and fished out the stomachs. Although the rats were always fasted during the night before surgery, their big, rubbery stomachs were nearly always stuffed with rat chow. I would slit the stomachs open, then suture the perforated flanges of the steel tubes to the thick, muscular gastric walls. I then punctured single small holes in the dependent parts of the rat bellies and slipped the tubes through (it's not a good idea to bring the tube through the main incision, if you do it will tend to make the incision break open later). Then I stitched everything up.

In a half-hour or so the rat would wake up. At first I was worried about the rats' having postoperative pain from the incision. I wanted to be humane, even though I was, technically, a vivisectionist! There was an experienced technician in the lab and she told me that if the rats were in pain, they would basically sulk and refuse to eat. Amazingly, after they awoke from the anesthetic my rats almost always started wandering about their cages, sniffing the wood chips and definitely consuming their fair share of food pellets. So they seemed to be okay. In fact, in short order I developed a healthy respect for the physiologic capacity of the rats. They could tolerate and recuperate from major surgery—like gastric operations—much better than their human counterparts. Despite minimal antiseptic precautions their wounds hardly ever got infected, either. For a while I considered abandoning my gut protein research and concentrating on the rats' remarkable resistance to surgical infection, but no one else in the lab was very interested. Although my ideas might have some merit, I was still just the kid, and definitely the low man on the laboratory totem pole. Somebody else had probably looked into it anyway.

I spent the next few months accumulating data from my rat patients. The first few weeks were tremendously frustrating, as I learned that the establishment of a useful experimental model is the most significant (and most difficult) aspect of scientific research. One at a time, in true Murphian fashion, every individual thing that could go wrong did go wrong, or so it seemed. The gastric tubes got clogged—constantly—with partially-digested rat chow. The rats gnawed their indwelling IV lines out. The whole animal vivarium was swept with a contagious, virulent respiratory virus. At one point the IV apparatus I was inserting in the rats was clotting off so rapidly and frequently that I was sure the dose of anticoagulant medication, heparin, that I was giving had been measured wrong. My foolhardy solution was to experiment by giving ten times the proper dose of the blood thinner to two rats in which I had placed these surgical IVs. The next morning I arrived in the vivarium to find that my two rats had both had profound strokes: one was milling about the cage but only moving its right side; the other was completely immobile but appeared to be fully conscious—it could breathe and blink, but that was about it.

I felt awfully bad about the two rats which I'd stroked out (God knows, the lunatic fringe of the animal rights gangs would have strung me up for that one, if they'd had a chance), yet, slowly but surely (as they say) I was getting to a point where I could make the experiment work— make it cough up useful data almost in spite of itself.

After a few months of this, enough data had been generated to reach a conclusion. Unfortunately, the information I had painstakingly gathered yielded the inescapable result that it was impossible to detect any CGRP-induced effect on the rats' gastric acid secretion. Intravenous injections of the protein didn't cause any increase or decrease in acid production at all. Either the hypothesis was wrong or the model was not sensitive enough; there was no way to tell which was at play, of course.

Frustrating as this was after months of work, the experience did teach a couple of valuable lessons. First it taught me first-hand respect for the Scientific Method: if you ask nature clear questions, she will usually provide clear answers in reply. Second, I learned something of practical use in any future academic career I might contemplate: negative answers to scientific inquiry are given scarcely any attention at all by the editors of scientific journals. I had learned that it was *not possible* to measure any difference in gastric acid output from rat stomachs after the IV administration of CGRP. This is "negative data," and although it might represent new information, it is not considered to be knowledge of similar importance as if a new phenomenon or effect in nature had been demonstrated (as, for example, if the CGRP *had* caused an appreciable increase in the acid production). No important journal would publish my negative result. Although I could understand why, and even shudder at what the medical journals would be like if every negative result were published, I couldn't help thinking that some poor, dumb bastard in another academic medical center might very well try the same thing I had tried and kill or stroke out that many more rats while wasting a year of his or her time (in fact, I wistfully wondered if I hadn't already walked in some other soul's star-crossed rat research footsteps myself).

I needed a new research focus.

Thankfully, the general atmosphere in the Research Laboratory was pretty lighthearted. For one brief shining moment, in a single conjoined office and lab, there were no sullen sticks-in-the-mud, and a general sense of hard-working good humor pervaded. Dr. Addis, the Chairman/Dean, would show up once every few weeks to continue some figure-head-supervision, but he was so out-of-touch with what we were doing that this soon grew uncomfortable and he stopped coming. It was a shame, actually: Addis' position of importance in administration had overwhelmed his original interests and focus—he had been a ground-breaking researcher in the past—and whenever he appeared in the lab, we would half-expect to see TV cameras behind him. I felt bad for him: he was a surgeon who was probably—in his heart—a scientist first; now he was a full-time administrator.

This left Ian Bennett in command of the lab. Ian—a spectacularly intelligent fellow—struck me as being in constant internal conflict, in a typically British sense. That is to say that he had both a classic perception of propriety (to which he endeavored mightily to adhere) and an utterly silly, infantile sense of humor lurking just beneath the surface. The ongoing task for him was to balance these two intrinsic characteristics throughout the course of the ordinary work day. I took it upon myself to make this task as difficult for him as I possibly could, primarily by making poorly-disguised appeals to Ian's acute appreciation of the absurd.

My first efforts at this were admittedly childish, but one has to get to know one's audience; comedians call it "finding the level of the room." I heard that Ian had occasionally dusted off the old gag of gluing a silver dollar to the floor and then finding amusement in monitoring the efforts that passersby expended in attempting to pry it up. I thought I might catch him at his own game, but it would obviously require some twist.

As it happened, the lab had recently acquired one of the early desktop scanners—primitive by today's standards but nevertheless fully capable of generating high-quality duplications. I realized that the proper varia-tion on Ian's scheme was to produce some counterfeit paper cash, then put it some place where he would casually encounter it. After some consideration, I focused on the details: a $50, or even a $20 bill would be too unlikely to be found lying about—Ian was very bright and would surmise the joke before it had a chance to be funny (which obviously depended on his being tricked for at least a few moments). I would make counterfeit $10s.

Some other details were rather more important: for example, I didn't want the joke to be so good that I ended up in Federal prison! It turns out that it's illegal to produce facsimiles of currency, but only if the copies bear a close enough resemblance to the real thing to reasonably fool a reasonable person: this is why novelty money that is tiny or enormous but otherwise an exact duplication is legal—no one could reasonably suppose that a $20 bill the size of a place mat (or a postage stamp, for that matter) is genuine legal tender. I decided to slightly increase the size of my *faux* bills and, moreover, print them on only one side—if the G-Men fingered me for a one-sided bill, I figured I'd do okay in court.

Beyond the actual mirth-making hardware—which was easy enough to make with the scanner—the prerequisites for this practical joke included a few other considerations. Although I suspected that Ian would be more easily tricked in the early morning (since he took a little while to get going at the start of the day—coffee or no), the lab office would be more heavily populated at lunchtime. When to pull the prank—7:30 AM or 12:00 noon? Ultimately, the noon hour won out—the thought being: what's the point of skewering the boss if everyone can't be there?

The final piece of the sophomoric prank was put in place when I stitched a length of fine fishing line to the counterfeit ten-dollar bill. As lunchtime approached, I surreptitiously reminded all the laboratory personnel that the gag was on, then placed the phony ten-spot just under the propped-opened door to the lab office, as if someone had dropped the bill and it had been swept under the door by one of the breezes that frequently coursed through the building. My idea was to tug the other end of the fishing line, which I held in my hand, and so cause the bill to hop along the ground (in Chaplinesque style) as if blown by some unseen and unfelt wind. I figured that Ian (whose frugality was well-documented) would chase the phony money, and so provide us lackeys with some good-natured humor.

At lunchtime Ian entered the office, where there was a microwave oven and a long table, and strolled right past my counterfeit/humor/land mine. He didn't even glance down.

"No problem," I thought. "He'll see it when he leaves."

I sat at my desk and listened to my stomach growl as I caught the scent of everyone else's lunches emanating from the break room. I tried to concentrate on my work, but I had to keep one eye on the door in case Ian escaped—the whole gag depended on my vigilance.

"Damn!" I thought. "Ian never takes this long to eat lunch!"

In fact, he was usually done in ten minutes. On this day twenty, then thirty minutes passed. I was stuck at my desk, distractedly editing some manuscript I was working on, one eye constantly focused on the break-room door. Finally I heard the rustling of some paper plates and the shuffling of chairs. Ian appeared at the break room entrance, headed toward the main office portal, where my prank awaited him....

He hesitated a moment as he looked at the floor in front of the door. My hand tensed on the fishing line. Without even bothering to look at me, in a bland tone Ian simply said, "Craig, I believe that some of your 'funny money' here is trying to make a run for the border...."

With that he was gone, out the door. In a split second he had seen the money, recognized it (or surmised it) to be fake, and had moved on: he'd basically seen through the whole ruse in about three seconds. Reflecting on my defeat I could only wonder at Ian's resourcefulness.

And plan his downfall.

During the several months I had spent on the fruitless acid-secretion experiments, I had somehow gradually gained the confidence of Ian and Dr. Addis. At any rate, when that work imploded, they allowed me to pick my own subject for further research, with the proviso that they each held veto power if I got too off-the-wall. I knocked around a few ideas for a week or so, trying to come up with a project that was both interesting and feasible—I'd continue to work almost completely on my own. One consideration that Ian provided me was the possibility of collaborating with another university: I might get to travel to another lab to learn new techniques, network with other investigators, etc. As appealing as this sounded, the only two locations that surfaced through the contacts of Addis and Bennett were Los Angeles (which I could drive to in less than a day, anyway) and Memphis. All things considered, staying in San Francisco seemed like the best choice.

I eventually settled on a project involving research into a poorly-characterized facet of rapid wound healing in the lining of the stomach and intestine. In this process, called "restitution," the cells which line the inner surface of the gut recognize the presence of an injury and rapidly move over the injured site to seal it off. The whole process is complete within a few hours and at first it even seems a little hard to believe, since nothing similar happens with the skin (which we're more familiar with in everyday life, of course)—at least nothing nearly as fast. Thinking that this sounded interesting, I began looking into what sort of methods had been used to investigate the process. It turned out that one experimental apparatus called an Ussing chamber—a bubbling glass contraption that looked like it belonged in an old Frankenstein flick—had been employed with moderate success by some researchers a few years before. I set up my chamber in an out-of-the-way cubbyhole in the back of the lab and devised a series of experiments. The plan was to remove the stomach from euthanized rats, strip the interior lining off of them, then measure the electrical voltage across the tissue to assess the progress of the restitution which I would induce. This, then, was the ticket—an interesting subject, reasonably straightforward experiments, cool equipment.

The only problem was that it proved next to impossible to get any results. The model worked perfectly, as with the acid experiments. I could easily measure the voltage across the cell layers, then damage the stomach lining (with grain alcohol!) and watch the restitution process take place over the next few hours. The voltage dropped to zero after I slammed the stomach with the booze—indicating that tiny holes were punched in the layer—then slowly returned to near-normal as the stunned (but living) nearby cells rolled over the empty regions to restore an intact surface. The whole shebang was displayed to perfection on my tracings of the voltage changes. The trouble was I couldn't get anything to alter the progress of the restitution! I incubated the stomach lining with all manner of biologically active organic and inorganic compounds. I tried different stuff to injure the stomach. I tried harvesting the rat stomachs differently, even killing them with different anesthetics. All of this took months, and it was exasperating. I had been in the GI Research Lab for most of a year, and I'd produced no meaningful research. It was very depressing.

In order to combat the depression, I focused on upping the ante in my efforts to chagrin poor Ian.

There is a period immediately following completion of their doctorate degree when Ph.D.s who are heading into the scientific field serve a sort of research apprenticeship. This is the "post-doc " period, and one of the post-docs in the lab was a remarkably abrasive native Chinese woman named Sunyi Yan. How she ever ended up at UCSF was anybody's guess, since she was so personally unappealing and professionally questionable (it's hard for me to believe that she was one of the "best and the brightest" from even so scientifically bankrupt a system as that of the universities in mainland China). After she left, it turned out that much of the data she had acquired during her two-year stay had been falsified—practically original sin itself in scientific circles, and utterly unforgivable—but no one was really surprised. Ian, in particular, detested Sunyi, and may have smelled a rat (a figurative one, of course— we all smelled genuine rats every day!) with regard to the validity of her research even while she was still working there.

In any case, Sunyi finally left to take a job as a pathologist in Detroit. Ian, shortly thereafter, embarked on a project which would dominate the next several years of his life. He became focused on a compound found, like CGRP, in the nerves of the gut organs. This stuff had the romantic, Dr. Jekyll-like name, "Substance P," and Ian was determined to find out everything there was to know about it. To this end, he had generated an antibody to the receptor molecules on the surfaces of the cells which bind Substance P. Accomplishing this was quite a feat, and even great efforts yielded just microscopic amounts of the antibody. Ian had staked months of upcoming work on the tiny cache of precious material, which was worth many thousands of times its minuscule weight in gold. Knowing this, the creaking wheels in my crazed mind began to spin.

As a practical joke, I determined to compose a fake letter from the dearly-Detroit-departed Sunyi, thanking Ian for providing her with a large amount (nearly all he had) of the antibody to the Substance P receptor. Thus it would appear that his work would be paralyzed indefinitely, and the cause would be the hated Sunyi Yan.

The first thing to do was find a willing patsy—someone who could play the role of the unwitting provider of the antibody to Sunyi ("I didn't know that I shouldn't have sent that stuff to her...."). As it turned out, this was easy enough, because all of Ian's assistants wanted to "get" him. The choice had to be able to take some Ian-abuse, yet keep the gag going long enough to milk some humor out of it. Folding under Bennett's heat too soon would ruin the joke. I picked the perfect subject in Patrick Garvey, a good-natured research assistant with the requisite backbone but also a valuable innate ability to BS.

Next I needed some convincing hardware: especially letterhead which would bear up under withering British scrutiny. Early on, I figured that an actual letter would be too tough: I'd need to fake a Detroit postmark, etc. The ideal alternative was a fax. With a facsimile transmission, the quality of the actual copy of the letter would be so low, anyway, that it could mask many of the suboptimal aspects of the forgery. Having settled on this, I set out to construct a fake letterhead with the word processor: an added touch of detail was to steal a logo (from another hospital, actually) and copy that onto the phony letterhead—God is in the details, but so is the crafty practical-joker. I then simply typed out a letter in Yan's broken English thanking Ian—and Patrick, the provider—for the antibody and remarking on how beautiful her roses were, a personal aside from her which I knew would further infuriate Ian. The crowning touch was to add a copy of Sunyi's actual signature—stolen from an old postcard—to the forgery.

I now had a rough draft which contained a printed fake letterhead and text, with glued-on phony logo and signature. All that remained to be done was to pass this through the fax machine—set to "copy"—and the masterpiece was finished.

The next Friday morning—I now knew that Ian was better prey early in the day—I placed the fax in Bennett's in-box. That morning we had a lab meeting, and I knew that he'd look at his mail immediately afterwards, in the office, with all around. The whole lab was in on the gag. This time it worked to perfection.

As the meeting adjourned, there was an ordinary amount of milling about. I waited for Ian to pick up his mail and begin to read, then shuffled past him with a mumbled "'scuse me." The secretary had added the perfect accent to the gag by burying the fake fax two or three pieces deep, but only below some meaningless junk-mail that he was bound to pitch as soon as he glanced at it. He finally got to the fax and gradually digested it. Garvey was still in the meeting room, casually polishing off a doughnut.

Ian's voice gathered a peculiar pitch and intensity as he fairly leapt out of his skin.

"Paaaaatriiiiick!"

Garvey was good. Real good. He was barely audible, with a mouthful of Krispy Kreme in the next room.

"What's up?"

"What's the matter?" the secretary asked, feigning genuine concern—although her face was blushed beet-red in an attempt to suppress her laughter.

"Patrick!" Ian ignored her. "Did you send some of the Substance P receptor antibody to Sunyi?!?"

"Yeah," Garvey wiped his mouth with a paper towel as he sidled up to Bennett, "she said you okayed it. I wondered why you'd want to give her almost all we have, though. Sheesh, that stuff was a pain to make...."

Garvey wandered off while Ian frantically instructed the secretary to contact Sunyi.

Uh-oh: I hadn't considered this. Not to worry, though; since she was in on the gag, the secretary wasn't about to actually call Detroit. She dialed a phony number, asked the appropriate questions, then hung up and told Ian that Sunyi had left for China—no one knew when or even if she was coming back.

This was exquisite. Improvisation by my co-conspirators was twisting Ian in directions I had never anticipated. Taking their cue, I chimed in, "Hey, Ian, you don't suspect that she took that stuff back to Beijing with her, do you? Damn, we'll never get it back now."

Poor Ian looked stunned and mournful, sort of like you feel when you've lost your car keys and your wallet. And your house. And your favorite dog. He began having what psychiatrists call "flight of ideas": generating grandiose schemes for intercepting Sunyi at customs or creating an international incident about the stolen biological material.

The torture went on for a few more minutes before our united front finally gave way: one of the research residents couldn't hold back any longer, and she began laughing hysterically. Soon the rest of us joined in. For some moments Ian still didn't realize that it was a put-on. He looked aghast at us as we apparently laughed at his calamity. Finally he caught on and, to his credit, began chortling with a combination of amusement and what must have been indescribable relief. He good-naturedly called me a bastard as I produced the rough draft of the fax from my desk drawer, then Ian disappeared down the hall to his lab and closed the door. Patrick later came in and said the first thing he did was go to the chemicals freezer and double-check the supply of the antibody!

A few weeks later, following achingly long effort, I was astonished to see an actual result in one of my Ussing chamber experiments. After I treated the stomach tissue with an antibody to a certain structural protein called laminin, the whole process of restitution seemed to be impaired—almost completely halted. Time after time, as I repeated the experiment, the repair which I previously couldn't alter at all simply would not occur. It was absolutely amazing and, more importantly for scientific purposes, absolutely reproducible. When I was sure of the validity of my experiments, I headed to Ian's office, where I could expect nothing but the most merciless scientific skepticism and scrutiny. Confiscating the startled Englishman to my work-bench, I brought him to a place where he could see the graphic tracings of my experiments (for a moment I wondered if he was recalling the events of the Sunyi prank; but that was weeks before…).

Ian glanced down at the printouts, examining them with his practiced—and therefore jaundiced—eye. It seemed like hours to me as he perused the simple documents. What was he expecting to see? The data were right there!

After he'd completed his examination, Ian looked back up at me. With a wide grin, he handed me back the printout sheet and uttered one word only: "Results!"

Results. They meant everything. They meant the possibility, even the likelihood of publication. They meant a good prospect for presentation at a national meeting (hopefully some place more exotic than Memphis or Los Angeles). Most importantly, they pointed my research efforts in a definite direction. Now I could follow this thread of information and trace it to its end. After I discovered the laminin result, my little Ussing chamber in the back of the lab became a paper-mill: although I had worked in the lab for almost fifteen months before I submitted my first article for publication in an international journal, over the next nine months I wrote five more. All were accepted to peer-reviewed journals. I presented my work in New Orleans and San Diego, and at a big meeting there in San Francisco. These efforts padded my resume (called in medical circles a "CV," short for the Latin *curriculum vitae*) handsomely, which helped immeasurably when I decided to enter the surgery match. My experimental work was very modest stuff, to be sure, but I did get the taste of what successful scientific research is all about.

I briefly toyed with becoming a full-time scientist permanently, especially when Ian was offered a prominent position at a university in Britain and asked if I wanted to come along. Ultimately, though, I decided that I wasn't really cut out for pure science. I wanted to be a surgeon. After three years in the GI Research Lab I re-emerged into the world of clinical medicine.

12

The Third Year—
On the Hot Seat

WHEN INTERVIEWING FOR RESIDENCY POSITIONS IN GENERAL SURGERY, one tries to take note of all the differences between the programs, so as to be able to make some sort of discerning and meaningful decision between them. If they were all the same, the only decision would be where one wanted to live which, given the time actually spent in the hospital, is probably the least important concern. By paying close attention, one can identify the important differences and make an informed choice. Nevertheless, there are remarkable similarities from program to program. One constant that I heard from the residents at essentially every program I visited was that the first and third years were the most difficult. I had eventually made it through the first, although there were several times when I nearly broke. Considering the prospect of another ordeal, reputed to be at least as harrowing, was not especially pleasant.

The senior residents at Ohio State confirmed what my own eyes had revealed to me about the third year. It was a bear. Everyone could see the third-years shuffling through the hallways at all hours of the day and night, the perpetual look of sleep deprivation—with which I was well acquainted—etched on their faces. But what was the reason for the exhaustion? What were the tasks that were so overwhelming? Although spared the mountains of paperwork and scut that flooded the interns, the third-year resident had his or her own considerable clinical crosses to bear.

The third-years (also known as the "junior residents," notwithstanding the fact that they had two full years under their belts) were primarily responsible for the consult service. Whenever an attending on another service wanted an official consultation from General Surgery, the residents on that attending's service called the clinical Gen Surg office. This office would figure out which among the three Gen Surg services was on call (Surg 1, 2 or 6) and page the third-year assigned to that group of attendings. The third-year (who quickly learned to recognize and despise the number of the hated consult line that constantly appeared on his pager—I still remember it now, 3-8777) would then take the basic information about the patient in question—name, location, diagnosis, reason for consultation—and go see the consult. If things were slow, you might be able to go right away; if you were busy (much the more common scenario) this might have to wait a few hours, unless the consult was an urgent one. The consults could come rapid fire, and each required a considerable amount of time to evaluate, especially during the early part of the year when one's confidence was lacking. The third-year on call might get a dozen consults during the day (and a dozen more overnight, counting the nocturnal ER hits), so it definitely didn't pay to get behind.

Another task of the junior resident was chart dictation. This was a thoroughly unrewarding task that was placed on the third-year resident for two reasons only: 1) it kept the attendings from having to do it, and 2) the first- and second-years were considered to be too inexperienced to do it right. Basically the hospital could not bill for services until the patient's hospital course had been summarized in a dictated letter, which I assume was sent to the payor. I always considered it odd that an organization with a multimillion-dollar budget, like a university medical center, would place the final responsibility for the reimbursement of services on a "junior resident." In any case, the third-year had to make his way to the bowels of the complex, where the medical records offices were, and locate a stack of charts with his name on them. He would then wade through the charts and attempt verbally to construct some sort of comprehensible narrative for the dictation department to put on paper. This was a task worthy of Sisyphus; no matter how much you dictated, the stack never seemed to get any smaller.

Another task that the junior resident was faced with, which eluded the intern, was helping to staff the clinics. As an intern I had dreaded clinic days, not because I had ever had to work there, but because these office hours corresponded to admissions and paperwork. For the junior resident, though, the clinic represented real energy expenditure. If there were three residents in the clinic and sixty patients (a fairly common proportion), you might have to see twenty patients whose histories and physical examinations you were completely unfamiliar with. To do this right takes considerable time and effort.

But the real focus of the third-year in any surgical residency is the acquisition of genuine, practical operative skills. This is the year when one is expected to attain and demonstrate mastery of the simple procedures—hernia repair, appendectomy, etc.—and gather more refinement in one's technique, in preparation for performing the complex operations reserved for the senior and chief residents.

Putting this all together, it's clear why surgeons consider the third year of residency to be so challenging. The sheer magnitude of clinical work which is shouldered, and the depth and scope of the skills and knowledge which are expected to be acquired, is daunting. Dr. Atcheson summed up the third year to me in this way: "Up until the third year you've been an information-gatherer. Now you must become a decision-maker."

As it turned out there were decisions to be made both in and out of the hospital that year. During the third year my daughter was born. During the third year my marriage came apart at the seams. During the third year I came within an inch of quitting surgery.

No doubt about it; the third year was a bear.

I started off these eventful twelve months with a rotation on the old stand-by, Surg 1. This time around I would have relatively little to do with the actual running of the inpatient service, though. That would be left to the Chief Resident and the intern. My primary focus would be seeing the many consults that came our way.

In a university hospital setting, consultations to a particular service are supposed to be divided equally, so that all the surgeons can share the work load and, moreover, all can develop a patient base. Now, as things happen, some surgeons get a better reputation among the referrers than others—not usually because of the quality of the operative work, though;

more frequently this is due to things like personality, how quickly the consult is seen, and so forth. The upshot of this is that the Surg 1 attendings, especially Dr. Atcheson, were constantly getting consulted directly, even when they weren't on call. In other words, the consulting service would specifically direct the referral to Dr. Atcheson, bypassing the usual system whereby that consult would go to whomever happened to be "on" that day. I don't know if the referring docs who did this thought they were doing the Surg 1 attendings a favor or not, but I do know that if they believed that, they were dead wrong. These guys were already so busy from their practices that they didn't need anything else heaped on their already too-full plates. But I suppose you never stop worrying about a rainy day, and "The Boys," as some of the women residents called the Surg 1 attendings, never refused a consultation.

One patient consult we all wished we might have refused was Steve Denham. Dr. Scott Marvin, Atcheson's fire-breathing young partner, was on call when Denham appeared in the emergency department with a rip-roaring case of pancreatitis. The story was that, while a bystander, he had been shot through the belly during a robbery attempt. He had survived the gunshot but the bullet had penetrated his pancreas.

Among the many witticisms attributed to Dr. Zollinger was the observation that, in order for a surgeon to be happy, he should "love his wife, be kind to animals and never operate on the pancreas." The reason is that with regard to surgery of the pancreas, unfortunately, the more you do the worse things get. Any kind of inflammation of the pancreas, or "pancreatitis," is potentially life-threatening, and all surgery on the organ results in some inflammation. Another frequent complication is a pancreatic fistula, where fluid from the organ leaks out through a hole in the skin. The surgeons who operated on Denham after his gunshot wound did the right thing in ignoring his pancreatic injury. They knew he might get a post-traumatic pancreatitis, or develop a fistula, but any surgery to repair the organ would have just about guaranteed one or both of those outcomes. Certainly there are times when the proper thing to do is remove some of a traumatized pancreas, but in Denham's case I think the proper decision was made. It just turned out that the "proper decision" wasn't good enough.

Denham not only developed traumatic pancreatitis, he developed a chronic form of it. I suppose there might be worse things to have than chronic pancreatitis, but I'm pretty sure that I haven't seen any. The surgeons of the early twentieth century were in awe of pancreatitis; in famous tracts they said it was the worst pain that a patient can experience. I've had patients with pancreatitis who cannot lie still without enough narcotic medication to render them unconscious. The only analogy I can draw is that talking to a patient with an acute episode of pancreatitis is like talking to someone who is on fire: they simply cannot stay stationary and maintain a conversation due to the intense, unrelenting pain. Denham lived this, day-in and day-out.

We had to admit him to the hospital every two weeks or so. The narcotics he needed just to be able to function had rendered him a helpless junkie: he was on methadone at home. We tried every non-drug intervention we could think of to control the pain and ease the pancreatitis: special abdominal "celiac" nerve blocks, skin-level electrical signal generators, TPN and fasting. Nothing worked at all. Sometimes we would admit him just for pain control, when the methadone wasn't enough and he needed morphine or, even better, fentanyl, a semi-synthetic opiate many times stronger than morphine. To compound matters, as the pancreatitis gradually ate away at him (in addition to its well-known role in insulin production, the pancreas makes digestive enzymes, and in pancreatitis these essentially digest the organ itself) his pancreas was becoming scar tissue. The predictable result was that Denham became an incredibly "brittle" diabetic – his blood sugar was rarely even close to normal. Hard on the heels of this, he developed terrible infections in both of his feet and had to have below-the-knee amputations of both legs.

The sad thing was that Denham had been a "regular guy"—with a wife, a good job—before he got caught in the wrong place at the wrong time. Now his life was a complete wreck. He looked like a "B" movie vampire, with colorless skin, massive black circles under his eyes and a near-skeletal physique. His only focus was obtaining narcotics, and like any junkie he would lie, cheat or steal in order to do so. Although she stayed longer than most would have, his wife finally left when she could no longer endure it. Her husband was long gone—replaced by a gaunt, hideous, hateful vulture. Ultimately Dr. Marvin had to refuse to continue caring for Denham when he altered some pain med prescriptions which had been written for him. I don't know what happened to Steve Denham after that, but I'm quite certain that he died soon after, whether from an overdose, a diabetic coma, or something else. In any case, the whole episode was simply awful, and I have no hesitation in stating that it was one of the more humbling episodes of residency—we could do nothing to help that poor man. I hope Denham is finally resting in peace.

Seeing dozens of consults a week, it was inevitable that I would have some triumphs and also make some mistakes.

I was asked to see one patient who was on the medical Gastroenterology service. They thought he had gallstones. After talking to him and reviewing his labwork, I thought he probably had pancreatic cancer. A few days and a few investigative studies later, it turned out I was right. Score one for Miller—although it's hard to celebrate one's diagnostic skills when they reveal that the patient has a fatal disease.

Another consult I saw as a third-year resident ended up getting me into trouble and, ultimately, having profound effects on the next several years of my life. Things began innocently enough, with a late-night page from the emergency room while I was on call. They had a patient there, a diabetic who had an infection in his leg. He was a derelict, and his leg had a wound that was draining pus. The ER attending told me that he didn't think the man would need to go to the OR; he'd just require some drainage at the bedside.

In truth, I had never seen anything quite like the infection in this man's leg.

There was a quarter-sized hole in the skin over his right shin, and when I pressed on the leg beneath it, great spurts of creamy yellow pus came gushing forth, straight through the hole. Amazingly, the pus was completely odorless. It was obvious that this guy needed to be admitted, but I felt that I should open up his shin-hole so that we could drain the rest of the stuff out of his leg and pack the infected wound. The ER attending helped me as we carved a three-inch incision in the derelict's leg. The cut we made caused the guy no pain, which surprised me at the time. The leg had hurt him considerably before it began to ooze: undrained abscesses can be excruciating.

Next I telephoned the attending at home and let him know what I was doing. He agreed with my plan and asked me to take him by the patient's room in the morning.

I admitted the man, put him on some antibiotics, and continued with the rest of my duties.

The next day we were busy as hell. All the attendings on the service were in the OR all day. I was still on call for consults until late that afternoon, and was getting paged seemingly every five minutes with a new emergency (it was a Friday, and a lot of services liked to dump their garbage on General Surgery before the weekend hit). As it happened, the attending in question didn't get out of the OR until after seven that night. When I took him around to see the consults, he was tired and in an understandably surly mood. When we came to the diabetic derelict's room, I took down the dressing. My nice, clean ER drainage incision was now black around the edges, and his entire lower leg was a startling shade of scarlet. Rather than improving, the infection had gotten markedly worse; the leg simply looked like hell.

The attending stalked out of the room while I redressed the wound. By the time I reached the nurse's station, he was already booking the OR. There was no question that the leg needed surgery immediately or it would have to be amputated. It might not even be salvageable at this point.

Even though I tried to explain to the attending that the leg was much worse than it had been when I'd admitted the man, he didn't believe me. He thought that I had blown an obvious diagnosis, and in so doing had put the patient in jeopardy. As I looked back on it, I realized that it would have been safer and easier just to have taken him to surgery the night before, but things hadn't looked that bad then. I was also tricked by the ER attending, who had poisoned my mind with the suggestion that the leg didn't require operative drainage. Still, it was my fault, and excuses didn't help me or the patient.

At surgery that night we removed a considerable amount of dead and infected skin and muscle from the derelict's leg, but it did survive.

The attending remembered my mistake as if it were a first impression.

The long hours at the hospital began to take their toll on my home life. My wife hadn't ever accepted the idea that the time spent at the hospital was necessary, or that the time that was further invested—taking call at home, which became more and more frequent as my seniority grew—was anything other than a punitive measure imposed by the faculty. The record would seem to invite her view and, truthfully, my sometimes frustrated responses to her anger may have betrayed my suspicion in this regard as well. In any case, we didn't communicate very well and a serious rift was growing between us. Neither of us was happy. The mistake we then made—a horrifically common one—was to perceive the other as the problem, rather than the ally. Outside forces were dismantling our relationship, and we should have teamed up against them; instead they divided us and, in true military fashion, conquered. Those forces then got help from a source I never anticipated.

I got a call to meet with Dr. Atcheson. Although he was my assigned "faculty mentor," this was unscheduled and certainly irregular. I was about to finish my Surg 2 third-year rotation and begin a period of six weeks in the lab, following up my research from San Francisco. I had spent several months gathering the equipment and resources for this and was, in addition, looking forward to some time off from the ungodly call schedule. There was another reason that I was looking forward to a few weeks away from the wards: my wife was pregnant. We were both ecstatic about this and, although we had a long way to go to patch things up, we both felt that some good time together would be just the thing. It had been a tough ride all the way around, no doubt about it; maybe things were going to go our way now.

On my way up to Dr. Atcheson's seventh-floor office, I decided that he was going to ask me about my research plans: he was sponsoring my efforts and we hadn't discussed them much. I wanted to tell him not to worry; just six months ago I'd received just about every surgical research award and accolade I could have, from a piece of work I had done on my own without any faculty "supervision."

Once I took a seat in Dr. Atcheson's office, I knew that something very different, very malevolent was afoot. Gone was the half-smile he always wore when we were in one-on-one situations. He looked grim. The last time I had seen a look like this, a teacher back at high school had been distractedly going through the classroom motions, possessed of the knowledge—as I was not—that my brother would be arriving in a few minutes with the news that our father had died.

There were no specifics. "Members of the faculty" were concerned about me. They thought I seemed distracted, sometimes argumentative. Careful to absolve himself of any contribution to the inquiry, Atcheson said that questions about my dedication to clinical service and patient care had been raised.

I was not at all ready for an attack on my ability and motivation in taking care of patients. I didn't realize it at the time, but that pus-filled leg was coming back to haunt me. After my initial, muted shock, I instinctively took a defensive posture. Goddammit, no one could say these things to me....

Rising in my chair, I demanded to know which members of the staff had made these outrageous remarks. Atcheson wouldn't say. I told him that this was America, and if he didn't tell me he would surely have to tell the lawyer I retained or the judge that oversaw the case I would bring. The constitutional right to know one's accusers is not given up by the choice (at the time, I thought, mistaken) to become a surgery resident. Atcheson seemed impressed by my indignation, even pleased, but he tried to calm me down.

"Craig, no one wants to fire you. I'm the Program Director, and I have no intention of that. We all think you're very bright and will make a good surgeon; we just want to get you some more experience. We want you to do Surg 1 over."

At that point in time, I would have rather had my eyes put out by sharpened, burning sticks than go through Surg 1 again. How would I tell my wife? We'd been hoping for this time to spend together, to find each other again, to get ready for the baby....

I refused. I told Atcheson that the nameless accusations were baseless as well, and that if he believed them he was going to have to fire me.

As he sat staring at his desk blotter, I began to consider my options after an aborted surgical residency. They weren't that bad, in fact. Since so many people had left the OSU program in the previous three years, whether by their own or the faculty's volition, I had had a chance to see exactly what it was that one could do in precisely the same situation. Most went into Anesthesia: the hours were certainly better, the pay comparable....

"Craig," Atcheson's voice brought me back to the issues at hand, "I understand that you're having some problems at home."

Now I was even more deeply offended, if that were possible. I'd never mentioned anything of the sort to Atcheson or any other attending. I felt like a German delegate at the Versailles Treaty in 1919—just thoroughly outraged. But I held my tongue.

"I want to do what I can to help," he continued. "You were probably looking forward to this time to patch things up with your wife."

"I was. I don't know whether your 'sources' told you, but she's pregnant."

"Congratulations."

"Thank you."

Atcheson glanced down at his desk, then announced, "Let's make a compromise. Go ahead with your research rotation, but take general surgery consults call every third night. You won't have to do Surg 1 again, and you'll get to spend more time with your family, but you'll also get some more experience."

Since I didn't relish the prospect of becoming an anesthetist, I accepted. I really had no other choice. I was thirty-one years old, halfway through a surgery residency, with no other marketable skills to speak of. Atcheson had me over a barrel.

The next day a friend of mine in the residency office showed me that, because another resident had quit earlier in the year, if I hadn't agreed to take call during my research rotation, the other third-years would have had to do so every other night, which was forbidden by the residency governing bodies.

Whatever their motivation, the unnamed malicious faculty members secured a warm body to take surgery call every third night. Soon enough, they also secured the demise of my marriage. And they made an enemy out of me. After that November meeting with Atcheson, I never considered the Department of Surgery to be any kind of professional family. There were friends within that group, of course, but there were also—clearly—some who could not be trusted. And no one could be allowed to see—or know of—any weakness whatever.

I have heard that in the military one has a permanent dossier kept by his superiors. This file supposedly contains anything remotely negative—substandard evaluations, disapproving write-ups, demerits—which might be useful in assisting the higher-ups should they decide to get rid of the subject in question. After this point in time, I became convinced that such files existed in the Department of Surgery, as well, and that any resident could be fired at any point for any reason: the dossier would be dusted off, and "proof" of a series of events brought to light. I had busted my ass for years, and narrowly missed getting canned—probably only Atcheson's personal loyalty prevented that—for no apparent reason. In an environment where I couldn't tell who might be trying to gather information against me, paranoia was to be the order of the day.

The next six weeks were probably the strangest of the whole residency. Ostensibly, I was to spend the daytime hours engaged in research, following up my work with the Ussing chamber from San Francisco. Every third night, I would take consult call like the other third-year residents. In practice, though, things worked a little differently.

Usually, the nighttime call was busy enough that I would get no sleep. It proved to me to be impossible to drag myself over to the lab and attempt to accomplish anything of significance on a post-call day. Perhaps more to the point, I realized quickly that I had essentially no hope of accomplishing anything of significance in the field of basic medical research in six weeks anyway. It had taken me more than a *year* of full-time work to get any results back in California! Once I came to that realization, I lost most of my interest in doing any lab work at all. Of course, the prospect of producing some paper which would bear the names of my tormenters and help to further their academic careers held little appeal at the time, too. I couldn't avoid actually going to the lab; the powers-that-were undoubtedly had eyes there, watching and waiting for me to screw up. What I could do was show up, start my *Frankenstein* Ussing chamber bubbling to make it appear as if experiments were underway, then bail out the back door.

On the other hand, when I took general surgery consult call every third night, I was at a heightened level of awareness. Any trace of nonchalance had been driven from me. When I got paged for a consultation from the ER or a medicine floor, I collected all the information about the patient in question and, before going to see them, spent a few minutes in the surgery library boning up on the presumed diagnosis. Once I had examined the patient, I carefully considered the diagnoses that I thought most likely, as well as the means of ruling each one out or in, and the appropriate courses of treatment for each scenario. Only after doing all this did I contact a more senior resident or an attending, at which point I concisely outlined the patient's history and physical examination, outlined my plan for defining the cause of the symptoms and provided my suggestions for treatment.

Since I was being driven by a sense of paranoia coupled with self-preservation, I made careful records of all the patients and all of my conversations with the senior residents and attendings. In these records I documented my own presumptive diagnoses and those of the more senior "colleagues," in addition to our separate treatment plans and the ultimate disposition of the patient—what, it turned out, they had wrong with them. My goal was to demonstrate my own capabilities *vis á vis* those of the higher echelon. In the six weeks I acquired over a hundred patients on my list. In only three cases were my diagnostic and therapeutic suggestions at odds with the others': in all three I turned out to be correct.

It was with considerable "I told ya so" satisfaction that I presented Dr. Atcheson with my records at the end of the rotation. He, of course, had no idea that I had been keeping such a list. But there, in long, handwritten columns, were the patient's names, the dates, the suggested diagnoses and treatments, and the ultimate outcomes. I had carefully noted the names of the higher-ups as well as the times and dates when they had given their opinions. The whole thing was incontrovertible.

Dr. Atcheson grinned broadly. He was obviously pleased. He asked if he could make a copy of the list, and I assented on the condition that I get the original back—this was my lifeline at that moment, and I didn't like to be without it for a minute! I got the clear impression that Atcheson was going to use my list as ammunition at some closed-door meeting in the immediate future. I think he was happy to have hard evidence that his boy—after all, he had personally placed me at the top of the rank list three years before—might make a good surgeon after all.

I wish I could say that the few extra hours out of the hospital did wonders for my marriage, but the truth is that the damage done was too great. By this point the two of us could barely speak without fighting, which was an enormous shame. We held things together through the birth of our daughter in January of that year, and even had a reconciliation of sorts during the next few months, but the handwriting was on the wall. We separated the next summer.

Nearly as soon as we stopped living together, we became fast friends again.

13

The Third Year—
Chops

As I've said, the third year is supposed to be the time when one really begins to spread his surgical wings and learn how to operate. For this reason I was excited about my rotation on the Surgical Oncology service, Surg 3.

Surg 3 was a very busy service, with more than twice as many attendings as any other general surgery service. The reason for this was that Ohio State had an enormous, brand-new Cancer Hospital which had been built partially through the funding of the monolithic National Institute of Health. The referrals poured in from throughout the Midwest, and they kept these guys (and women) hopping.

Dr. William Neher was the Chief of the Division of Surgical Oncology. He had done his residency at OSU in the '70s, so Neher must have been considerably older than he appeared. In truth he looked like a movie actor in his mid-forties, with tanned, chiseled features; dark, curly hair—graying, as if scripted, at the temples—and a dazzling smile. Predictably, all the nurses and female patients were nuts about him. As it happened, one of Neher's specialties was breast surgery, so the waiting room of his clinic was composed of an odd mish-mash of the fitfully anxious and the cooingly wanton—often in the same patient.

More to the point as far as I was concerned, Neher was known as a technically skillful surgeon, one from whom much could be learned if one were attentive. Since I had been a musician in a previous incarnation, I understood the value (or, really, the necessity) of the mastery of technique. Unlike many musicians, I had also enjoyed the process of practicing technique—endless scales, arpeggios, inversions, picking and fingering exercises—because I recognized its value in terms of providing the player with an ability to express himself as fully as possible. Musicians call technical skill in the playing of an instrument "chops." Now I was eager to work on my surgical chops, and two months with Dr. Neher seemed like a good way to start.

My first operative case with Dr. Neher was a breast biopsy. This procedure is performed on lesions in the breast which are suspicious for cancer, when other modalities (like needle biopsies) haven't been conclusive. Sometimes the lesions are lumps which can be felt; other times they are mere specks of calcium on a mammogram and the radiologists have to mark them by inserting needles to guide the surgeon. This particular lesion happened to be palpable. After prepping and draping the patient, I waited for Neher to finish scrubbing. He came into the room, got gowned and gloved, and stepped up to the left side of the operating table. I had stood hopefully on the right side, which is the usual surgeon's position. Wordlessly, he took a sterile marker and drew a small curved line—technically an arc—basically parallel to the outline of the nipple.

With my eyes glued to the purple line he'd drawn, I held out my right hand for the scalpel. As the nurse moved toward me with the knife, I saw Neher's hand flash out and grab it.

"Oh no!" I thought, "he's left-handed."

As I watched in horror, Neher performed the entire minor operation. I held retractors and cut suture, much as I had done as a medical student seven years before. He worked so fast that there was nothing I could digest, no tricks I could pick up. The entire thing was over in less than ten minutes. Neher then broke scrub and immediately went to the phone to dictate the details of the operation for the medical record. At least he wasn't making me do that, I thought. But as I listened in awe, he described the history of the patient, her physical examination, the x-ray findings and then the complete operation in about 45 seconds. It was the fastest I had ever heard a person speak in my entire life. Then he was gone. I was still putting the dressing on the wound. Neher hadn't spoken a single word to me, nor mentioned me as an assistant in his dictation. I don't think he knew my name, although I had been a resident for two-and-a-half years.

Once again I had learned that just because a surgeon is skillful, and works in an academic medical center where residents are trained, it does not mean that he is a good teacher. It's a lesson that was repeated with disappointing regularity throughout residency.

In time, though, I came to have a good relationship with Neher (and he did learn my name). His lack of effective teaching stemmed, I think, from a few sources. For one thing he was too busy; his clinic and O.R. schedule didn't allow him much time to spend slowly and carefully instructing residents—but that should not have been allowed to happen since he was also being paid to teach. Neher was probably also a kind of "control freak." Some surgeons are like that; they cannot give up any of the operation to the resident or even to a partner. That's okay, but this type of surgeon just shouldn't be in academic centers.

Ultimately I did learn quite a bit from Neher about technique—it was true that he was extremely skillful in the O.R. He showed me little things that I have used and will continue to use throughout my career, like how to hold a clamp in the left hand and put a stitch in with the right, how to gracefully pass a tie around the end of a hemostat (even good surgeons look awkward doing this—Neher showed me how to look like Nureyev), how to hold a scalpel for precision and how to hold it for speed. How did it come to pass that Neher taught me these things?

I got in his good graces because of *West Side Story*.

Neher liked to play some interesting music in the operating room. He adored John Denver, Disney soundtracks and (ack!) Barry Manilow. Most of the O.R. staff did their best to stomach this stuff and, I admit, it was especially tough fare for a one-time rock'n'roll guitarist such as myself. Neher's favorite O.R. musical selections, though, were Broadway show tunes (for what it's worth, he was otherwise very textbook macho). One day Neher had the circ nurse put in a CD that was a potpourri of numbers from these musical plays. He was demonstrating his superior knowledge of this rather specialized field by quizzing the operating room personnel *en masse* on which musical the particular song that was playing had been taken from. My knowledge of Broadway musicals was (and is) less than encyclopedic, but, to my amazing good fortune, as the CD advanced it seemed to touch on each of my minor points of knowledge, and I chimed in repeatedly with the correct answer: *West Side Story* ("A Place For Us"—that had been sung at my wedding), *Fiddler on the Roof* ("Sunrise, Sunset"— a real favorite of my grandfather), *Jesus Christ Superstar* ("Everything's All Right"—I'd seen a live production a few weeks before). If it had been a parlay in Vegas, I'd have broken the bank.

After that Neher figured I must be okay, and he showed me the techniques and tricks that he had at his disposal. But he still really did all the cases himself. It wasn't until I was a Chief Resident on his service, nearing the end of residency, that he allowed me to do a big operation— a thyroidectomy—on my own. As the assistant he was absolutely breathing down my neck, and I was sweating bullets, but everything came out all right.

I wasn't at all sure how "all right" things would be with my next third-year rotation, which was adult Cardiothoracic Surgery.

My only previous experience with this service was as an intern. At that time, it had been an every-other-day-call nightmare which had been almost devoid of educational benefit. Without exaggerating, I think it is accurate to say that the 'terns on Cardiothoracic (there were two at a time, trading that every-other-night-call) were just tools to allow the attendings to concentrate on the money-making aspects of their practices: operating. I can certainly say that I personally never learned a thing from those attendings while I was an intern; if they could have cared less about education, these "professors" couldn't have shown it.

About the only one-on-one interaction the interns on "CT" had with the attendings consisted of an incredibly demeaning annual holiday ritual to which the chief of the service submitted us.

Dr. Liebowitz was a tiny, nearly completely bald individual with a gargantuan nose and an ego to match. He looked and sounded almost precisely like "Mr. Burns" from the Simpsons; in fact, if you met him after seeing that show, you'd have sworn he was emulating the character. Like Burns, Liebowitz was just about universally despised—in this case by all the doctors and nurses in the hospital. His megalomania—and its nasty, insulting manifestations—transcended the whole division. Luckily, as interns we rarely even encountered him, except in December.

Every Christmas, Liebowitz had his secretary send out cards to the residents who had been on his service during the previous academic year, inviting them to come to his office to receive Holiday gifts. Having only seen Liebowitz infrequently, we interns hustled up to the Great Man's office as soon as we got these invitations—rather like we had found the gold chocolate bars that would admit us to Willy Wonka's factory. The secretary would let us in, then mention that Dr. Liebowitz had bought bottles of wine ($7 vintages, as it turned out!) for us. The catch was that we had to actually face Liebowitz in order to get the wine.

The third-year residents got the same invitation, but they all ignored it. They knew better.

You read about the care with which such historical figures as Napoleon and Mussolini fashioned their offices and the approaches to them, all with the object of inducing fear and awe in the visitor and the supplicant. Liebowitz had clearly read these same accounts, and he had structured his office, with the pitiful bottles of off-brand holiday wine behind him, in much the same way. His secretary's desk occupied an antechamber, and after that one entered an oblong room, with bright, northeast-looking windows to the left and oak bookcases to the right. Intriguingly, the bookcases were loaded with TV monitors that were wired to display the vital signs and continuous EKGs of his patients in the ICU. (Later I learned that one of Liebowitz's less-enamored fellows had figured out a way to jostle a patient's bed just enough to make these EKGs look exactly as if the patients were in a lethal heart arrhythmia— to screw with the boss's head.)

My fellow intern (a tremendously bright and hard-working fellow on the Urology tract named Ed Wilson) and I came across our Liebowitz holiday cards at precisely the same time while on a visit to the mail room. We decided to beard the lion in his den, together. After being ushered in by Liebowitz's condescending secretary (her correct title would be "administrative assistant" but, knowing how much she would disapprove, I will persist with my present term) we were faced with The Nose himself, accompanied by one of his smirking Fellows. He asked how we were enjoying the rotation. We said it was swell, sir (I'm paraphrasing here). Then he looked at Ed and asked what field he was going into. Wilson said Urology, and Liebowitz replied something to the effect that he was too smart to "only operate on dicks." Ed looked for a moment as if he might deck Liebowitz, who was about five inches and forty pounds smaller than him. Grinning like an exhumed corpse, The Nose then asked me what I was going into. I replied General Surgery. He answered (with pathetically meager wit, I might add) that I, on the other hand, wasn't smart enough for that—maybe I should think about dick-surgery.

Both Ed and I independently weighed the pros and cons of flattening the detestable Liebowitz. Independently we reached the conclusion that, unlike the Burt Reynolds situation in *The Longest Yard,* it wasn't worth clocking the warden.

This was our tariff for getting the seven-dollar bottle of wine. Both Wilson and I, expecting a holiday-season handshake, and a thanks for a job well done, had instead been subjected to moronic, junior-high level humor at our expense.

As a result, this was the sort of crap I knew to look forward to as I embarked on another Cardiothoracic rotation. At least I also knew enough now to ignore the Christmas card from Liebowitz. As it happened, though, I never got one. The Nose had made enough enemies by then that his own venom had come back to poison him, and a new, female Dean of the College of Medicine had heard about his bullshit and summarily fired him. Couldn't have happened to a nicer man, we all thought.

Unfortunately, among his colleagues, Liebowitz' personality and his egotism were the rule, not the exception.

Dr. Bratt, for example, was one of the cardiac surgeons. He had been hired at Ohio State after losing his job at another academic medical center following a messy sexual harassment lawsuit. Unlike a number of heart surgeons, Bratt had virtually zero personal charisma. He was thin and gaunt (one resident said that he had a "body like a hamster") and in both physique and demeanor personified everyone's impression of what must have become of the kid who got his lunch money taken from him at school. Not surprisingly, Bratt projected a compensatory false bravado which, in his case, went to hilarious extremes. He had convinced himself that he was one of the world's greatest surgeons. At one point during my third-year rotation, Bratt and I were traversing a hospital hallway when

I was astonished to hear him say—completely out of the blue, "You know, Craig, I don't think there's any question that I'm—technically—one of the ten best surgeons in the world. I firmly believe that...."

At the time I didn't know Bratt well at all and I responded the way any sensible person would to such an offhand remark—I laughed. I was thinking that that was a good line and I'd have to remember it. There was only one problem: Bratt wasn't kidding.

He stopped dead in his tracks and looked at me like I had leprosy.

I looked back at him and thought, "My God, he's serious—and he does have a body like a hamster."

Dr. Bratt insisted on playing the most venomous, atonal heavy metal grunge music in the operating room, at the loudest volume. Even I, who had been a rock guitarist in my pre-medical life, found the music he played to be noisome garbage. Tellingly, Bratt had no knowledge of the bands he insisted on playing—frequently he couldn't even recall their names, once the disk began. This told me that the effeminate, gaudily unpopular Bratt had perused the campus record stores and paid off some multi-pierced denizen to select a sort of metal potpourri for him to proffer as his own to the O.R. crew. The post-adolescent cry for attention— "Look! I'm cool!"—could hardly have been more obvious. He reminded me of the Chris Rock comedy routine about the old guy in the night-club—fighting to retain a youth and virility which has vanished—or which, as in Bratt's case, never existed.

Even the most wide-eyed, ingratiating junior medical student recognized what a pretentious, sexist asshole Bratt was. The operating room nurses considered him a loathsome creature, even before they found out about the previous harassment lawsuit.

All of this made the situation which was about to develop that much more delicious, at least for the distant observer.

As it happened, Bratt had met and, improbably soon thereafter, married a young woman internist—who was just out of residency there at Ohio State. She had a bit of a gold-digger reputation and the wide-spread understanding was that she had married The Hamster out of regard for his bank account, rather than his person. The tasty aspect of all of this derived from the fact that this woman had just recently been divorced from one of the more charismatic surgical chief residents, Dr.

Rick Ho. Ho, a diminutive Asian (he couldn't have been taller than five-and-a-half feet) with an unlikely Adolph Menjou moustache and tragically moussed hair resembled a sort of fusion of late-1980s club-hip and *Bridge on the River Kwai* authoritarianism. He was a slick surgeon and slicker womanizer (which, naturally, had led to the demise of his marriage to the internist) who had scored—along with a not insubstantial number of nurses—the Cardiac Surgery fellowship at Ohio State.

As a result Bratt and Ho, linked by common attributes and a common wife (as it were), had to spend the next two tears in near-continual contact and mutual discomfort. They were both insufferably self-absorbed jerks, and so this provided great amusement to the community of onlookers (I suspect none was more amused than the shared internist-wife, although I have no evidence for this aside from an appreciation of the baseness of human nature). We all imagined the conversation which might ensue when Ho had to call Bratt at home with a problem when he was in bed with the community-wife. What if *she* answered the phone?

"Hi, Beth. It's Rick. Is Bratt there?"

"Yes, he's asleep. Do you want me to wake him?"

"In a minute." Ho was slick, remember. "What are you wearing?"

"I don't think I should be telling you that, Rick."

"Is it that black-lace teddy I bought you for Christmas last year?"

"No. He doesn't want me to wear things that he didn't buy me. He's kind of jealous."

"You always looked great in that teddy...."

Unfortunately for us, Bratt simply forbade Ho from calling his home. If there was an emergency, one of the junior residents had to make the call. In true adolescent fashion, and with possible risk to his patients put aside, he absolutely refused to have Ho call the house where he and the common-wife lived. So none of the potentially great soap-opera scenes were ever acted out, to the best of my knowledge. Circumstances forced them to operate together at times, and I always wished I could have snuck in or been a "fly on the wall" for those sessions: the tension must have been exquisite. Supposedly Bratt refused to let the technically-talented Ho perform any substantial part of the operations. He had to retract and cut ties—med student tasks.

A few months into the year the whole mess was defused when Ho married an attractive but well-traveled (by the residents, that is) blonde

Oncology nurse. He still wasn't permitted to call Bratt's home for any reason, but I suspect that his interest in doing so for other than professional causes had diminished, anyway. Nevertheless, the idea of a married, settled-down Ho was hard to accept; that just didn't fit his persona. He had ploughed too many fields. Sure enough, after finishing his Cardiac fellowship, Ho elected to pursue still further training in pediatric heart surgery at another hospital, out-of-state. Knowing him, all I could think was that he knew he was heading to a spot—a Children's Hospital packed with women of child-bearing age—where the hunting grounds would be fertile. God help his wife, who must have thought that she had finally found one who'd made the commitment, after so many samplings of the surgical resident populace.

A large part of the third-year experience on the Cardiothoracic Surgery service was given over to the critical care of the postoperative patients, which took place in the surgical intensive care unit. The way the SICU suite was arranged, four pods of 10-12 beds each surrounded a kind of "nerve center," which doubled as the nurse's station and a central monitoring point. A high-tech feel pervaded this spot, which reminded me of the bridge of the starship *Enterprise*. While on this service, I spent countless hours perched on a chair in the Cardiac surgery pod's nerve center, glowering over monitors and keeping a close eye on the postoperative patients. Usually things went smoothly, but there were some notable exceptions.

A "Code" is the most frightening event which can occur in a hospital. In this situation (sometimes known as a "Code Blue") a patient has experienced some catastrophe and is in danger of imminent death. A frantic, general call for help over the public address system summons all physicians in the hospital (or at least in the vicinity) to the patient's bedside. Once there, the docs must ascertain the cause of the patient's collapse and, hopefully, institute measures to correct the problem. Most often the event has been a cardiac one—that is, related to a serious heart problem—and the best hope is for rapid diagnosis and intervention. So frequently is this the case with codes that now all medical school graduates must be educated and tested in the protocols of "Advanced Cardiac Life Support." ACLS is a collection of algorithms (essentially flowcharts intended for rote memorization) by which such emergency cardiac events can be diagnosed and treated in a systematic and timely fashion. This takes the element of thinking out of the approach to the emergency situation. Ordinarily, thinking would seem like a good idea but, as we all know, it takes time. By simply memorizing what to do when faced with the most common scenarios the physician can act in a reflexive sense, saving precious seconds.

As it happens, by an overwhelming majority most patients who are "coded" do not survive their hospitalization; if, indeed, they even survive the code. For this reason, the ones who do survive stand out in one's memory.

Wolfgang Breuner had undergone coronary artery bypass surgery. In this operation the vessels which normally carry blood to the heart muscle itself—but are blocked by atherosclerosis—are circumvented, usually using grafts of the patient's own arteries and veins. The goal is simple: to prevent myocardial infarction, "MI"—a heart attack. Breuner had had this operation and the procedure, and then the first 24 hours after it (spent as a matter of course in the Intensive Care Unit), had gone splendidly. His initial recovery had been entirely uneventful. In fact, he was due to be transferred out of the ICU on the morning of his first postoperative day. That morning, then, sitting in the *Star Trek*-like atmosphere of the Surgical Intensive Care Unit, I was engaged in the seemingly interminable paperwork involved in the simple transfer of Breuner to the regular floor. Feeling post-call pangs, I wondered if I could sneak away from the ward long enough to secure one of the free bagels that a local merchant had been donating to the surgeon's lounge. These were no ordinary bagels; they came in all imaginable varieties and flavors; the cream cheese lay in buckets. There was even a free coffee/hot chocolate vending machine. To a hungry man the visions were intensely seductive and I was momentarily overwhelmed by them....

Suddenly a frantic cry, accompanied by the wailing and clanging of half a dozen electronic alarms, arose from Breuner's room: "Dr. Miller, can you come in here now please !!!"

I rushed into the room as the curious gathered and the "crash cart," containing all the emergency cardiac medications, was wheeled in. Breuner looked dead. He was glassy-eyed, with a fixed, unblinking stare. He was completely unresponsive. He had no pulse and no spontaneous respirations. His EKG was a flatline.

I began CPR and called for the intravenous administration of epi-nephrine, a heart and blood pressure stimulant (more commonly known as adrenaline) and atropine, a drug which accelerates the heart rate and can sometimes generate a cardiac rhythm when none is present. These drugs were given by the nurses as I continued to compress Breuner's chest, the force of my thrusts the only impetus to circulate the medica-tions. I stopped the compressions long enough to see what his EKG tracing looked like. Nothing. I began again. We prepared to place an endotracheal tube in order to more effectively manage Breuner's pulmo-nary function. I had a med student draw an arterial blood sample to check the adequacy of the patient's respiration.

Now in the ICU a code situation is supposed to be so commonplace that it should attract little extraordinary attention: in fact, some patients in "The Unit" are so sick that they are essentially in a state of continual coding, with powerful IV heart and blood pressure medications main-taining their vital signs around the clock. Nevertheless, in a university hospital setting there are so many of the uninitiated—residents, medical students, student nurses, student pharmacists—that a sudden life-and-death struggle, even in the ICU, always attracts a crowd. As I continued CPR on Breuner, I glanced around the room, primarily hoping that someone more senior—a cardiac surgery fellow or attending—would appear. Of course, there was no such luck—they had been summoned by page, but were all scrubbed in the OR in big cases—I was on my own. But I did notice that the room was full of youthfully anxious, excited faces, all trying or wanting to be useful—this was like something from TV to them: an especially good episode of *ER*, I guess. I briefly recalled my own first exposure to a code situation and the awe in which I held the residents who were "running" it—it had seemed so cool.

As I ran Breuner's code, though, nothing seemed remotely cool about it. Instead, I had the unmistakable feeling that death was not only close by, it was right in front of me, prepared to claim this man. Of course, without CPR he'd have been dead already. While the code lasted the whole thing felt like a battle—a knock-down, drag-out fight, with bloodied noses and busted lips for all. A well-conducted code is just like that—it's a conflict with mortality and it usually sways back and forth—for a few seconds you feel as if you have the upper hand while the patient rallies in response to your treatments. Moments later he takes a sudden turn for the worse as the disease process gets the upper hand. The tug-of-war goes on for what seems like an eternity, although the issue is really decided in the first few minutes. If the memory of that first code I witnessed back in med school had come back with sufficient accuracy, I would have recalled that that patient did not survive. As I've said, few did.

As I got ready to place the endotracheal tube, I stopped the chest compressions to assess the EKG again.

A gaudy turquoise cursor bounced on the screen in response to the motion of my hand leaving Breuner's chest. The oscilloscope at the core of the EKG then took a few cycles to integrate the signals coming from the electrodes on the patient's chest. A few moments later, that same turquoise blip began to leap leisurely across the dark screen, tracing out a near-normal electrical signal. Amazingly, Breuner had generated a spontaneous cardiac rhythm. It was slow, but it was there. In minutes his heart rate had returned to normal, he was breathing on his own and he had good pulses. I looked down at Breuner, drenched in perspiration and the sudden, heady excitement of the successful code. He was awake and reasonably alert, glancing about dazedly.

"Mr. Breuner," I asked, "How do you feel?"

"Woozy," he replied in a clear voice.

The jaded ICU nurses, who had surely seen it all, cheered and slapped me on the back as I left the room. I thought to myself that having those ACLS protocols etched into my memory sure paid off. Breuner had been as dead as the pharaohs, and now he was back to normal (or close to it). It was a real high point of residency.

My wife said I should have asked Breuner if he had ascended into any bright light while he was gone. I should have, too.

Transplant surgery is another subdivision of general surgery, although it really comprises a separate existence unto itself. By that I simply mean that the "nuts and bolts" of transplantation have very little to do with those of any other surgical specialty. Solid organ transplantation evolved from first tentative attempts in the early 1900s to become a profoundly scientific, broad-based clinical specialty.

There are twenty or so major organ transplantation centers in the U.S., and ours was one of these. This fact provided for a fair amount of misery for the surgical resident staff, for reasons which may be made clear presently.

Now the evolution of the surgical transplantation of solid organs is a fascinating story, and there's no denying that it has yielded significant benefits to society. Hearts, lungs, kidneys, livers, pancreases and even intestines have been transplanted, with varying degrees of success. Sometimes the results are wonderful. For example, when a kidney transplant goes smoothly, everyone wins in a big way: the patient gets to live a relatively normal life away from the dialysis machines to which he has been tethered, society is spared the enormous cost of that dialysis, and the surgeon enjoys the satisfaction of knowing he has made the difference. There are drawbacks to life with a transplanted organ—chief among these a permanent reliance on immune-suppressing drugs—but they are minor by comparison to the burdens imposed by end-stage organ disease. In some cases, of course, the alternative to transplantation is death. Nonetheless, it must be acknowledged that when a transplant goes bad, it goes awfully bad indeed.

A case in point is that of Noah Brees. Mr. Brees was a 65-year-old African-American man with kidney failure which had arisen, as is often the case, from years of poorly controlled diabetes. He had been on dialysis for several months prior to getting word that there was a kidney available, due, of course, to the misfortune of some unknown soul with a giving spirit (or, more likely, a generous next-of-kin).

Hemodialysis is a grueling ordeal in the best of circumstances. It typically consists of multiple needle sticks into surgically-created arterio-venous shunts in order to gain access to the circulation to draw out, then cleanse, the toxin-laden blood. This takes many hours, and must be repeated several times a week. IV line infections, clotted shunts and other unpleasantries are the norm. Peritoneal dialysis, consisting of frequent circulation into one's abdomen of electrolyte solutions to effect the same result as hemodialysis, is somewhat more convenient but wrought with its own complications. It was no surprise, then, when Mr. Brees jumped at a chance to put an end to these travails and undergo kidney transplantation.

The operation itself proceeded uneventfully. The technical aspects of renal transplantation have been refined over the years to a point where the operation is pretty much cookbook surgery, with little call for improvisation. This is all for the better, of course, as it allows for a speedy procedure and technical flaws are kept to a minimum. Mr. Brees's transplant took a little less than two hours to perform. On the table, his new kidney (which had been kept in ice, perfused with a chilled electrolyte solution since its harvesting) perked up when it received its new blood supply, and immediately began to produce urine. Cause for optimism abounded. The patient was taken first to the recovery room, then to the specialized postoperative transplant unit, where his clinical course could be followed closely. Soon he was doing well enough to be discharged. On the whole, he appeared to be doing remarkably well. However appearances, so the old saw goes, can be deceiving.

Transplanted organs are obviously foreign tissues and the recipient's immune system would naturally try to destroy them as such. In fact, safe suppression of this immune response in order to permit function of the transplanted organ has been for decades the Holy Grail of research associated with transplantation. With the discovery, investigation and mass production of such drugs as cyclosporine, mycophenolate and azathioprine the goal has been approached, but at a cost. Each of these medications produces its own litany of serious side effects and, as one might expect, all of the immunosuppressive compounds share the adverse characteristic of predisposing the patient to infection. By interfering with the body's ability to recognize and destroy a foreign organ, we interfere with its ability to do the same thing to a dangerous virus, bacterium or fungus. Broadly speaking, these drugs induce a susceptibility to infection not dissimilar to that which accompanies AIDS.

Given large doses of powerful immune-suppressing drugs to protect his new kidney, Mr. Brees got infected.

After his discharge, Mr. Brees had gone home and tried to resume his normal life—without, of course, the ball-and-chain of thrice-weekly dialysis treatments. Naturally he felt a little poorly—he was recovering from major surgery, after all. A few days passed and he seemed to rally. Then he developed very high fevers, over 104 degrees Fahrenheit. Dripping in sweat, he had called the transplant office, where the well-trained nurse coordinators instructed him to high-tail it for the emergency room. The transplant team saw him there, immediately admitted him and placed him on intravenous antibiotics. They also instituted an all-out search for the source of what appeared to be a virulent infection. Mr. Brees underwent ultrasounds, CT scans, blood, urine and sputum cultures, the works.

Unfortunately, not only did all the diagnostic tests come back negative, Noah got worse. His blood pressure dropped, and the team was forced to place him in the intensive care unit for resuscitation and close monitoring. Once there, and now in a substantially debilitated state, Mr. Brees was a set-up to develop more infections. This he promptly did.

Noah's breathing grew labored, and he was placed on a ventilator. Soon he developed a dreadful pneumonia, and had so much fluid around his lungs that he had to have chest tubes placed in both sides in order to drain it off. He stayed on the ventilator so long that a tracheostomy had to be done to prevent permanent damage to his vocal cords from having the endotracheal tube in place.

Reluctantly, the transplant docs took him off his immunosuppressive medications. They knew that this would mean the loss of his transplant kidney, but they were trying to save his life at this point.

Horribly, even this didn't slow Brees' inexorable spiraling. The original source of his infection had never been identified, but it seemed likely to be within his abdomen somewhere. There is an axiom of surgery which states that undrained abscesses will never resolve—all the antibiotics in the world won't cure them. It seemed likely that Noah was harboring an abscess somewhere—drugs with powerful activity against bacteria, viruses and fungi were having no significant effect on his clinical course—and the belly looked like the best bet.

An abdominal exploration was done. As one might guess by this point, it turned up nothing. What it did accomplish was the penultimate saber stroke in a series of medical *coups de grace* which were administered to Brees. For some unknown reason, after the operation the concentration of blood-clotting cells called platelets decreased to virtually nothing. Noah began to bleed from everywhere: his IVs, his tracheostomy, his chest tubes. One of the transplant attendings made the serious mistake of cutting open the skin over a collection of blood in his groin, and the raw surface oozed uncontrollably. Nurses spent entire eight-hour shifts holding pressure over this bleeding site.

Soon the transplant kidney died amidst Brees' system-wide mobilization of immune activity. He was back on dialysis. Mercifully, though, this wasn't for long.

After discussions with Noah's family, it was decided to leave him off dialysis. No headway whatever had been made in the battle to fight off his infections, and his inability to clot his blood had led to the requirement for daily transfusions. As the toxins accumulated in his system, Brees' drifted into incomprehension. Soon he was comatose, and then he died.

Based on the hideous case of Mr. Brees, I coined a new medical term—a diagnosis, really. It was a reference to the indefinable myriad of deleterious consequences which seemed to arise from profound, medically-induced immune suppression. This new entity I termed "FUTS," which was an acronym for "Fucked-Up Transplant Shit." If anyone ever died from FUTS, it was Noah Brees.

14

The Senior Year— Little Problems

IT WAS JULY 1 OF A NEW ACADEMIC YEAR, and I was now officially a "senior resident." I didn't feel particularly different, not especially learned or wise, but three years had passed since the whole ordeal had begun and I supposed that some knowledge and ability must have come my way. Surprisingly, there was little apprehension at the prospect of increased responsibility. In fact, by the end of the third year I had been chafing under the burden of being a junior resident with little decision-making authority. Since I was six years removed from medical school, I imagined myself that much more mature than my classmates and I no longer cheerfully accepted being under the thumb of younger, though more senior—within the hierarchy—residents. During my final third-year rotation, on renal transplant surgery, I had managed to irritate the attending staff considerably with what they perceived to be my disinterest in the vagaries of their patient care protocols. In actuality, I was simply bored with taking orders and being a mere information-gatherer (as Dr. Atcheson would say). I needed more responsibility and authority. In time, I would get them. But first I must return to Children's Hospital for a third and final time.

Ultimate house-staff authority was still in the future for me because, although I was now the senior-most general surgery resident in the hospital, there loomed above me two Pediatric Surgery fellows, each spending two years after general surgery training in the acquisition of the specialized skills associated with the surgery of infants and children.

Due to a peculiar form of what is known as surgical "inbreeding" (simply the hiring by a program of those who have already been trained in that program) both of these fellows had recently completed their general surgery training at OSU, so of course I already knew them. They were each distinguished by startlingly individual traits of physique and personality.

The senior fellow was Salim Fahd, a tall, lanky native Saudi Arabian with a gentle demeanor but the fierce physical appearance of a psychotic terrorist. In fact, "The Terrorist" was one of his many nicknames (others included "The Glide," the meaning of which escaped me then and still does, and "His Royal Highness," which I believe stemmed from his considerable familial wealth). Fahd was an intelligent and capable fellow, and had successfully shed a considerable amount of what had been (in his previous incarnation as a general surgery resident) an abrasive—in fact, imperial—personality. Although he was gentle and kind with the children, they never really warmed to him much, probably because he was somewhat frightening to them with his thick accent, shoulder-length hair and Barbary Coast goatee. All that was missing was a gold hoop earring and scimitar. The other fellow was a diminutive Indian named Ravinder Puri. Puri stood no more than 5'4" even with the addition of some singularly unconvincing (but menacingly—to him—lofty) elevator shoes. Perched atop these "stature-enhancers," Puri was unconsciously forced to affect the prancing gait of a tube-topped street-walker in six-inch pumps. This contrasted, to great comedic effect, with the Pythonesque mantis-strides of the six-foot-three Fahd, and when they rounded together they always left a trail of giggling floor nurses in their wake. Puri had been trained in the U.K. initially but, desirous of the American life-style—and greater pay afforded Stateside surgeons—had chosen to be re-trained in the U.S. (foreign residencies, even those of western Europe, are not recognized by the American medical establishment). Puri spoke with a peculiarly melodic mix of Indian and English accents which gave his frequent didactic monologues a bouncy, amusing quality which he probably didn't appreciate himself.

These two really ran the Pediatric Surgery service during my tenure, but I hovered underneath, occasionally making suggestions, which might or might not be acted upon (the latter, naturally, was the more common occurrence).

The general surgery of infants and children evolved during the post-World War II era, ushered in by a handful of giants who dominated the field for decades. Chief among these was Dr. Robert Gross of Boston, whose reputation was enhanced further by his successful training of many of the pioneers in the field. One of these trainees was Dr. William Clatworthy, who came to Columbus in the 1950s to found the Pediatric Surgery service at Children's Hospital beneath the watchful eye of Dr. Zollinger at Ohio State. Under the guidance of Gross and, for the most part, his disciples, the specialty of pediatric surgery gradually came to encompass a rather well-defined range of diseases and conditions. This is to say that, in contrast to the situation with adults, there is general agreement among pediatric clinicians of all description as to those conditions which require surgical intervention in children.

When such a condition is identified, other differences between adult and pediatric surgery patients become uncomfortably clear to the novice surgeon. The obvious one is the most profound. In a word, size does matter.

As an intern I had scrubbed on many pediatric operations, and as I glanced over my case list from three years before it seemed to me that I had accumulated a pretty fair experience in pediatric surgery at that time. Why was it that I didn't remember much about the operations?

When I entered the OR at Children's again, this time as a senior resident, the reason for my amnesia became crystal clear: I hadn't remembered much because I hadn't seen much. In any pediatric surgery case, the second assistant holding a retractor is condemned to mindless, sightless labor for the duration of the procedure, similar to the "heart-holding" of the cardiac surgery internship. You can't see anything except someone's back.

One back I became intimately familiar with belonged to Dr. Douglas Kane.

Kane was a tall, burly old-timer with a perpetual scowl partially hidden by a burnt-orange moustache. He also had a gravelly baritone voice which would have been perfect for reading narrative on an old radio melodrama. Now that I was no longer just an intern "back-looker," but the senior resident, I got to spend some time in close contact with Kane. This would prove to be time well spent.

At Columbus Children's Hospital at this point the pediatric surgeons were divided into two groups: an academic group of three surgeons, headed by a Dr. Clooney, who held full-time appointments as faculty in the University, and a private group headed by Dr. Kane, also consisting of three surgeons. The groups had what must have been a strained relationship, to say the least. Although they cooperated enough to share on-call duties, they were obviously in direct competition, economic and otherwise. Even more conducive to acrimony, Dr. Kane had been a part of the academic group for years and had been passed over for that head job when Dr. Clooney had been hired, a snub that had rankled him enough to precipitate his quitting and then setting up the competitive private group. Amazingly, both groups participated in resident education with enthusiasm. It was probably the only common ground the two camps shared.

Despite the ugly turn his career had taken as a Professor of Surgery, Dr. Kane was never really purged of the academic bug. He still liked to teach, and was one of those rare examples of a surgeon who can communicate techniques of dexterity. There were other reasons for paying attention to Dr. Kane, though. He had trained under Dr. Zollinger and was one of those living glimpses into the mixed glories of the surgical past. For example he could call a scrub nurse "sweetheart" without there being any hint of impropriety (if I had said the same thing, the reams of write-ups for sexual harassment would have felled many aged trees). But he could also operate with utter coolness in the most extreme of circumstances. Above all, though, Dr. Kane was legendary among the residents for his particular artistry—and odd field of expertise—in the otherwise morally bankrupt field of "pimping."

Pimping is a term with a specific meaning in medical education, a meaning that has no demonstrable origin—and no clear counterpart in common usage. It is the asking of a student or resident, by an attending, of some question within the broad field of medical knowledge. The implication is of repeated needling, a probing for pockets of ignorance; in fact, pimping is a sort of evil twin or mutant outgrowth of the Socratic method. It is used as much to harass as to teach.

King was superb at pimping and liked to focus on a particularly arcane corner of the physician's mental notebook: fluids and electrolytes.

Of all the stultifying aspects of medical education, beyond the mind-numbing memorization of bones, muscles and nerves, beyond the sleep-inducing organic chemistry reactions, beyond even the incomprehensibles of renal and respiratory physiology, lay the ultimate cure for the insomniac medical student: the study of fluids and electrolytes.

I don't mean to suggest that knowledge of this arcane subject is without worth; on the contrary, it's indispensable—at least in its basic form—to the practicing physician and, particularly, the surgeon. It's just so god-damned boring.

But Kane was a master. I believe he had actually taught himself the normal serum concentrations of all the solutes known to be present in the human. Beyond even this, he knew how to calculate the replenishment of these if they happened to be deficient—regardless of the size of the patient! (I might be giving him a bit too much credit here—he was a pediatric surgeon, after all, and was used to altering medication doses for small patients). I'm not just talking about the major players here, by the way—the sodiums, potassiums, chlorides—he knew the daily selenium requirement per kilogram of body mass!

So Kane was a legend for his fluid and electrolyte pimping, frequently done on rounds but just as often in the operating room. Trying to win with him was hopeless. If you got a few questions right, he would just keep going until he found one you didn't know (this was not generally a long process for him). A typical OR exchange might go like this:

"So ... Dr. Miller," he would begin (the dramatic pause after the "So" mirroring the strategic lull in the procedure which allowed some time for him to contemplate my downfall). "What do you imagine this infant's magnesium requirements will be in the next twenty-four hours?"

I had learned by this point not to answer immediately. Knowing I would be wrong no matter what I said, I paused to give the impression that I was legitimately attempting a reasoned calculation. After keeping up this charade for ten or fifteen seconds I provided my answer, just hoping to be somewhere in the numerical vicinity of the true number (then he might think I was just lousy at arithmetic).

Kane's response to wrong answers (honed, no doubt, from thousands of examples over the years) was immutable. Again the pause was used for ultimate dramatic effect.

"That ... is incorrect."

I thought he was great. Pimping idiosyncrasies aside, he was fearless and skillful in the operating room. He could also teach. I may have learned more about surgical technique from Dr. Kane than any other surgeon with whom I trained. If my own child needed an operation, I would send him to the old man in a minute.

A real plus about rotating at Children's Hospital was the Resident Building. Astoundingly, within the complex there was an entire structure dedicated to the house-staff: call rooms with functioning locks and showers, a fully-loaded kitchen, a game room (Foosball and Ping-Pong, anyway) and a Great Room with a big-screen TV. Not even the anesthesiology residents at "The U" had it that good. Better even than all this, every night at ten some greasy food would arrive from one of the local pizzerias or chicken outlets, for free.

After a while I learned to avoid the TV room for a few reasons, though. First, I was an outsider: there was a maximum of eight surgery residents in the hospital at any one time, and there were easily twenty pediatrics residents in that room alone at any given time, day or night. Second, they insisted (women and—ahem—men) on watching the most effeminate program they could identify on their interactive cable system. Usually I just walked away, bemused, but one Sunday afternoon I sauntered in and suggested to the accumulated throng that we watch that day's football game—a little contest called the Super Bowl—instead of the Martha Stewart Hour, or Bob Vila's Country Kitchens or whatever the hell it was they were glued to. They all gasped and refused. Prepared for this, I then had my surgery residents, including some strapping bar-bell boys from the Orthopedics Division ("The game's on, dudes!"), make a well-orchestrated entrance. Outweighed if not outnumbered, the Pediatrics residents made the correct choice in terms of self-preservation and vacated the space.

If it had been possible, I would have liked to have avoided the Pediatrics nurses, too. Although some were pleasant and could get along with the residents, the bulk (a fairly descriptive term for some of them, by the way) were abrasive and surly, typically with no provocation.

As an example, while a senior resident surgical consultant, I was asked by the pediatric medicine service to see a young fellow with multiple medical problems who, among other difficulties, had significant fluid in his abdominal cavity. The pediatricians wanted a sample of the fluid to help with their diagnosis and treatment. Although I was pretty sure of the diagnosis myself, I served my role as consultant and—having agreed with the need for tapping the fluid—proceeded routinely. After obtaining consent from his parents, I anesthetized and sterilized the unconscious child's abdomen and proceeded with the "paracentesis," as the procedure is called. But I had made one significant mistake: I had failed to find the child's nurse and notify her of what I was doing.

In fact I *had* made an effort to find her; not so much because I believed that she would be of assistance but more to keep the lines of communication with the medical service—tenuous as they were—open.

That wasn't enough. It didn't even have the chance to be enough, as it happened. The nurse found me in the middle of the procedure and basically treated me the way I would have expected to have been treated in adolescence by my mother if she had found me with a cache of porno magazines. What was I thinking? If there was a problem, why didn't she know about it? Why wasn't she "in the loop?" She tried to make me feel guilty for having performed a necessary procedure in her absence! My answer was perhaps unnecessarily combative, I admit; something along the lines of, "Sorry, I'm new here; I didn't see you on the unit and I don't know where the coffee break room is...."

This nurse took it upon herself to file an official complaint about my egregious actions with the hospital administration. Characteristically, she fabricated events that she hadn't even been around to witness in an effort to make me look bad: reporting that I hadn't sterilized the child's abdomen in the institution's standard way (whether I had or hadn't she couldn't possibly know, since at the time she was ragging on a Marlboro and knocking back a mug of Folger's Crystals to the televised strains of the *General Hospital* theme.)

The official ramifications came down to the Terrorist Fahd asking me in a hallway one day if I had aspirated fluid from a child's abdomen without sterilizing the skin first. Emboldened by my knowledge that the local and national scarcity of senior surgical residents rendered me a valuable commodity I told him that #1, it wasn't true and #2, for asking me that question he could kiss my ass.

Looking back, though, I realize that the Terrorist was just doing his job. It was the nurse—who was at first absent, and then accusatory—who had genuine issues to deal with. Unfortunately she was not only not an aberration at Children's Hospital, she was the prototype!

That brings us to the fundamental question: why would someone with an inherently unpleasant disposition take upon themselves the care of children—of children!—as a profession? And if that observation is wrong and they aren't inherently unpleasant, why did they behave that way in such unmistakable terms in their interactions with the house-staff? Obviously, not all of them had begun their careers as confrontational bitches. What had gone wrong with the Pediatrics nurses?

Unquestionably part of the problem was that most of these nurses suffered from a self-aggrandizing delusion that they were the "patient advocates." This is a term that is actually used in nursing circles, and refers to the concept that the nurse is primarily responsible for the safety of the patient and the protection of that patient's rights (I personally believe the true duty of the nurse is more appropriately defined—succinctly—as the care of the patient). Although this definition of "patient advocate" sounds nice, it actually carries with it an ominous hidden meaning. After all, if the nurse's duty is defined as the protection of the patient, the clear implication is that there are individuals who are potential sources of harm. Without the embodiment of a threat to the patient, the role of patient advocate is meaningless.

The peds nurses had focused in on two groups as such potential threats: the physicians (especially the residents, who were constantly around and thus in their eyes capable of much mischief) and, incredibly, the parents.

While I could grudgingly forgive the nurses for being so zealous in their self-appointed roles as protectors of the sick children as to be endlessly confrontational with the residents, and no doubt mistakes were avoided because of their watchfulness, I could never fathom their treatment of the parents.

There are certainly parents who are neglectful of the needs of their children, and some who are frankly abusive—we saw them, I'm sorry to say, and the results of their misdeeds—but the number is not large. Most parents of seriously ill or injured kids are frantically concerned for their well-being, some to the point of emotional breakdown. In this setting, the pediatrics nurses seemed to have promulgated an unwritten rule: all parents are child abusers until proven otherwise.

The hospital had a policy of allowing the parents of a sick child to stay in the child's room overnight, certainly a most humane consideration and one which I'm sure is in existence in most children's hospitals in America. While the nurses gave lip service to their approval of this, it was most enlightening to listen to their incessant gossip about the parents as they were changing shifts in the morning. As an intern I would write my progress notes in the patient's charts at the nurse's station during this part of the day, unobtrusively eavesdropping. I loved this; it was like a living classroom of pathologic psychology:

"What do you think of that Stevens mother? I think she's a boozer."

"Ever notice she always smells like cigarette smoke? If I catch her smoking in that room, I'm calling Security. No questions asked, buddy."

"He's not any better. Does he ever wear anything but a T-shirt? They're nothing but trailer-trash."

"Social services should get involved. That's no way for that little girl to grow up."

I'm really not exaggerating. It went on like this for forty-five minutes, each set of parents being verbally eviscerated, their flaws—real or imagined—dissected by these tremendously vitriolic nurses. In fact, parental character assassination had become a kind of sub-cultural unit of social exchange among the nurses at Children's Hospital: if they could talk about nothing else among themselves, they could always agree that the residents and the parents were low-lifes. What a conversation-starter!

Tom Griner was another of the Pediatric Surgery attendings, a member of Dr. Kane's private group. A slight, bespectacled fellow with a full, dark beard and moustache, Griner's most prominent physical feature was a rather unusually large and round head nearly devoid of hair. Almost everyone who met him (and voiced an opinion) remarked that he resembled one of Jim Henson's muppets, although there was never any general consensus as to which one. Griner's odd appearance was well-matched by a charmingly nasal caterwaul of a speaking voice, which sounded precisely like that of the Martian from the old Bugs Bunny cartoons. Factor in a superficially blank personality and the initial impression of the man was typically not very favorable, except in so far as it provoked amusement. As an intern I could barely look at him without giggling, and when his Martian-commander voice then gave me a patient care order, I nearly always had to feign a severe coughing fit to camouflage my laughter. I was coughing around him so much Griner must have thought I had TB.

But this awkward appearance had some advantages to it. Most importantly, the kids really took to Griner, probably because of his vague resemblance to something which might be sitting on their shelves. Even the sociopathic nurses cut him some slack.

But we were all misjudging Griner badly, and on many fronts.

Now that I finally was operating with him, I realized that Griner was a deft and skillful surgeon. His judgment and restraint were admirable, and I appreciated his tact in asking my opinion and appearing to value it (I had managed to get past—for the most part—the mental image of the Loony Tunes Martian when he spoke).

But the real shock about nerdy, mild-mannered Dr. Griner came when, in ordinary OR conversation, I accidentally stumbled on the topic which was his great interest and passion: serial killers!

Griner had a knowledge of mass murderers and serial slayers that bordered on the encyclopedic. Now, it should be admitted that most people have an odd fascination about death and its many manifestations, which is not surprising since we all must face it eventually. There's even a common phrase which is used to describe this ordinary interest in the macabre: morbid curiosity. A fairly large fraction of the population is captivated by fictional murder mysteries and real-life courtroom dramas, too, suggesting that the more specialized topic of death by human intent is not a rare interest, either. But it is, I have to assert, an unusual individual indeed who takes up a passionate amateur interest in the study of repetitive killers.

The Gentle Reader may recall a minor uproar a few years ago generated by media reports of a company which was distributing serial killer trading cards. The concern was that putting murderers on cards like baseball stars would contribute to society's overall glorification of violence (can't you see the kids on the playground exchanging cardboard pyschopaths? "I'll trade you a Bundy for a Dahmer." "No way! You give me a Bundy AND a Gacy and I'll think about giving up my Dahmer..."). Well, Griner owned the entire set. He had purchased them in their entirety. Why? I have no idea. How? An even better question. Did the backs of the cards provide him with any information that his extensive reading had omitted? I seriously doubt it. He just wanted to own the cards because he was a serial killer fan and they were serial killer cards.

The guy was an awesome repository of hideous information. He knew all the details of the different murders and, once unleashed, delighted in relating them. At one point I noted that he had actually been present in some of the cities (Philadelphia, Milwaukee) where the killers he described had been working, at the time of their sinister efforts. When I asked him about it, I half-hoped that he would become indignant and defensive, thus revealing himself to be the true killer (in the true murder-mystery dime novel fashion). Unfortunately (I think!) he said that yes, he had lived in those cities during those times, and furthermore that was how he had developed such a macabre interest: the sordid events were transpiring in his figurative front yard.

All of us were a little disappointed that our local nerd-muppet-surgeon wasn't a mass murderer after all, but those are the breaks. Of course, there hadn't been any serial murders in Columbus since Griner had moved there, anyway. Then again, a sufficiently brilliant serial killer could go against type and change his *modus operandi* with each murder, couldn't he? Probably, but that was not the case with Dr. Griner, who just happened to be a very bright man with a very odd appearance and a very strange hobby.

Interestingly, Griner was the most vehement opponent of the well-publicized euthanasia attempts of Jack Kevorkian that I ever encountered. During his research Griner had discovered facts which, to my mind, strongly confirmed what the Michigan prosecutors were asserting at that time. These facts ran contrary to the image that a sympathizing popular press was generating. Kevorkian wasn't some kindly, paternal general practitioner who wished to ease the pain of suffering, helpless patients but a possibly deranged, certainly deluded menace to the community. Kevorkian, as all docs knew, was a pathologist: a physician without a clinical practice who never saw living patients and only saw patients at all when they arrived in his lab as disembodied specimens or cadavers. Griner's research had uncovered a particularly chilling bit of information, which was not general public knowledge and which sealed the deal for me: as a pathology resident, Kevorkian had collected photographs of the open eyes of cadavers, staring lifelessly into his camera lens. He had scrapbooks full of such photos. Dr. Death was the right nickname. Griner knew about him in detail because he put him on the list with Gacy, Bundy and the rest.

Unquestionably the best part about rotating through the Pediatric Surgery service was getting to spend time with the kids. I had no children of my own when I began residency, but was getting to be of an age where I was starting to think about the prospect. So I was paying more attention to the little folks. It's amazing how much more appealing they are as one approaches 30—there's no question in my mind that some pre-programmed genetic time-bomb goes off in this period, instantly altering the prospective parent's perception of small children and infants from being mere sources of grief and consternation to objects of tremendous appeal and delight.

In any case, one of the few aspects of senior residency at Children's Hospital that I enjoyed was the children. When we were dealing with them, it must be recalled, they had some sort of diagnosis or symptoms which required surgical intervention, so theirs was not a typical, carefree child's life. Most of them reacted to their lot with confusion and fear, as most adults do—the difference being that, unlike adults—they have society's tacit approval to express these emotions by crying and complaining. But they are almost universally more courageous than adults, sometimes heartbreakingly so.

Little Justin Hayward was only five years old (he was one of the last few to be burdened with the astonishingly common names of either Jordan or Justin during this period). He had been throwing up for about two days when I was asked to see him in consultation in the emergency department one summer night. Over the previous few hours he had developed abdominal pain, which had begun around his umbilicus and then gradually shifted down toward his groin on the right. He had a slight fever and, according to the blood work drawn by the ER docs, a slightly elevated white blood cell count with a normal urinalysis. An abdominal x-ray the ER guys had done was negative (they were uncommonly on the ball this evening). Without actually examining him, I could say that he had as classic a presentation of appendicitis as it's possible to have, which is why the ER physicians had summoned the surgery team. Armed with his chart and the knowledge I've just described, I entered Justin's examining room.

It may be a personality flaw on my part, but when another doctor provides me with a diagnosis before I even see a patient my first thought is to disprove that diagnosis. At least that way, if I'm right, I won't compound a mistake by propagating that misdiagnosis. Plus, as a surgeon, I'm the one who will be inflicting trauma on a patient (as any surgery does) if the suggested diagnosis requires an operation and I want to make sure that all other possible diagnoses or other therapeutic options are exhausted before I do so. One other thing: the other guys often are wrong.

So, despite the strong suggestion of appendicitis which my "chart biopsy" provided, I walked into Justin's room with a healthy skepticism.

The patient in question was perched supine on the examining table, a small spread-eagle figure draped in blue hospital linen. Dark circles rimmed dark eyes which were fixed on the ceiling as his chest rose and fell with measured breaths. I introduced myself to the parents as I kept my eye on Justin. They were about my age, bore a remarkable resemblance to each other, and had clearly slept as little as their son over the past forty-eight hours (I briefly reflected—to myself—that I supposed they had slept about as much as I *normally* did in any forty-eight hour period). I quietly approached the boy, avoiding the IV pole from which a bag containing electrolyte solution and antibiotics hung. Introducing myself to Justin, I asked how he felt.

"Okay."

His two front teeth—as far as I could tell, the only ones he had— were biting into his bottom lip.

I grasped his hand and felt his pulse. The hand felt warm and the pulse was fast, but I was used to the slower heart rate of adults and my skeptic's mind compensated for this: probably a normal heart rate for a five-year-old; I'll double-check the normal pulse rate for a kid his size when I get back to the front desk. A fever could be from anything. Granted, the history was good for appendicitis but the physical examination would be the final arbiter.

After warning Justin, I listened to his belly with my stethoscope. It was eerily quiet. Normally the sounds of the constantly-active intestines yield easily-audible coos and gurgles. Then I placed my hands on Justin's abdomen. He grimaced slightly. I pushed gently up near the edge of his ribcage.

"Justin, does that hurt?"

"No."

Continuing, I pushed on his belly down toward the umbilicus (the belly button) and the groin. His face twisted uncomfortably. Justin's abdomen was exquisitely tender to any kind of examining touch, and tender in the proper area for appendicitis. I repeated my question.

Again he replied, "No."

The little fellow refused to verbally acknowledge pain. He hadn't learned how to hide facial expressions, which was what gave him away, of course, but he absolutely would not admit that anything hurt. I smiled weakly at the parents, who in their anxiety were missing an amazing display of courage on the part of their son. Their distraction was, of course, perfectly understandable. I brought them out into the hallway.

"I think Justin has appendicitis. We should take him to surgery right away."

The father looked relieved, the mother more concerned. They asked about the usual things: prognosis, possible alternate diagnoses, length of hospital stay. I called the attending, Dr. Clooney, and booked the OR time. During the half-hour that it took to get things arranged to get him to surgery, Justin never let down his guard, never displayed any weakness. He reminded me of a pint-sized Shane.

At surgery, not surprisingly, he had a perforated, gangrenous appendix. It had probably ruptured a good day earlier. His entire lower abdominal cavity was full of murky, infected fluid. He had frank peritonitis. The pain he had felt in the ER must have been excruciating.

Justin had to stay in the hospital for a little less than a week, while we gave him IV antibiotics and allowed his incision (which we couldn't close because of the infection present) to heal partially. True to form, he never complained about any pain during his in-hospital convalescence. And it's not as if he didn't feel it; you could see him wince and his little eyes well with tears when we had to change the dressing—he just would not acknowledge that the pain was there. His parents had no idea where this utter stoicism had come from. Just a tough little SOB, I guess. One night I stood over his bed with his dad while he slept. I remarked that if we had all been living one hundred years before—with no antibiotics and, more importantly, no one to do an appendectomy—Justin would have died. Now that I look back on it, I'm not so sure....

One of my fellow residents didn't particularly enjoy the experience of working with children. To him, their inability or unwillingness to articulate their symptoms and cooperate in the diagnostic and therapeutic process was exasperating. For these reasons he liked to compare pediatrics to veterinary medicine. Although there is some validity to this view, I preferred to consider the small patients just a different challenge: sometimes it gets old when the patient clearly communicates what's wrong with him. With the kids, you had to be a little slick sometimes.

Kelly Hobson was four years old. She had sandy hair and chocolate-brown eyes, which were stained with tears when I first saw them. As with Justin Hayward, she had been brought to the emergency department by her parents for belly pain. The ER docs were likewise concerned about appendicitis, although Kelly's symptoms weren't nearly as classic as Justin's had been. It was late afternoon when they called me. After reviewing her chart, lab work and x-rays, I was doubtful that she had anything much beyond a stomach-ache. But the most important and revealing segment of the diagnostic process for the surgeon is the physical examination, and I could hardly make a definitive statement about Kelly until I had (as the ER guys put it—I personally hated the phrase) "laid hands" on her.

Whenever I walked into a pediatric examining room (or any other, for that matter), I liked to gauge the whole scene first: I found that I could pick up a lot of information about the family dynamic just by observing the position and posture of the individuals. Were the parents close together or on opposite sides of the room? Was the child avoiding the parents or clinging to them? How about the siblings? These kinds of things don't provide much help in actually making the diagnosis, but they can aid in the communication process immeasurably—and communication is essential in all patient care. You have to *notice* things or you'll miss the boat sometimes. I'm afraid that many surgeons just focus on the disease, and that does the patient and their family a disservice.

Little Kelly reminded me a great deal of Justin when I got a look at her. She looked tired and scared. Her parents were a mixed bag: the father looked embarrassed and a little pissed off at being there; the mother wore the universal expression of maternal worry. It turned out that Kelly had had belly pain since the morning, but she hadn't vomited or had any fevers. I talked with Kelly and her parents for a few minutes, making no movement in the direction of the little patient. Knowing that she would be reluctant to allow me to examine her, I then tried to distract her with conversation as I slowly approached her. She wasn't really buying it, though: by the time I reached the bedside she'd rolled herself into a ball and glared menacingly at me.

"Kelly," I said quietly, "you know I have to feel your stomach. I have to see if I can make it all better."

"NO!" she replied.

I paused a moment.

"Do you want your mommy to hold you while I feel your belly?"

Screwing her tiny face up indignantly, with her little brow furrowing, she repeated her answer.

"No!"

The mother attempted to intercede, as they always do (usually with success). "Now, Kelly, you have to let the doctor examine you. How else can he help you? He wants to make the ouch go away. You have to let him try…."

Even this sensible plea was ignored, if anything even more emphatically. The father threatened a spanking but this, too, was met with a stone wall (I don't think Kelly considered that much of a threat, for whatever reason).

At this point I recalled a sequence from the autobiography of a pediatric surgeon which I had read back in medical school. The scenario was similar, and that surgeon had tried a clever ruse to get the child to allow him to do his examination. The story had a too-good-to-be-true ending, but the technique sounded reasonable. I decided it was worth a try.

Behaving as if I'd given up on the idea of examining Kelly, I distracted her with a few minutes of idle talk, then announced suddenly, "I can do something that you can't do. I can tell what you had for breakfast just by looking at your stomach."

"No, you can't," she answered. "You can't see *inside* my stomach."

"Oh, yes I can."

"No, you can't."

"Well, let's just see. Lift your shirt up and I'll tell you what you ate for breakfast. I can't see through shirts."

When Kelly did this I leaned down, right next to her belly, and stared intently. I kept this up for several seconds.

"Hmmm," I said. "This is harder than I thought. I can almost see your breakfast, but not quite. The lights in this room just aren't bright enough."

Kelly looked puzzled as I continued.

"This right here"—I put my right hand just below her rib cage and gently pushed on her—"looks like toast."

Kelly was grinning. My show continued.

"This over here"—I brought my hand below her belly button—"feels like cereal."

The little patient was enduring my exam without an apparent twinge—her symptoms were unquestionably not due to appendicitis or any other diagnosis which might require an operation. She probably just had gastroenteritis.

With a great flourish I made an end of my performance.

"You had cereal and toast for breakfast. A little orange juice, too."

Kelly looked up at her mom, her eyes wide and questioning. How does he do that? she was asking wordlessly.

"He's a doctor," the mother said, smiling. "He can tell these things. That's right, Dr. Miller, we had cereal, toast, and orange juice. The only thing you didn't mention was the melon we ate."

Feigning confusion, I glanced back at Kelly.

"That's funny," I said. "I didn't feel any melon in your stomach."

Kelly cast a guilty look in the direction of her mother, and thrust out her bottom lip.

"I'm sorry, mom," she pouted. "I didn't eat my melon. I think they're yucky."

When the Pediatric Surgery rotation came to a close, I gathered up my books, scrubs, toothbrush, razor, etc., from the call room and prepared to head back to the main University Hospital campus. The final stint at an outside hospital was now over. The rest of residency would be at "The U." There was a definite sense that the last lap was underway, even if the home stretch was not quite in view. If I thought that the hard part was over, though, I was soon to learn otherwise.

15

The Senior Year— Glorified Plumber

WHEN MY TWO MONTHS ON THE PEDIATRIC SURGERY SERVICE WERE DONE, I rotated onto Vascular Surgery back at the main University Hospital. Of course I had already been on this service as an intern and a second-year resident, so I knew what I was in for: Vascular was one of the most challenging rotations. All the patients seemed to be at death's door: they almost all had heart trouble, many had diabetes, hypertension and other, significant co-existing conditions, in addition to the peripheral vascular disease that had brought them to the care of the vascular surgeons in the first place. Once again this was a service with a fellow—another Ohio State product, too—a native of Greece called Kosmo Kouras.

Kosmo was of average height, with curly black hair and perpetually tired-looking eyes. He spoke English well, but with a heavy accent (oddly, another of the residents was also Greek by birth, and his accent was completely different from Kosmo's). He had the peculiar habit of beginning nearly every sentence addressed to a fellow resident with the words : "Listen, let me tell you something, my friend,…" (This was easy to pick up on and Kouras impersonators abounded amongst the junior residents.)

But Kouras was comparatively hands-off with regard to interference in my day-to-day running of the service. He only occasionally rounded with the team. This was of vital interest to me, because I needed badly to spread my wings and exercise some autonomy in patient care activities. Kosmo also kept out of my way in the OR, only assisting the attendings on the most complex cases. Fortunately, there were enough of these to keep him happy, and he only rarely "stole" operations from me.

There were only two attendings on the vascular service at the time: the chief, Dr. Richard Treves, and Dr. Chet Tovar, who had overseen my first foot amputation two years before.

Dr. Treves was in his early fifties, tall and slim, with gentle dark eyes and carefully-coifed black hair graying at the temples. Always impeccably dressed (usually in a charcoal or navy suit), but with his imperial appearance and professional perfectionism softened by an unusual gift and appreciation for humor, he was a delight to be around. He had a superb, almost Twain-like grasp of the humorous anecdote, which he would unfurl from time to time when you least expected it. Treves had a habit of cocking his head to one side when he verbalized an observation, and frequently wore a wry but inoffensive grin, as if he were the only one who got the joke but he didn't want to lord it over you. He was remarkably well-traveled and well-read, and seemed to have a grasp of nearly every subject which might come up in conversation. In the operating room Treves was even more impressive. He was a truly gifted surgeon, one of the technically best I've ever seen: he exhibited complete mastery over any situation he encountered. Although he could be a rough-and-tumble character in the OR—especially if the vascular surgery fellow was not operating with the appropriate elan—Dr. Treves pretty much summed up, for me at least, everything that a gentleman-scholar-surgeon should be. At that time I considered him—even more than Dr. Atcheson—a nearly-complete role model.

Dr. Treves had grown up in the South, in Nashville in fact—and it must have been under privileged circumstances because he was acquainted with many famous country music performers, including "Bocephus," Mr. Monday Night Football-theme song himself, Hank Williams, Jr. (who was a boyhood neighbor). Still, Treves had not the slightest trace of a southern twang in his voice, and it always surprised people to find out that he had grown up in Tennessee. Later he went to college and trained in surgery in New England (and Old England, too; there he spent a year at a hospital which specialized in chest surgery).

It was from his days in training that Dr. Treves's legendary story-telling prowess emerged.

As an intern at one of the most prestigious Boston academic hospitals, Dr. Treves had had the mixed privilege of being the frontline, grunt-level member of the surgical house-staff. In this capacity he had encountered any number of locally and nationally famous individuals, from Boston sports stars to international political movers and shakers. My personal favorite Treves story involved the 1970s U.S. Secretary of State, Henry Kissinger. Treves was always careful not to reveal any medical secrets as he told stories from decades past, but from what I could gather Dr. Kissinger had been brought to Boston to have some potentially surgical ailment evaluated. He was placed in some sort of VIP building adjacent to the main university hospital. Being the thorough sort, the young intern Treves had insisted on performing a complete physical examination, including a rectal exam.

Rectals are no fun. No patient likes getting them and no physician without a serious psychologic derangement likes administering them. Yet they are an invaluable—in fact, indispensable—aid to the diagnosis of many serious problems: prostate cancer, colon malignancies, rectovaginal fistulas … but, despite the intellectual acknowledgment of the amount of information that can be gained from the rectal exam, it never seems appropriate to stick one's finger into a stranger's anus.

Imagine then, if you can, the amount of testosterone the young Dr. Treves must have mustered to ask the Secretary of State to bend over and take the greased glove!

By Treves's account, Dr. Kissinger complied without much coercion. He was a diplomat, after all, and must have realized that he had little ground on which to maneuver (it makes you wonder what the nearby secret service guys must have been thinking, though). A few seconds later, Treves was "two knuckles in," as we used to say. According to my Chief of Vascular Surgery, the Secretary of State silently accepted his fate for a few wiggly moments, then turned his head to say, in his unmistakable baritone German accent, "Do you have any idea how many presidents and prime ministers in the world would love to be doing what you are doing right now, doctor?"

The first major case I did with Dr. Treves was an abdominal aortic aneurysm, a "AAA." These are abnormal dilatations of the aorta, and their cause is poorly understood. They seem to arise in patients with an abnormal balance in the enzymes which build up and break down arterial structural proteins. Atherosclerosis plays a role in their development, too. These two factors—atherosclerosis and an imbalance in the production of structural enzymes—probably merge in some unknown way to create aortic aneurysms.

AAAs usually have no symptoms, and they are most frequently found either by accident or during a careful physical examination. They've been compared to intra-abdominal time-bombs, since they have a tendency to rupture without warning. When this happens, the result is usually death. Albert Einstein died of a ruptured AAA, as did the actor George C. Scott. Because of the risk of rupture (which increases with the burgeoning of the diameter of the aneurysm) the vascular surgeons repair AAAs once they get bigger than about five centimeters (two inches) across, provided the patient is well enough to tolerate the operation.

Richard Conners was a healthy 62-year-old man who, as they say, never had a sick day in his life. One afternoon at a delicatessen he had been leaning with his belly against the counter, ordering a pastrami sandwich or something, when he noticed that he was bouncing back and forth. After a few moments he recognized that something in his abdomen was big and pulsating. A worried trip to his general practitioner had led to an ultrasound and then a CAT scan, and now he had the brand-new diagnosis of a seven-centimeter abdominal aortic aneurysm. Mr. Conners was referred to Dr. Treves, and told that he should have the thing repaired. Initially he was understandably skeptical: this aneurysm was causing him no pain, why not just leave it alone? Treves pointed out to the patient the high risk of rupture and, especially, the overwhelming likelihood of death in the event of such rupture. The operation would be relatively straightforward in his case, and the risk of the surgery was pretty low. After a few days of hemming and hawing, Conners agreed to the operation.

For some reason, Treves was in an especially good mood the morning of Conner's surgery. In any case, the aneurysm was an uncomplicated one—it didn't involve the arteries to the vital organs or to the pelvis and legs. This held out the promise of a relatively quick procedure. I thought Treves might be ticked off that he would have to operate with an inexperienced resident doing his first aortic procedure (rather than the fellow, Kosmo) but he didn't seem to mind at all.

We made a midline incision and entered Conner's abdomen quickly and easily. Treves swept the bowel out of the way and wrapped it in some towels. The aneurysm was now staring us right in the face. It looked like some sort of shiny, pulsatile, headless snake. I hadn't expected that it would be twisted around on itself. Maybe it looked more like a gnarled old tree than a snake. In any event we rapidly dissected out the normal parts of the aorta above and below the aneurysm and selected appropriate clamps for controlling the vessel. Treves asked the anesthesiologists to give Conners some intravenous heparin to keep his blood from clotting (he always asked in the same, humorously idiosyncratic way: "Please administer 5,000 units of bovine heparin sodium into the vein of your choice.")

Once the heparin had had a chance to circulate, we clamped the aorta and opened it with the electrocautery device. The small amount of blood still within the aneurysm leapt out, and we quickly suctioned it away. The aneurysm sac was full of a rubbery brown material.

"Oh my God," Treves shouted, "someone's shit in this man's aorta!"

The scrub nurse, having seen this trick of Treves's, just shook her head at his childishness. The brown mass was accumulated blood clot, which had built up on the wall of the aorta over the years as the aneurysm grew. Treves looked at me.

"Well," he said, "get that crap out of there."

I reached my hand down and scooped the mass up. Treves pointed out that delivering the clot intact was considered a badge of honor. I didn't know if he was feeding me another line of BS or not, but I tried to keep the thing from fragmenting. This was tougher than it sounds, because it was much more adherent to the aortic wall than to itself. I almost had it out when the damn thing broke in half. Treves chuckled as I handed the disgusting handful to the scrub nurse.

"Check the Apgars on that, will you?" he chortled. Apgar scores are used to rapidly assess the health of a newborn.

The next step was to oversew the multiple bleeding points on the inside of the aorta. Once this was done we brought up a tube-shaped graft made of synthetic Dacron and simply sewed it to the normal segments of the aorta above and below the aneurysm. We reestablished blood flow to the legs by carefully releasing the clamps—frequently the blood pressure will drop too rapidly if this is not done in a circumspect fashion, as the circulating blood encounters a markedly decreased amount of resistance. Conners, though, didn't turn a hair—he was a healthy bastard. Next we closed the aneurysm itself over the graft—like a jacket of living tissue, to help protect the synthetic material from eroding into the soft bowel and to minimize bleeding, too. After closing the abdominal wall, we stapled the skin shut with sterile metallic clips.

The whole case, my first abdominal aortic aneurysm operation, was done in an hour and fifteen minutes, skin-to-skin. We rolled into the recovery area at the same time as the hernia cases. I preened like a hot-shot, but there was no question that Treves had been the real speed-demon. As I reflected, though, I realized that he had actually allowed me to perform every essential step in the operation. Maybe I was getting the hang of this stuff.

Chet Tovar had finished his general surgery and vascular training at Ohio State in the early 1990s. As a disciple of Dr. Treves, he tried valiantly to emulate him as best he could. Truthfully, this was without much success. For starters, Tovar was a big man. A few inches shorter than Treves, Tovar outweighed him by close to one hundred pounds. As a result, whenever the two appeared together, Chet was not going to benefit from the contrast. Moreover, Treves had an effortless command of nearly every subject that came into polite conversation, from partisan national politics to twentieth-century American literature to college football. Tovar's interests were genuine and present, but not nearly so catholic; again, the comparison was unfavorable. Finally, Treves was such an excellent technical surgeon that the best Tovar could hope to do was equal his results – he couldn't make any gains here, either. Despite all this, Chet worked hard and earned a measure of respect from the other medical and surgical faculty, and he received his share of referrals.

Another aspect of Tovar's personality that mirrored Treves's was his sometimes violent temper. Unlike Treves, though—who confined his tirades almost exclusively to the operating room—Chet might let any situation get the better of him. One cartoonish legend had it that as a Chief Resident (several years before I arrived) he had become so incensed on a certain occasion that he actually popped the buttons off his carefully-fastened white lab coat. The means by which this could occur aren't entirely clear to me, but there were plenty of witnesses and they were all adamant that it did happen.

For some reason, in the intervening years since I had been an intern—at which time he had seemed to harbor some deep-seated personal hatred for me—Tovar had performed a complete 180 and acted like we were best friends. At first I thought he must be bullshitting and that I'd better watch my back, but he never shifted gears again. Why he had been such a bastard and then, even odder, taken a shine to me will remain a mystery, I guess.

This new-found camaraderie would not protect me in the operating room, though. Tovar was one of those (and they're fairly common in surgical circles) tyrannical fiends when he operated—constantly berating the assistants, nurses and anesthetists. In fact it was as if he had taken a page from Dr. Klein's book of anachronistic acrimony, although the two didn't even know one another. Tovar had developed some techniques in infantile acting-out which were all his own, though:

As his frustration mounted (maybe the resident wasn't moving fast enough, or the instruments were being handled awkwardly), Chet would silently pump his clenched—but empty—fists in front of his body, careful to maintain sterile technique. Later, sweat would begin to appear on his brow. In a few minutes, if things were progressing badly, a tremendously high-pitched, wordless whine would emanate from his tensed throat. By this point the residents and nurses would be so unnerved by Tovar's body-english brow-beating that their performances were bound to suffer (I can recall one time when, while I nervously tried to suture a hole in a small artery closed, he screamed at the top of his lungs at me, "Goddamnit, stop shaking so fucking much!") The next step in a Chet meltdown was something that really had to be seen to be believed: he would actually hop up and down repeatedly, exactly like a temperamental toddler, although this one weighed 275 pounds!

Because of Chet's volatile nature I always loathed having to call him with late-night emergencies. He could be awfully nasty when awakened. Still, when a patient needs an emergency vascular operation, it pretty much means they are either going to die or lose a limb if you don't act, so I never hesitated to wake a sleeping Chet.

One night, a graying old fellow named Chuck Schroeder showed up in the ER with an acutely swollen right shoulder. He'd been exercising—doing jumping jacks, he said—and felt something "pop." Instantly the shoulder had swollen and soon thereafter his right hand had turned cold and blue. The guy was upbeat and smiling, but you could tell he was scared (I personally wanted to know why the hell he was doing jumping jacks at two in the morning). You could also tell that Chuck had already had some sort of surgery near his right clavicle, or collarbone. The intern on the service, Bert Cress, was appropriately holding pressure over the swollen site to prevent what we presumed to be a problem with bleeding into the soft tissues from worsening. When he briefly removed his gloved hand I could see a surgical scar. As it turned out Schroeder had had a bypass graft from the right axillary artery (which courses from just below the clavicle into the armpit) to the femoral artery in the leg, after an old aortic graft had gotten infected and needed to be removed. Tovar had been the surgeon who had done these operations, so I gave him a call.

"Dr. Tovar? Hey, it's Craig. Sorry to wake you up."

"What—what is it?"

"There's a patient of yours called Chuck Schroeder here in the ER. You did an ax-fem on him about six months ago."

"Right. What's the matter? Did it clot off?"

"That and more, sir. Looks like he must have ripped the graft off the artery at the axillary end. He was doing jumping jacks and felt something pop."

"Jumping jacks? That dumb fuck. I told him to take it easy on that arm. Does he have a pseudoaneurysm (an accumulation of flowing blood in the soft tissues alongside an artery)?"

"Yeah, no question about it. I've got Bert holding pressure on it now. His hand's cold, too. I'm sure the artery's either compressed off or thrombosed."

"Probably both. Book the OR, all right? I'll be there in ten minutes."

"Will do."

By the time Tovar arrived we already had Schroeder in the operating room and were beginning to induce anesthesia. The speed with which the OR front desk handled the whole affair was astonishing—it usually took half an hour before anyone from anesthesia even laid eyes on an emergency surgery patient in the ER. At first I thought I was beginning to have some clout at the hospital, after four years of med school and three-and-a-half of residency. In fact, though, it was Chet. He had called the OR desk about a nano-second after hanging up with me, and begun raining down brimstone on the heads of the staff. With such a fire lit under them, they had moved rapidly.

Bart was still holding pressure on Schroeder's clavicle as we prepped him out. While Tovar and I scrubbed, I noticed that Chet seemed amazingly good-natured about having to explore this man's axillary artery at three in the morning. He was even whistling under his mask. I didn't dare say a word, though, in fear of breaking the spell, which had probably been brought on by a sudden infusion of black coffee.

After we had been gowned up, Chet insisted on making the incision himself. I was more than happy to oblige him, because I had no experience with the surgical exposure of the axillary artery and frankly didn't see how we could hope to get control of the vessel. It seemed to me that Schroeder was in real danger of bleeding out once we opened the pseudoaneurysm, before we could find the artery and get a clamp on it. Tovar cut through the old incision and straight down into the aneurysm. This was, I think, an accident, since we were nowhere near being able to see where the artery itself was.

A great geyser of fresh and clotted blood burst out of Schroeder's shoulder, hitting Tovar directly in the face. We both thrust our hands into the wound to staunch the eruption, while Chet regained his senses. He never wore glasses in the operating room, and was supremely lucky that the blood missed his eyes. His entire mask and neck were literally dripping with blood. There was blood all over the room—even on the ceiling. Tovar seemed stunned—after all, twenty minutes before he had been asleep in his bed, now here he was caked in blood, with his fingers stuffed in a man's shoulder, trying to keep him from bleeding to death.

We were in a bad spot. The actual hole in the artery was well away from where there was any exposure at all. If we moved our hands to try and find the hole, the incision instantly filled with blood, blocking our vision and easily outstripping any attempts at suctioning it away. I thought we'd have to crack Schroeder's chest in order to get a clamp on the artery. With his experience and training, Chet had another, better idea. He took a balloon-tipped catheter and inserted it into the aneurysm, in the general direction of the heart. Then he inflated the balloon. The bleeding lessened considerably. I did the same thing with another catheter, but this time pointed the tip toward the arm. After I inflated my balloon, the entire field was dry. The balloons had occluded both the forward flow from the heart and the backflow from the arm. Now we could carefully do the required dissection to get the artery freed up and, ultimately, fixed.

Sure enough, Schroeder's vigorous but ill-advised exercise routine had torn the suture line which attached the Goretex (a form of teflon) graft to the axillary artery. Once we had dissected the vessels out sufficiently to place clamps across them (no small feat in a scarred-in area such as this) we removed the occlusion balloons. The balloons were in the way of what we would have to do to repair the tear.

We ended up replacing part of the graft that was badly damaged, and reattaching it to a segment of uninjured axillary artery. The previous hole was sutured closed. When we took off the clamps, everything flowed perfectly, and Schroeder's right hand immediately began to get pink again. There's some truth to the statement that vascular surgery is really just like glorified plumbing: all you have to do is get the pipes hooked up right. Of course, if the plumber screws up, you get a wet floor; if the vascular surgeon does, you get a dead leg or a dead patient.

Although we had to transfuse Schroeder a few units of blood, he did well and went home in a couple of days. The worst part of the whole experience for Tovar was the fact that he had been unable to change his mask during the operation, since every step had been crucial and he couldn't even back away from the table for a moment. He told me later that the masks definitely weren't waterproof—with that first blast he'd gotten a pretty good mouthful of blood, and tasted it for days.

On the Vascular Service we operated on Tuesdays, Wednesdays and Fridays. Monday was reserved for an early morning case conference and then an all-day Vein Clinic. Thursday was the main General Vascular Clinic.

Without question, the Monday Vein Clinic was the most painful of these exercises. A steady stream of patients would circulate through the office from 8:00 in the morning until 4:00 in the afternoon, and basically none of them had interesting problems. In fact, you were doing well if the patient's presentation didn't gag you half the time.

About two-thirds of the Vein Clinic patients were women with varicose veins. These came in a number of different flavors. Some were nearly-invisible "spider veins" that upset the aesthetic sensibilities of middle-aged women who were clinging forlornly to a rapidly-vanishing youth. Often as not I couldn't even see the tiny spider veins, but Treves was slick at obliterating them with injections of concentrated saline from a minuscule needle. More understandable were the concerns of the patients with the grossly bulging varicosities. Sometimes these were asymptomatic—they just looked like hell. Other times they caused pain or phlebitis. If these patients didn't respond to treatment with compression stockings, we would offer them surgery. The operation would usually consist of dividing the main superficial vein near its termination in the groin, then painstakingly excising the rest through tiny incisions over the entire length of the leg. Although this procedure sounds unappealing, few patients refused it once it was out on the table and, truthfully, it was a very effective treatment: if the operation was performed correctly, the problem was almost always solved. The patients were exceedingly grateful, too. A woman who is able to wear a skirt after years of being ashamed of the appearance of her legs can be very appreciative, indeed. Often, one successful varicose vein operation would beget several more, as the patient showed off her new look to her friends!

Another group that showed up on Mondays had problems with "venous stasis ulcers." In this situation (as with varicose veins, by the way) the one-way valves in the leg veins have become ineffective for some reason, and blood pools in the calves and ankles. This leads to swelling as the fluid components of the blood seep through the vein walls and out into the tissues (often some proteins will seep out, too, and stain the tissues brown). Since the skin is pushed farther away from the arterial, oxygen-containing blood, cells in that skin begin to die. Eventually, ulcers develop on the ankles and shins, and they don't heal—and usually become infected—because they can't get the oxygen they need to combat these problems. These ulcers can be wide and deep, and usually seep large quantities of tissue fluid.

The treatment of venous stasis ulcers is remarkably simple—the problem usually is that the patients either don't seek care for months or the primary care physicians that they do go to haven't had the proper training to help them.

A physician named Unna inadvertently figured out the answer in the 1800s. He dressed the wounds of his leg ulcer patients with tight bandages caked in zinc oxide. Unbeknownst to Unna, the zinc compound had antibacterial effects, and the tight wrap behaved exactly like a compression stocking, improving the return of venous blood from the leg and, thus, augmenting the delivery of oxygen to the tissues that needed it to heal. After a week or two in the simple dressing that came to be known as Unna's boot, nearly all venous stasis ulcers will heal.

So a large number of referrals came to the Vein Clinic with stasis ulcers, most of whom only needed Unna boots. Placement of an Unna boot is actually reimbursed rather well, for being such a simple thing, and

I suspect that the primary care physicians referred the stasis ulcer patients to the vascular guys just because they didn't know that they could make decent money from them. Truthfully, though, some of these enormously swollen legs with great, weeping sores could scare the hell out of you—the family docs were doing the right thing by passing them along.

Beyond the aneurysms and vein problems, the main tasks of the vascular surgeons were to prevent strokes and to save legs.

The carotid arteries are the major source of blood flow to the brain. When they become narrowed by atherosclerosis, these arteries place the individual at risk for having a stroke. Frequently the narrowings draw attention to themselves by causing temporary stroke symptoms which resolve, but as often they are entirely clinically silent. In recent years, research has demonstrated that a conceptually simple operation known as carotid endarterectomy is capable of nearly eliminating the risk of stroke in this setting. In this procedure, the artery is opened and its diseased lining stripped out. Although the operation itself can cause stroke, this risk is small, and in recent years many thousands of patients have been spared the devastation of a debilitating "cerebral infarction."

Satisfying as a successful carotid procedure can be, little in surgery can equal the sense of accomplishment that comes with the restoration of blood flow to a leg that is compromised.

Atherosclerosis has a predilection for appearing—and wreaking its particular form of havoc—in certain predictable regions of the body: the coronary and carotid arteries, for example. One of the other common sites where the disease frequently arises is in the femoral arteries of the leg. Ordinarily, blockage of this artery is reasonably well tolerated—provided it occurs over an extended period of time. This is because the gradual narrowing allows the smaller arteries to take up the slack left by the main, diseased one. These "collateral" arteries can generally provide enough blood flow to keep the leg alive, although the patient may experience pain with exercise—the smaller vessels can't keep up with the demand for oxygen of exercising muscle. Patients in this condition are usually not offered surgery: with exercise and modification of some risk factors—principally the cessation of smoking—the symptoms can be controlled and even improved.

When the arterial diseased has progressed somewhat further, the arteries may not provide enough blood and oxygen to meet the demands of the tissues even at rest. In this case, the patient is in imminent risk of losing their foot or leg, and surgery is necessary. Most often, the procedure offered is a form of arterial bypass, wherein the blocked segment of artery is circumvented with either a segment of the patient's own vein or a prosthetic material.

James Boyd was in this very boat. A seventy-year-old, reformed smoker, Boyd had developed several ulcers on his toes which wouldn't heal, and he was tortured by unremitting, burning pain in his pale left foot. His family doc had ordered some blood pressure measurements in his legs, and these had confirmed that very little blood flow was making it to Boyd's lower legs. There was virtually no blood pressure in his left leg at all. After he had been referred to Dr. Tovar, Boyd had undergone angiography. In this procedure, the radiologists had injected contrast into his arteries to define their anatomy and help us plan a bypass. It turned out that he was a good candidate, and we scheduled Boyd for the OR.

In the operating room, we dissected out the femoral artery in the thigh above the level of the blockage and found the "target vessel"—below the occlusion—in the calf. After removing the major superficial vein in Boyd's leg, we stitched it to these two arteries and restored flow, completing the bypass. The vein worked perfectly as a conduit, and we closed the incisions. There were normal pulses in Boyd's foot for the first time in years, and it turned a bright pink.

That night, I watched him like the proverbial hawk. His foot-pulses didn't change over the next several hours, so I began to ease up a bit. Being a fourth-year resident, I didn't need to remain in the hospital while on call, so after a while I somewhat reluctantly wandered out. At home, I had just drifted off to sleep when the hated pager sounded its shrill cry. Sure enough, the nurse had lost the pulse in Boyd's foot, and the intern couldn't find it, either.

After a few choice words muttered beneath my breath, I rolled out of bed and headed out into the night. Maybe the nurse and intern were wrong—they hadn't been in the OR and didn't know for sure where to feel for the pulse. As soon as I walked into Boyd's room, though, I knew that this was a forlorn hope. There was a large, El Marko black "X" over the precise spot where the pulse should have been—the nurse had marked it while it still could be felt, as they sometimes did. I double-checked but they were right, of course. We listened with a hand-held ultrasound device which could tell whether there was blood flow or not, and I was further convinced that the damned graft had clotted.

The disappointment in this was multiple. First of all, Boyd had to go back to the OR, and right away. This entailed waking Tovar up with the bad news, once again after midnight. Secondly, I was once again screwed out of a night's sleep—and Treves had a full schedule of elective surgery I was supposed to help him with the next day. Mainly, though, Boyd was now at increased risk for complications ranging from wound infections to losing his leg—all because the graft had failed.

Once again, I conjured up the appropriate cuss words, then made the necessary phone calls.

It turned out that the way we stitched the vein to the artery below the knee was awkward: it had narrowed the path of blood flow. This would have caused trouble either sooner or later, so I guess it was best we picked it up when we did. After revising this, we took Boyd back to his room. As important as anything, Tovar didn't make any effort to cause me grievous bodily harm during these events, for which I again thanked my lucky stars.

Boyd did fine after this, and his ulcers as well as his foot pain went away. Overall, it was a big save, despite the necessity for re-operation, and afterward Boyd was as happy as any patient I'd ever seen.

The practice of the vascular surgeons fascinated me. The actual technical aspects of the procedures were the most elegant I had seen, and the genuine, tangible results of success in these procedures was very gratifying. Some of the other residents likened vascular surgery to a kind of glorified plumbing, since it entailed the establishment of fluid flow through tubes and so forth. In fact, the plumber may have a harder job, since metal and plastic tubes don't heal up the way arteries and veins do. In any case, I found the whole practice fascinating, and decided, after some soul-searching, that vascular surgery would be a nice fit for me. Learning to be a vascular surgeon would mean another year of training, as a fellow, but I thought it would be worth the extra time to earn the right not to have to operate on people's asses, to be quite honest.

16

M&M—The Crucible

PROBABLY THE SINGLE LEAST ENJOYABLE ASPECT of residency for me was the M&M (Morbidity and Mortality) Conference. This was a weekly gathering of the entire Department of Surgery, and attendance was mandatory. The purpose was to discuss the deaths and complications (to surgeons, the word "morbidity" is synonymous with "complication") which had occurred on the surgery services during the previous week. In another era there was a popular saying that surgeons buried their mistakes. At Ohio State, we aired them publicly and with sometimes painful candor. The idea was that if there was anything to be learned from a case that had gone bad, we would uncover it. While this sounds noble, the reality of the conference was something less.

The conference was held on Thursday mornings at 7:15 AM. Two days before, the senior-most resident on each surgery service was expected to provide the Residency Office with a complete list of the operations which had been performed on his service during the previous week, along with a separate list of all the deaths and complications which had occurred. These would be put into a standard format by the secretaries and printed up for distribution at M&M. All the residents and attendings would then have this information at their fingertips during the course of the conference.

The format of M&M was always the same: the chief resident on the service in question would go to the front of the room and announce that service's name, the number of operations which had been performed, the number of patients who had been discharged and admitted, and whether there had been any deaths or complications. These last would then be

171

described in detail. During the course of this presentation, the resident would be fair game for any questions—specific to that case or with regard to the disease and its treatment in general—from the gathered attendings. This had the practical effect of providing considerable stimulus to the resident to learn all he could about the case and others like it.

Although in principle the conference was a good idea (in fact, it was required for the program's accreditation), in practice it often became little more than an opportunity for some of the more pathologic attendings to publicly humiliate the residents.

Dr. Eleanor Daniels was a good example of this.

When I was a medical student, she had been a senior resident, and our paths had crossed when we were assigned to the same rotation for several weeks, the busy General Surgery service over at Grant Hospital. Although I had enjoyed the experience of being a part of the surgical team (and, especially, assisting in the operations), the two of us never quite hit it off, to say the least. She seemed to have it in for me, another of those few who just take an active dislike to you immediately and with no apparent reason. Short and moderately overweight, with a head shaped like a large, rounded peanut and a tangled mass of short black hair, she displayed the kind of shocking arrogance that nearly always derives from crushing insecurity. Judging from her reputation as an operator amongst the nurses and other surgeons, there was good reason for this self-doubt. Daniels' period of residency spanned the entire decade of the 1980s, supposedly due to a combination of clinical inadequacy and an inability to coexist peacefully with her colleagues: allegedly, she didn't "play well with others." It was with considerable surprise (and disappointment), then, that upon my return to Columbus for residency I encountered her as an attending in the Division of Transplantation. (There were rumors that she had been hired after finishing residency to keep her close by, since she was supposedly felt to be in need of indefinite supervision.)

Needless to say, we took up right where we had left off: she tormented me and I tried to ignore her. She had been a major player in the attempt to lynch me in my third year.

Since I was only on the transplant service for a few weeks each year, Daniels had what must have seemed to her a barely adequate opportunity to berate me. But as I advanced through the program and became a senior resident, I began having to represent my service at the weekly M&M

showdowns. These conferences allowed her a regular forum to vent her spleen in my general direction.

We residents presented the complications but, in the main, the decisions which led to the clinical problems had not been ours. These decisions had been the attendings', of course. Nevertheless we were forced to testify, in a sense, as if we had been the final arbiter in these cases. It was absurd. Even more absurd was the behavior of the attendings like Daniels who played up this charade with venomous vigor, dissecting our supposed thought processes and clinical decision-making with verbal jabs and not-too-subtle innuendoes. Some of the involved attendings would make a point of showing up for conference to deflect the criticism of the residents and defend their own actions, but just as many stayed away when a particularly unpleasant case was due to be discussed.

I can recall presenting the case of a man who had had a partial pancreatic resection for cancer, the massive Whipple operation. Being, at that time, the third-year resident on the service, I not only hadn't assisted during the surgery, I hadn't even been present in the O.R. The man had had a relatively minor complication postoperatively, a wound infection. Still, for the sake of completeness, I suppose, it needed to be discussed. The big mistake I'd made, though, was in reporting the patient's diagnosis as "metastatic pancreatic cancer." Dr. Daniels picked right up on it.

"Dr. Miller," she hissed through clenched teeth, "did you really perform a Whipple operation on a man with metastatic cancer?"

Ouch. Why hadn't I just typed in "pancreatic cancer?" The problem was, no surgery would be of any benefit to a patient with this type of tumor which had already spread to other sites, let alone the biggest operation we could do. Most of the little time the patient had left would now be spent recovering from a major operation. I glanced around the room. The attending and fellow who had actually operated on the patient were notably absent. The bastards.

"Uh, yes, that's right."

"Well, would you mind telling us the indications for resection of pancreatic cancer?"

Minding wasn't an issue, of course; remembering them was. Luckily, I could recall them reasonably well and I listed them.

"You didn't mention metastatic cancer."

"Yes, I know."

"And yet you operated on this patient with unresectable disease?"

The exchange was highly unpleasant. No one in the room seriously believed that I, the junior resident, had had anything to do with the foolish decision to operate on this man. Yet I was forced to take the fall. I wanted to shout out, "Look, I thought it was stupid, too! Why don't you bitch at the idiot who actually did this?!" But that simply wasn't done: if possible, it would have rained down even more abuse on my head. You have to remember that I would still have to work with the attending who had made the call: publicly accusing him of malpractice would not tend to enhance the enjoyability of that interaction. I was between the proverbial rock and a hard place. The best reply I could muster was, "I can't comment on the thought processes underlying the decision to operate on this man; his case doesn't merit surgery by the criteria I understand."

This seemed to satisfy her.

These sorts of surly exchanges occurred on a weekly basis.

If I never achieved a sense of mastery over the M&M environment, I at least managed to avoid letting it overpower me, as it did some others.

Ron Rausch, the Surg 1 chief of my internship rotation, had a unique approach to the presentation of complications: he defended nothing and collapsed like a house of cards on questioning. He was the one who had been to West Point and he invariably called the attendings "sir" or "ma'am." He may have been so accustomed to the culture of not talking back to superiors that the thought of defending his actions never occurred to him. I hated to watch him at M&M, though, because he was a good guy and a hard worker, and when he presented complications, the attendings were like sharks around a bobbing, bloody bucket of chum. At the first serious question Rausch just gave up, falling on his sword and basically admitting, whether it was true or not, that he had fouled up.

Another resident who suffered badly in the crucible of M&M was Emily Owyang. While a junior resident she was so nervous during her presentations that she actually read them from prepared speeches, as if M&M were a political stump. The attendings did not permit this for long, though, since she really did need to learn to think on her feet. Eventually she developed her own style, which was an effective defense as it turned out. She discussed her complications in a voice so remorseful—almost tearful—that the attendings basically didn't have the heart to thrash her.

One of the best at M&M was Katherine McCormick, who was a chief when I was an intern. Her strength arose from a stunning ability to lie about nearly anything, large or small, in such a glib manner as to arouse absolutely no suspicion, and with apparently no conscience at all. Because of this dubious gift and her undeniably high intelligence I still consider her to be one of the most dangerous people I have ever encountered. But her skills worked wonders at M&M. She would present her complications, omitting facts or embellishing as she saw fit. Sometimes the attendings would smell a rat, but none could come close to pinning her down. She was a true master of improvisational lying. At one point she actually invented a diagnosis: someone had seen that she had done a rectal operation and wondered what the indication had been. Being the intern on the service I knew the answer but she had apparently forgotten.

"That was done for a rectal toriatoma," she said.

I went cold. There was silence in the room. No one had ever heard of this diagnosis. Of course, that made sense since it doesn't exist. But in the back of everyone's mind was the possibility that a "toriatoma" was a rare tumor they had just never seen or heard of themselves.

"A what?"

She repeated the phony diagnosis. Silence again.

Dr. Mike Wagner was present, an expert in surgical oncology. I could see him rifling through his mental filing cabinet, searching for the elusive "toriatoma." Coming up empty, he decided that Katherine must be bluffing.

"What s-sort of a t-tumor is that?" he asked. Wagner had a stutter and usually tried to avoid speaking in an off-hand way at these conferences (when he had prepared talks, the stutter vanished). Unfortunately for him, Katherine knew this weakness and immediately realized that she could exploit it, since he was the only threat in the room. She was also extremely fast on her feet.

"It's a malignancy of the vascular smooth muscle cells of the rectum."

I was amazed at the speed and originality of her bullshit. It sounded completely plausible.

Wagner still looked unconvinced. Although Katherine's story sounded good, not much had slipped under his radar over the years and he was having a hard time believing that an entire type of cancer was unknown to him. But his protests were going to be extemporaneous, and difficult to follow due to the stuttering.

"I-I don't th-think there's s-such a … I-I'm not s-sure I r-recall—"

Katherine, expertly feigning a look of annoyed impatience, broke in, "It was a rectal toriatoma: the biopsy and the path report were all consistent with toriatoma. The margins were negative and the patient won't require either chemo or radiation therapy. Let's move on to the next case, OK?"

Awe-inspiring, that's all I can say. On her feet, in front of experts in the field, Katherine had made up the diagnosis of a cancer which didn't exist, just to justify performing an operation which, by the way, was perfectly reasonable for the real diagnosis. Then she had stuck to that line of B.S. and ridden it all the way to the fabricated finish line, making the expert appear ignorant of his own forte. I couldn't have done anything similar in a thousand tries. Mighty impressive. Not the sort of individual I personally would want as my surgeon, though.

I met Katherine's newlywed husband once; a big, well-to-do fellow with a winning smile but not too much going on upstairs. What a ride you're about to take, I thought.

Dr. Atcheson was in charge of the M&M conference; he "ran" it. He called upon the representatives of the service, he asked the lion's share of the questions (but, unlike Daniels', his were fair and invariably had a teaching point), and he decided when the resident had had enough and would be excused back to his or her seat. He was usually benign but could get testy if he was in a bad mood. About mid-March Dr. Atcheson would get the results of our standardized resident in-training examination back from the national clearinghouse. These were rarely what he thought they should be. The M&Ms in the few weeks following this tended to be particularly harsh. No question, the boss knew how to put the metal to you if he had to.

I learned lessons from the incessant pounding of M&M, though. Of course the desire to avoid public embarrassment was a strong incentive to read up, and my surgical knowledge base was strengthened considerably. Less respectable attributes were bolstered, as well. Although I never could approach the abilities of Katherine McCormick, I had, nevertheless, also discovered ways to conceal or modify facts which might otherwise cast the service in a negative light. For example, by the time I was a Chief Resident I never would have put "metastatic pancreatic cancer" as the diagnosis of a patient who had had a major resection. Something like that was just asking for trouble. It was possible, with experience, to disclose all pertinent information without exposing oneself to abuse. These were purely tactics of self-preservation, though; not ones of deliberate misinformation.

By the time I was the senior resident on the liver and pancreas transplant service I had mastered quite a few of these tactics. They would come in handy in my final battles with Dr. Daniels.

Dorothy Cudgel was a diabetic whose long bout with this disease had ultimately led to kidney failure and dialysis. She was considered by the transplant team to be a good candidate for a combined kidney and pancreas transplant procedure, an operation which might cure both her kidney failure and her diabetes at one stroke. Unfortunately, following her operation Dorothy's transplant kidney had failed to function. Tests indicated that the surgically-constructed blood supply had clotted off; "thrombosed" in the technical terminology. She was taken back to the O.R. and the clot was removed. Tragically, in the second postoperative period the graft thrombosed again. This was too much for the donor kidney and it died. For whatever reason, the donor pancreas survived with no apparent ill effects.

It was my duty to report the facts in the case of Mrs. Cudgel at M&M. As I prepared to present the case I began to consider what Dr. Daniels might say to make me look bad. How could she trip me up on this? Experience began to pay off for me. If I had been a mere junior resident, I would not have known that the transplant office kept records of their patients which were far more detailed than the ordinary hospital charts which the residents had access to. I knew that Daniels would review these and attempt to use information in them to undermine me at the conference. This time around, though, I would have the advantage: she could not have known that I had my own contacts in the Transplant

Division, and that through these I had been able to peruse, at leisure, all the records that Daniels had seen. I had a trump she didn't even know existed.

For the first time in residency I looked forward to Thursday morning. It couldn't come soon enough for me.

The transplant service was technically Surg 5 and, since Dr. Atcheson liked to have the services present in numerical order, I had to wait nearly an hour before my turn to address the Department came around.

I told the story of Mrs. Cudgel and her clotted graft in all of its exquisite detail, watching out of the corner of my eye as Dr. Daniels quivered about, like a mongoose about to strike. I didn't have to wait long.

"Dr. Miller," she interrupted me, "what type of dialysis was this patient on before her transplant?"

There are two types of dialysis available these days: peritoneal dialysis, in which a solution is placed into the abdominal cavity which cleanses the blood, and hemodialysis, in which the blood is drawn directly out, filtered through a machine, and returned to the circulation. Although neither can be regarded as ideal situations, of the two, peritoneal dialysis is by far the more preferable.

"She was on peritoneal dialysis," I replied.

Daniels had this peculiar habit of glancing around the room while she was interrogating you, rather like a distracted lizard; in another reality she'd have made a good prosecuting attorney.

"Peritoneal dialysis," she repeated. "And why was that?"

This was a very odd question, but I was beginning to get a feel for where Daniels was headed, so I did my best to clear the path for her.

"She was on peritoneal dialysis because it was the best option for her. It allows a more normal life by allowing her to dialyze at home at night; she didn't have to spend 15 hours a week at a hemodialysis clinic."

Daniels took the bait. She'd been watching too many reruns of *L.A. Law*.

"Wasn't she on peritoneal dialysis because she had a clotting disorder? Didn't she have a hypercoagulable state (a condition where the blood clots in an abnormally aggressive fashion)?"

I could sense the room, which was mostly residents and students, starting to cringe on my behalf. Obviously Daniels had known something I hadn't known, and now I, the resident, was going to be made to look awfully bad.

But the reality was that I had as complete a knowledge of Mrs. Cudgel's medical history as it was possible to have: from the Transplant Division's own files I had, in a hard copy in my lab coat pocket, the entire, comprehensive pre-transplant work-up.

Pausing a little for dramatic effect, I bowed my head, as if Dr. Daniels had exposed a resident in yet another moment of weakness (in effect, I did my best Ron Rausch impression). Then, rising, I paid my own homage to *L.A. Law*.

"No, Dr. Daniels, there is no suggestion of a clotting disorder in her medical history. She was on peritoneal dialysis for the reasons I've described."

The conference room grew quiet. During my entire residency, in only one other instance did a resident openly challenge an attending at M&M in this fashion. Daniels looked uneasy; at this point she may have suspected that I had her trumped. Still, true to form she followed through, "leading with her face," as a boxer might say. "If you had read the pre-transplant work-up on this patient, you'd know that she has a clotting disorder. You should have known about that before the surgery. You should have known that she was at high risk to clot her graft."

The room was absolutely silent. Outside the door, you could clearly hear the clinking sound of silverware on plates in the cafeteria. Dr. Atcheson, who was silent throughout the exchange, peered up at me, narrowing his eyes as he awaited my response.

It may have been the high point of my residency, from a purely personal standpoint, when I reached into my lab coat pocket and produced the handful of 81/2" x 11" sheets, folded twice over, and held them up in the air.

"Dr. Daniels, here is the pre-transplant work-up," I said. "There is no mention of a clotting disorder, or any suggestion of one. Would you like me to read it aloud?"

As Daniels glared at me, Dr. Atcheson defused the situation by calling for the next service to present. When the conference ended, the other residents clustered around me as if I'd scored the winning touchdown in the big game.

Daniels never asked me another question at M&M.

17

Danger

EVERYONE INVOLVED WITH THE CARE OF PATIENTS these days is aware of the risks of transmissible disease, especially the fearsome blood-borne viral diseases like hepatitis and AIDS (which we called "The Big Dreaded"). Given the invasive nature of our chosen field, those in the surgical disciplines were especially alerted to the jeopardy in which we were putting ourselves and our families. But exposure to blood and other bodily fluids is almost inevitable in surgery, and all we could and can do is to try and minimize these inherent risks as much as possible.

In the operating room surgeons breech their gloves all the time. There's just no technology available which has produced a sterile glove that will both provide inviolable protection and still allow the tactile sense that all surgeons require to operate smoothly. Some surgeons wear two pair of gloves, reasoning that the outer pair might be torn but the inner will still be protective. Most find this to be no solution, though— once again, it's just too hard to feel the tissues with any degree of subtlety with two sets of gloves on. Besides, if a knife or a needle will penetrate one set of gloves, what's to stop it from perforating the next pair? Thankfully the really nasty diseases need a good foothold: just smearing some HIV-infected blood on normal, unbroken skin is very unlikely to transmit the disease (although I still wouldn't recommend that particular behavior). It takes a good, strong inoculum like a puncture with a hollow needle containing infected blood, or a good-sized gash bathed in the tainted stuff. That'll get the job done.

For these reasons the best bet to avoid contracting a blood-borne disease during surgery is to be scrupulously careful. The best way to approach the problem is an offshoot of the "Universal Precautions" protocols devised by Public Health experts in the 1980s: treat everyone as if they are infected. Assume that the patient has a deadly, communicable viral disease that you, too, will catch if you touch their blood—then trust me, you'll be careful handling that scalpel. Of course it's hard to do this when you're removing the gall bladder from a 75-year-old grandmother, but you're best served if you operate on her as if she were a pockmarked, strung-out heroin addict.

Although these concerns were never far from my mind during these years, there were two instances when they took the forefront.

Rosanne Stoker was a very unfortunate woman. When I met her in my internship year she was being admitted to the hospital for severe malnutrition and dehydration. Having been diagnosed with pancreatic cancer, she had had part of her pancreas and intestines removed in the awe-inspiring Whipple operation. Like many after this procedure, she had difficulty with near-constant nausea and vomiting and had ultimately required placement of a permanent intravenous line for the administration of fluids and nutrition. The good news was that her cancer was cured, not an inconsiderable achievement in the face of a malignancy as aggressive as pancreatic cancer. The bad news was that, due to her problems with taking in adequate amounts of food, she now weighed sixty-five pounds. Worse news for me as I admitted her was that the indwelling IV line she had in her neck was not functioning.

Long-term IVs are best placed in large veins such as those under the collarbone, in the neck or, in exceptional cases, in the groin. Smaller veins will eventually collapse and clot off if a catheter is left in place. Larger veins stay open longer. Since they're deeper, they're less likely to get infected, too.

Rosanne's neck and collarbone veins (the jugular and subclavian veins, respectively) had clotted off because they had been used so many times already. This was why her old IV had ceased to work and she had become dehydrated and malnourished, unable to receive the proper supplementation which she needed because she could take so little by mouth. She lived with her husband several hundred miles away, in rural West Virginia, and when she showed up for an unscheduled appearance, it usually meant that things had gotten awfully bad. Such was the case this time. The long-term IV had stopped working, but her husband had tried to see her through the difficulty, feeding her broth and whatever else she could hold down. In a few days he realized she was heading in the wrong direction and he made the long drive to bring her to Columbus.

The first order of business was to provide her with decent intravenous access, so that we could resuscitate her with fluids and, eventually, provide her with calories via IV nutrition, called TPN.

Since I was dubiously blessed with the knowledge that Mrs. Stoker's jugular and subclavian veins were inaccessible, I found myself staring reluctantly at her groins, the site of her other large, approachable veins, the femorals. I didn't have to look very hard, since most of this lady's anatomic structures were clearly visible beneath her skin. Poor Mrs. S looked like a photograph from Auschwitz or Andersonville brought to life. Her cheeks were sunken and her eyes protruded, her skin hung from her limply like a drapery. All of her bones showed through the skin like an anatomy text. She truly looked like a corpse, and every time I walked into her room I thought, "this time, she's dead." Then I would speak her name and the corpse would move, turning its head to the source of the sound, and speak in reply.

And this patient needed a femoral vein catheter.

The senior residents were mysteriously absent as I set up to place the intravenous "central line"—so-called because the femoral vein, like the internal jugular and the subclavian, led directly into the central circulation, unlike a "peripheral" arm vein. In retrospect, it was because they were trying to instill confidence in the new intern—let him do an easy central line, soon enough he'll be able to do them all on his own—but that wasn't clear to me at the time. What was clear was that the patient had been "prepped" with antiseptic iodine solution and draped with sterile paper and there I stood, unutterably alone. The prepackaged central line kit with its sterile polystyrene bubble-compartments occupied my attention for quite some time, while Mrs. Stoker waited patiently. I stalled for a few more minutes, numbing up the skin with about six times the adequate dose of local anesthetic. Finally I realized that I was on an island, alone. Those bastards were missing on purpose.

I decided to take matters into my own hands (since there was no other alternative). My gloved forefinger felt for the strong pulse of the femoral artery, which lies right along the vein, just to the outside of it. Knowing the vein was right next door, I inserted my needle through the surprisingly tough, leathery skin. In an instant I was in the vein, dark red blood creeping up the needle and into the barrel of the syringe. There was a feeling of inexpressible joy. I had placed a few central lines before, but always under the very close supervision of the senior residents and never in the femoral vein. Now I had flown solo and hit a home run, mixed metaphors aside. The next step was to slip a flexible wire through the center of the puncture needle, remove the needle, and slide the catheter over the wire and into the vein. Mission accomplished! Now to stitch the line in securely....

Reaching back to the polystyrene kit where I knew the silk skin stitch to be, I glanced up toward the window, where a majestic multicolored autumn sunset was painting the normally bleak North Columbus skyline like a Renaissance master. An overwhelmingly sweet sense of self-satisfaction was immediately punctuated by the unmistakably pungent sensation of a needle piercing my right forefinger. Not lightly, either.

"Fuck!" I shouted.

"What's the matter?!" came the understandably anxious voice of Mrs. Stoker from beneath the sterile drapes.

I held my hand up to the light and gasped as I saw my own blood welling up under the surface of the latex glove. I looked down at the central line kit. Which needle had I struck? The obvious answer was the local anesthetic needle, which I had used to numb up the skin. It was poking rudely up through the accumulated detritus of the kit, as if sniffing out its prey.

"Damn," I thought, "A hollow needle!"

This was not good news. It was common knowledge by the late 1980s that hollow needles were more dangerous in terms of the transmission of blood-borne diseases than solid needles (like those used in placing sutures) because the blood of the (possibly infected) patient remains within the hollow center of the needle, poised to be injected into any unfortunate who stabs himself with it. This, of course is precisely the mechanism by which hepatitis and HIV have been transmitted between intravenous drug abusers.

"Sorry, Mrs. S," I answered, still holding my injured hand as if it were a piece of road-kill. "There's no problem. I just stuck myself."

"Oh, you poor dear," she said—despite her *Creepshow* appearance, Mrs. Stoker was a sweetheart—"Are you all right?"

"I think so...."

About 35 million thoughts run through one's head at this particular point in his career. Chief among these: "God, I hope she doesn't have AIDS," "Why the fuck am I doing this with my life?" "Why weren't the senior residents around to help me?" and "God, I hope she doesn't have AIDS."

I took the drapes down from Mrs. Stoker and looked her in the eye. I knew she had had pancreatic cancer, had suffered from the postoperative gastrointestinal complications of the massive Whipple operation and lived in the hills of West Virginia, about as far from the urban vices which had given rise to and then harbored HIV as it was possible to be in North America. Still, with her emaciated appearance, she looked to me at this time far more like an AIDS patient in the final stages than the malnourished war-crimes victim she had resembled before.

"Mrs. Stoker," I began, "I'd like to run some blood tests on you. I stuck myself on a needle that I used to numb you up."

At this point her husband entered the room, summoned by my profanity of a moment earlier. The complete physical opposite of her, he stood a good 6'3" and must have been 275 pounds. He was also fiercely protective of her, even if his judgment was sometimes ill-advised.

"What's that!?" he bellowed.

I repeated my request, this time pointing out that they had the right to refuse any blood draws I ordered, particularly those meant to identify communicable illnesses with social stigmata, as HIV was at that time.

Mr. Stoker grew quiet and his voice mellowed.

"We don't have any of them diseases," he said quietly, "but you can do whatever tests you need to."

Mrs. Stoker sat up and agreed: "Yes, Doctor, you're doing so much to help us; you mustn't be worried...."

Although it was a great relief, after that exchange it was no surprise when all the tests came back negative the next week.

I made another mental note to be careful. That mental notebook was becoming cumbersome.

The mental notebook may have grown so weighty, in fact, that I set it by the side of the figurative road one spring morning in my second year of residency, when I was operating on some inmates of the Corrections System of the Great State of Ohio.

As I've mentioned elsewhere, it was our dubious privilege at The Ohio State University Medical Center to care for the prisoners of the State Penitentiaries. One of the general surgery services, Surg 6, was designated as the prisoner service, and while on that service the residents operated on those prisoners who needed surgery—with a pretty fair degree of autonomy, as it happened. When it came to their private patients, the attendings almost never let the residents perform key parts of procedures unsupervised. With the prisoners, however, that was the norm—at least if the resident had some competence.

And so it was that on this Spring morning a very green second-year surgery resident bearing a remarkable similarity to this humble author found himself operating with the assistance of only an awestruck third-year medical student. True, the cases to be performed were minor—excisions of small soft tissue masses, for the most part ("ditzels," these were called—another slang medical term with a thoroughly obscure origin), but I felt like Ben Casey anyway. This was the first time I was the senior man on the surgery team in the OR: I was the Operator, the final authority. Well, not quite, but that's how it felt—and a welcome change it was from being the grinning lackey.

The first two procedures went smoothly. I removed lumps and bumps and sent them to the pathologists for evaluation, although it was abundantly clear that they were benign growths. The attending on service appeared very briefly in each case and signed some paperwork. He surreptitiously conversed in low tones with the circulating nurse—I'm sure to get some confirmation that I wasn't performing abject butchery—and left the operating room with loud, sarcastic praises as to the genius-level surgical skill of Dr. Miller.

I was getting comfortable. At that point in time I didn't realize, as I now do, that this is the first sign of real trouble ahead.

The third case was another ditzel, this one about the size of an acorn and perched on the very crown of this prisoner's head, emanating from the soft tissue of his scalp. I had not met him before this (the operation had been scheduled by another resident some weeks before), and he was already anesthetized by the time I returned to the OR from depositing the second patient in the recovery room. While I scrubbed with my by-now-seasoned medical student, the nurses shaved the prisoner's scalp and prepped it with Betadine. We returned and, after donning the gown and gloves, got set to start. Having dealt with similar ditzels in the past, I knew that this one was most likely either a lipoma (a benign proliferation of fatty tissue) or a sebaceous cyst (a subcutaneous collection of sebum—the greasy material which derives from hair follicles). I had learned to be somewhat wary of the latter, as there had been a recent experience in a similar setting in which I had inadvertently perforated the cyst. That cyst had been under considerable pressure, and my penetration of it had allowed a large amount of the rather revolting contents to burst forth directly in my face. I was never so thankful for eyeglasses and a surgical mask as at that time. But I had learned a lesson: don't pop the damn thing if you can possibly avoid it (it all needs to come out anyway; if you just drain it, it'll come back).

It was for these reasons that I took special care to make a wide skin incision circumferentially around the lesion. I carefully excised the mass, leaving it intact, and passed it off the operating field to the scrub nurse. As she placed it in a jar of formalin and labeled it, I began to close the elliptical incision. The amusing thought occurred to me that if it was, in fact, a sebaceous cyst the pathologist might inadvertently cut into it and spray himself with the fetid contents. That'd be fun to watch.

Thus distracted by my sadistic mental image of some wretched path resident caked in viscous, cheesy sebum, I was once again caught unaware as the sewing needle, locked in the hand-held driver, dove clean through the prisoner's scalp and into my left thumb.

The aforementioned "F-Bomb" expletive was soon heard again, this time to echo through the operating room and, no doubt, the adjacent hallways. My right hand reflexively dropped the needle driver and grasped the left in the same, helpless "roadkill" pose I had struck in Mrs. S's room. Once more I caught the ghastly site of my own blood welling up beneath the latex. Stepping back from the field I pulled my gloves off. The circulating nurse picked up on the problem right away (I guess there was a reason the attending had trusted her judgment of my abilities—she knew what the hell she was doing) and doused my injured hand with Betadine. I gripped the hand and forcefully tried to make it bleed more, knowing that the effusion might carry any infectious agents out with it. At least it was a solid needle. The prisoner's wound was nearly closed, so I let the student put in the last few stitches as I headed for the Employee Health office.

After my previous experience I knew the drill. Blood draws from me and the patient (if he consented). A few forms to fill out. Some counseling if the patient was HIV positive.

By the time I got back the prisoner was in the recovery room. I was involuntarily shaking as I approached him. We've all heard the stories about the depravity which permeates the prisons. Was there any chance this guy was clean? He looked relatively non-threatening as he sized me up in his still half-groggy state. I told him what had happened, as he listened intently. The story seemed to shake him out of any residual anesthetic effects. I finished by asking him if he had any of the well-known risk factors: a history of IV drug abuse, anal intercourse, etc.

I was as much afraid of the sound of his replies as of their content. Of course it's a ridiculous stereotype, but if he had answered with a high-pitched lisp I think I would have collapsed. Instead an irate baritone burst out with righteous indignation.

"I never shot up and I ain't no goddamn faggot!!"

I felt like hugging him, but after his proclamation the prisoner's reaction might have landed me in the ER!

He agreed to the testing and I basically put the episode behind me. I knew that the Employee Health office would contact me if anything turned up positive, and a week passed without a word. I was helping out in the Vascular Surgery clinic, already on another rotation, when I received a page to an unfamiliar hospital number. When the voice on the other end of the line said, "Employee Health," it was my turn to feel like collapsing again.

The prisoner had been exposed to hepatitis C, a viral disease without a vaccine. The other tests, including HIV, were negative. Did this mean I was likely to get hepatitis? Should I be treated prophylactically, as in HIV exposure? The Employee Health rep couldn't give me any answers, so I had to do some quick research on my own.

Basically, if I didn't get sick, I needed to get my exposure status checked in six months with another blood test. It's possible to have chronic infection with hepatitis C and be symptom-free, with or without liver disease itself. As it happened, I didn't get sick and my exposure status never changed, but I did worry about it constantly for those months.

A good friend of mine in the Urology tract got stuck with a needle used on an HIV patient that same Spring. The initial blood test he underwent showed that he had become infected. He had to wait a week before the more sophisticated and expensive confirmatory test proved to be negative. How he managed to continue with his day-to-day routine during that week is beyond me.

18

Death

DEALING WITH DEATH is unquestionably the most difficult aspect of being a physician. Most doctors treat death as defeat: the goal is to prevent the death of the patient and if you don't—if the patient dies— you've been defeated. The more insightful physician might realize that the real goal is to prevent suffering, but even in cases where death brings an end to a patient's suffering in a more complete way than any doctor's interventions could, it still never seems like an ally.

Like everyone else, physicians carry within themselves their own impressions of death from the impact it has made on their lives outside the profession: its first appearance in the distant memory of our childhood as a hushed word spoken among tearful grown-ups, one of whom we never see again; its savage brutality coring out a defining moment in our youth as a parent is taken unexpectedly; its melancholy permanence driven home in our adulthood as a friend our own age succumbs. These perceptions lurk behind the scenes in the psyche of all physicians, coloring their clinical decisions as they relate to the lives and deaths of their patients.

My first significant clinical confrontation with death occurred when I was still in medical school. I was on the Pulmonary Medicine service then, learning amongst a group dealing with the severest of lung diseases. By random chance I was assigned to follow the course of a patient named John Harding, who by odder chance happened to have been born within a few days of me, in the same year. We were both 24. We both had been born in May of 1965 in central Ohio. As I shortly learned, we had had similar childhoods, had similar interests (sports, cars, girls, rock 'n' roll), and similarly hated being confined in the hospital. In fact, aside from his small stature there was no particular distinguishing feature between the two of us that any outside observer would have been able to detect. But there was a major difference between us: I was in ostensibly good health, and John Harding had a progressive, incurable lung disease.

John had an inherited form of pulmonary fibrosis, a devastating disease in which the normal tissue of the lung is replaced by non-functional fibrous connective tissue. As the disease follows its inexorable path, the ability of the patient's lungs to perform their primary task of providing oxygen to the body is crippled. The only possible hope was a lung transplantation, at the time still experimental.

Some of the symptoms John was experiencing could be treated, with medications and with supplemental oxygen. He had been hospitalized many times. But the underlying disease process could not be stopped or even delayed, and as it happened when I began to follow him, he was in the hospital for the last time.

Neither of us knew that at the time we met, though. He was admitted because of some breathing difficulty, that's all, and he had had that for years, and had been admitted for it, too, as a matter of fact. Some O_2 by facemask, a few doses of medication and he'd get back to the skirts and the Nascar. That's what he told me when I did his admission history and physical, at any rate. But this time things didn't improve by much with the simple measures and, truth be told, the pulmonologists had nothing else to offer. They were hoping that a lung transplantation would be available soon but only two or three centers were doing them, the results were early and mixed, and the wait list was long. If John didn't get better on his own this time (and as the days dragged on, not only did he not get better, he got worse), then it might be the end.

We talked about this on rounds, and the pulmonary medicine attending discussed it with John's family, but we all agreed to keep John in the dark. Although I won't ever hide knowledge about a patient's condition from him now in my own practice, and I had misgivings at the time in John Harding's case, I thought it was the right thing to do then and I think the same now, in retrospect. He held his own for about a week, breathing concentrated oxygen through the face mask and taking the inhaled medications which soothed his symptoms but couldn't come close to altering the course of the progressive scarring of his lung tissue.

It was a brilliantly-sunlit spring afternoon when the effort finally became too much for John. Although he was breathing 100% oxygen, the monitors showed that the hemoglobin in his blood was barely 50% saturated with it. This was a situation not compatible with life for long. The torment might be briefly extended by placing an endotracheal tube and employing a mechanical ventilator, but the outcome would be the same. The pulmonary attending, Dr. Kurek, appeared and he reviewed the situation with the family, away from John. Kurek had taken care of John for years. They agreed among themselves to abide by John's wishes: if he wanted to be on the ventilator, they would stay with him. If he wanted to make an end of it today, they would be there with him.

With the family all around the patient, in addition to the medical team and the nurse, Dr. Kurek approached John, whose effort to take a single breath was, by this point, stupendous. He had to lift himself off the hospital bed and vigorously thrust his chest and shoulders forward just to take a breath in. With each exhalation he would collapse back into the bed and his entire chest seemed to cave in to the floor. He was trying to make these exertions upwards of 40 times a minute, and he was running out of gas. There was no way he could verbally answer a question, but Dr. Kurek tried anyway.

"John, I think we've come to the end of the line here. If we put you on a ventilator, we can buy a few days, but that's about it."

John's eyes were glazed as they stared unblinkingly at the ceiling. His unbelievably rapid and labored breathing continued. But you could tell he was listening and comprehending.

Kurek continued.

"We can either put you on the ventilator or make you comfortable and end it now, John. I'll do whatever you want."

Every member of the family was in tears. The nurse was holding one of her hands in the other so hard that her knuckles were white. She held a small vial in the white-knuckled hand. I was numb as I experienced the most intense drama of the human condition that I had ever witnessed.

Kurek's voice was the only source of stability, the only cause at this point to believe that anything existed either inside or outside this room. But that voice was about to ask the question that everyone, with the possible exception of John Harding, dreaded.

"John?"

Kurek's voice faltered. He stared at the floor and I could see tears welling in his eyes.

"John, do you want me to put you on the ventilator?"

Several seconds passed as Harding's frenzied efforts to catch his breath persisted. Then he unmistakably stopped those efforts long enough to shake his head emphatically no.

Kurek paused for a moment and I watched him swallow with difficulty and blink.

"John, do you want me to make you comfortable?"

Still working impossibly hard, still unable to speak, Harding nodded.

Kurek, in his own turn, nodded to the nurse. She moved to the side of the bed and silently administered a few milligrams of morphine from her white-knuckle vial. Just enough to eliminate the awful feeling of anxiety that smothering to death brings on. In a few minutes Harding was dead, passing peacefully because of that morphine. The medical personnel silently left the room, to allow John's family some time with him, alone.

Although these events have passed through my mind countless times, I have never been able to find the right words to describe my emotions that day. I believe I learned much from that experience which I carry with me yet, things too complex and meaningful for words. I hope so.

Harding died in the late afternoon that Spring day, and rounds were already over. I had stayed to be close when I saw, early in the day, that the end was near. Now the end had passed and I could go home.

A strong impression which remains etched in my memory is the incredible exhilaration I felt at being alive as I drove home the day John Harding died. The weather had been rainy and depressing for weeks. Now it was a brilliant sunlit day, the birds were singing loudly, and no one I saw or talked to could have any understanding as deep as mine of how wonderful it was to be alive.

No training is provided to the surgical resident in dealing with death, whether it be helping the patient's families cope with the spectrum of feelings and practical problems which may arise with death's coming, or learning how to assimilate and appropriately channel his own emotions about the process. In this regard medical schools have made much more progress in the education of their students, most of whom are tailored for primary care roles as internists or family doctors. As a result, in my opinion there are no physicians who are more poorly prepared for the death of a patient than surgeons. This is manifested in a number of ways.

In my experience as a resident the attending surgeons almost universally tried to wiggle out of situations in which they either had to tell a patient he was going to die or tell a family the patient was dead. Eventually I used this fact to my own advantage by offering to do the dirty work myself. Not only did this free the reluctant attending from his ethical responsibility to transmit the bad news (thus scoring me points in the eyes of the attendings, whether they consciously realized it or not), but it also gave me experience in how to approach this most delicate of subjects. I wanted the experience because I was so disgusted by the gutless quivering of the otherwise chest-pounding faculty with regard to this issue that I resolved never to duplicate their behavior when I was in practice on my own.

Another way to deal with death was simply to ignore it as a possibility, a perception not as deranged as one might think in the era of mechanical ventilators, cardiopulmonary bypass machines and post-modern critical care.

A case in point was that of Phyllis East.

Phyllis came to the hospital to have her heart fixed. She had a severe form of coronary artery disease, that great scourge of modern society in which the blood vessels that supply the heart muscle (the "coronary" arteries—so-named because they resemble a crown as they descend along that organ) are clogged with waxy, atherosclerotic plaque. She needed surgery to avoid a fatal heart attack in the near future, which was a strong probability if not frankly imminent. The cardiac surgeons took her to the operating room and performed an operation in which three blocked coronary arteries were bypassed by grafting some of her own vessels to the arteries above and below the blockages, a "triple bypass" as the popular press would say. The operation itself went smoothly.

Phyllis' postoperative course, however, was nightmarish. Before we were even able to remove her endotracheal breathing tube and get her off the mechanical ventilator she had begun to show signs of a devastating complication. There was unmistakable evidence of "thromboemboli." This is the dreaded situation wherein bits of blood-clot form within the bloodstream at some site of injury and/or low flow. These bits then travel as far in the arterial system as they can, being carried passively by the flow of blood, and lodge in some small artery too tiny for them to squeeze through. Stuck in these small arteries, the emboli block the flow of blood (and thus the supply of life-sustaining oxygen) to the tissues beyond them.

Almost before our eyes, Mrs.' East's toes became black. Over the next few days her feet and calves died, and she had to have both legs amputated above the knee. Then she threw clot to her gut. We opened her abdomen and resected feet after feet of blackened, fetid intestine. Her kidneys failed, and she had to go on dialysis. Clots went to her liver, and she grew startlingly jaundiced as this organ succumbed.

The heartbreaking element in this tale is that only one major organ system did not suffer a profound insult, the most susceptible of all: her brain. Phyllis remained fully awake and alert through virtually the entirety of her death by inches. Mercifully (for her caregivers) she stayed on the ventilator with an endotracheal tube in place, unable to verbally articulate her thoughts as the days dragged piteously into weeks and her organs shut down one by one. But her eyes, piercingly yellow from the bile which her choked liver could not metabolize, told the whole horrid story. She lay nearly motionless in the bed, the rhythmic pulse of the puffing ventilator and the constant hum of the intravenous pumps surrounding her. Turn off any one of the IV drips and she would die in minutes. Pull the endotracheal tube and it would be seconds.

Everyone wanted her to die, the residents, the nursing staff, the family. I spoke with her shell-shocked daughters daily, and they repeatedly begged me to stop all the tests and surgeries and just let her go. I sympathized with them, because I knew that their memories of their vibrant, loving mother would be forever polluted by the image of the jaundiced, disfigured, ventilated cadaver decaying before their eyes. But we were all powerless because the two individuals who did not wish her death were the ones in charge of making the decisions: the attending surgeon and Phyllis' husband, the daughters' stepfather.

Both these men were blinded by emotion. The husband truly loved Phyllis and just wanted her to be back home with him. He did not see that she was already gone. The surgeon, ordinarily a level-headed, highly intelligent and capable man, in his great need to keep her alive completely lost sight of her quality of life. I think he felt tremendously responsible for the misfortune which had befallen her, and he refused to give up even when further intervention was absurd and, in fact, probably immoral. At one point, when her death was clearly imminent, he even went so far as to describe her as being "salvageable." Salvage what!? I thought.

One evening before she died I stood in Phyllis' room just looking at her and contemplating. I felt indescribable pity. Amongst the wave of emotions which swept over me, the strongest which I can form into language was, "Lord, please don't let me die this way." Looking at her dulling eyes, set in that sunken yellow face, I was sure she was thinking the same thing.

As difficult as it was to face the agonizing death by inches that Phyllis East suffered, at least all of the healthcare workers and the patient (as well as her family) had time to grasp what was happening, and prepare themselves for the inevitable outcome. This is by no means the case with all patients who die under the care of surgeons. Sometimes the end comes before anyone has a chance to realize that anything significant is happening, let alone to prepare for it.

In no setting is this fact driven home with more finality than the trauma bay of the emergency room, as it was for me and the others involved on a winter night in my fourth year of residency. I was rotating at an outside hospital where we gained extra trauma experience.

Celeste Findlay had been partying most of that cold night, dancing and bar-hopping and generally raising alcohol-fueled hell with her companion. It was a Saturday night, and the couple were driving from nightclub to nightclub. They may have been celebrating something or just letting off steam. No one ever got the chance to ask her that, or to ask whether she noticed from her passenger seat that her friend had mistakenly turned onto an exit ramp as he tried to merge onto the interstate.

The head-on crash was devastating. Her friend was dead at the scene. The emergency squad extricated Celeste with some difficulty and raced her to the hospital, just a few blocks away.

Back at the hospital, the PA loud speaker announced the imminent arrival of a Level 1 trauma, and I drowsily slipped out of bed. It was 2:30 AM, closing time for the local bars. On Fridays and Saturdays, especially, this point in time was followed hard up by an influx of trauma as drunks crashed their cars or started fights. By the time I reached the emergency room most of my team was there. We all put on gowns, gloves and lead aprons (these last due to the number of x-rays which are shot in rapid succession when the patient arrives). The ER operator, who maintained radio contact with the squad while it was en route, popped her head in the room long enough to tell us that we were going to get a bad one: the paramedics had lost the patient's vital signs.

Now this piece of information may generate a variety of emotions in a trauma team leader. The immediate thought is along the lines of, "Oh, we're going to have our hands full," after all, if the patient has no vital signs one will have to try to identify the reason(s) why and correct them—with precious little time in which to do so. The second consideration, though, is, "The injuries are probably not survivable; we don't have much to lose." This concept comes from the almost uniformly bad outcome of patients who present to the trauma room in cardiac arrest—those who are salvaged are in the minuscule minority.

My own thoughts drifted toward the second of these examples. In my memory I briefly lingered over the previous cases I had been involved with in which trauma patients had arrived at the ER in full arrest. No, I recalled; none ever came back. Then the wailing of the siren brought me back to the tasks at hand as the ambulance backed up to the ER doors, the spinning lights casting multicolored spirograph patterns on the frosted windows.

In seconds the paramedics were wheeling Celeste's gurney into the trauma room. She was so covered with blood from head to toe that I couldn't immediately tell what race she was. Someone said she was 30 years old. While one of the paramedics performed chest compressions, the other was rhythmically pumping a lavender plastic bag which was driving oxygen through an endotracheal tube protruding from the patient's nose. They explained that they had placed the tube at the scene in order to protect her airway, since she was unconscious. As we moved Celeste from the gurney onto the trauma bed, they continued to describe the harrowing journey from the crash scene and her loss of vital signs. I noted that the patient's chest was not moving as the bag was being squeezed. I told one of the surgery residents to remove the tube from her nose; it was probably in her esophagus.

Celeste had clearly suffered multiple facial fractures, and to attempt to place another breathing tube through her nose or mouth would be both hazardous and next to impossible. But she was not breathing on her own and an airway had to be secured.

"I'm gonna cric her!" I shouted, grabbing a bottle of Betadine and a scalpel ("cric" is pronounced with a long "i"). Dousing her neck with the brown antiseptic solution, I made a rapid cut across her throat, through the skin and the superficial muscle fibers beneath. Spreading the yielding tissue with a clamp, I identified the cricoid cartilage of the trachea. Just below this lies the soft cricothyroid membrane, the easiest way into the trachea. I made a slit in the membrane and inserted a plastic endotracheal breathing tube. In a few seconds I had it stitched in place, and now Celeste's chest rose and fell with the bagging of the respiratory therapist.

But still there was no pulse, although her continuous EKG displayed apparently normal electrical signals. This is a state known as "PEA," or pulseless electrical activity, and in a trauma setting it usually indicates severe blood loss with consequent inadequate circulation. It's also a retrievable situation if the volume of the vascular space can be replenished, even with simple IV fluids.

To this end I quickly placed a subclavian central venous line, followed by a femoral venous line. We poured in the fluids and the uncrossmatched, type O blood. Still she had no pulse when we stopped the CPR chest compressions.

I placed a tube into each side of her chest, and several pints of blood gushed forth each time. Although this revealed serious intrathoracic injury—not a good omen by any means—relieving the pressure on her lungs and heart caused by all the blood in her chest might have helped. But it didn't.

We were running out of options.

The CPR continued, hopefully perfusing her brain in case our efforts were rewarded and, against all odds, she survived

My last shot was to try a pericardiocentesis. In this procedure a needle is blindly inserted into the pericardial sac, the tough fibrous sheath in which the heart lies, in order to drain off any fluid which may be compressing the heart (a condition known as "pericardial tamponade"). As desperate as this measure may sound, I had already saved the lives of two people in my residency by using it. The most important step was to think of trying it.

Unfortunately for Celeste, about the only place in her body where she didn't have blood was her pericardium. As I slid the needle beneath the breastbone, nothing came back. It was dry as a desert.

Incredibly, the attending, a genuine fool and several notches below the typical caliber of trauma surgeon at this hospital, had arrived and begun preparing to perform a DPL. In basic terms, this is a procedure in which a catheter is inserted through the skin of the abdomen into the belly to determine if there is internal bleeding. It's a quick way to find out if the patient needs their abdomen explored at surgery. In this case, however, abdominal exploration was out of the question: the patient could not even generate a spontaneous heartbeat!

To no one's surprise, there was indeed blood in the patient's belly. I finally had to say something.

"Should we book the OR now, Doctor?"

The attending glared at me but stayed silent. He wasn't on staff at my hospital and if I needed a defense the medical record would speak for itself, so I had little to be concerned about.

The room was packed and I never found out who said it, but in a clear voice some bold soul expressed all our feelings: "Why don't you go home and crawl back into bed, asshole?"

Celeste's EKG had degenerated into ventricular fibrillation. Although in her state it was almost certainly the last electrical gasp of a heart which couldn't keep up with an obscenely battered body, it was a pattern that could potentially respond to electrical shock: "defibrillation." We tried a few rounds of this, then finally gave up when there was no response. Celeste's pupils were fixed and dilated. It was over.

I knew none of the trauma nurses or ER docs who helped me with that trauma code, but looking at each other we all knew that we had given it the best try we could. After losing a patient, it was a very strange ambivalence I felt when I overheard one of the trauma nurses say, "that's the best surgery resident I've ever seen." I didn't know whether to laugh or cry.

As I pulled off my sweat-soaked gown and blood-soaked gloves, profoundly humbled—despite the nurse's kind appraisal—by the ease with which death from violent injury could triumph over my pitiful attempts at intervention, a social worker came up to me with a look on her face of utter grief.

Celeste's husband was in the waiting room. He had left their three small children with their grandmother when he heard about the accident from the police.

The thought never occurred to me to have the attending talk to him.

I asked the social worker to take Mr. Findlay to a private room while I cleaned up a bit. I deliberately did not rehearse a speech as I washed my hands at the scrub sink. Nothing trite or formulaic would do in this setting.

The door creaked gently as I entered the conference room. Mr. Findlay was dressed in a plaid flannel overcoat, blue jeans and boots. He had tousled brown hair and a thick moustache. He had been weeping and his eyes were crimson. Had someone already told him? No such luck.

"H-How is she?" he stammered.

From time to time as one progresses through residency one gets to feeling that he can handle anything that is thrown at him. It's called confidence, and mine was melting like the snow on the soles of Findlay's olive rubber boots. Nothing that wasn't trite or formulaic came into my mind.

"I can honestly say that we tried absolutely everything we could—"

The man's knees buckled and he nearly collapsed. I knew that physical contact was the wrong thing to do, but it was a struggle not to put a hand on his shoulder. I tried to continue: "The injuries were just too severe ... too severe. I'm sure she never knew what happened."

Findlay sobbed into his sleeve as he told me about their three young children, about how they would be motherless from now on. About how he was all alone. How would he tell her mother, who was home watching the children? There was no doubt that, unlike most, this man immediately realized the full impact of the accident. Or so I thought.

He looked up at me.

"What I don't understand is that she hated driving at night. She never drove at night. Where was she going at two in the morning?"

I felt my blood grow cold. The police hadn't told him the details of the accident, only that his wife had been hurt and that she had been taken to the hospital. He didn't know there had been another man in the car with his wife.

A realization seemed to come over him.

"Oh God," he said, his eyes suddenly a thousand miles away, "I hope she wasn't going to see that bastard Tony again...."

I excused myself, telling Mr. Findlay that the social worker would return in a few minutes to go over some things with him. Shuffling numbly back into the ER I ran into a highway patrolman who was doing some paperwork. He looked up as I passed.

"She didn't make it, huh Doc?" he observed.

"No, she ran out of luck tonight," I replied. Stopping in front of him I asked, "Hey, do you have an ID on the one who died at the scene?"

"Yeah," he said, flipping through some sheets, "Pallone. Anthony Pallone."

19

Trauma:
Life in the Big City

DURING MY YEARS IN PURE RESEARCH I recognized a certain paradox: for the most part, research in surgical disease produces non-surgical solutions to problems. For example, up until the 1980s gastrointestinal ulcer disease was a common indication for abdominal surgery: ulcers caused bleeding, intestinal perforation and obstruction, all problems which frequently, if not invariably, required surgical intervention. Research into the cause of ulcer disease, much of it performed in labs run by prominent academic surgeons, led to the discovery of potent anti-acid medications like Zantac. Partly as a result of the widespread use of these medications, operations for ulcer disease are now rare.

Surgical research, then, often eliminates the need for surgery. But there remains one area of medicine which, regardless of any technological advances or laboratory research we can immediately comprehend, will remain a surgical domain.

Trauma.

Trauma will always be a surgical concern because, of course, no amount of biochemical laboratory manipulation will help a patient with a bullet hole in his intestine, or a tear in his aorta. These simply need to be fixed. Only trained hands can solve these sorts of problems; no drug will do the trick.

Having said this, I would be remiss if I did not point out the enormous amount of time and effort which has gone—and still goes—into refining the treatment of trauma patients. Research is ongoing and fruitful; rarely, though, does it shift the actual management of significant injury away from surgical intervention. Advancement in imaging technology, such as CT scans and sophisticated ultrasound machines, have enabled us to avoid unnecessary operations which would have taken place in earlier decades, but no one, as yet, has developed a "trauma pill."

At Ohio State, surgical residents acquired their experience in the management of trauma in three separate settings: at the University Hospital, at a local private institution called Grant Hospital, and at Children's Hospital. All of these facilities were designated as "Level 1 Trauma Centers," a distinction which hinged on a number of convoluted criteria but whose practical significance boiled down to the fact that the most seriously injured patients could be treated with rapid, major surgical intervention. At all three hospitals the personnel and equipment were always at hand.

University Hospital had a dedicated trauma service, Surg 6, and an expert trauma director named Larry Murphy. Tall and beefy, with tufts of thick black hair crowning a ruddy, classically Irish face, Dr. Murphy vaguely resembled a young Tip O'Neill on a successful Grecian formula program. He also possessed a piercingly acerbic wit, which he could bring to bear to great amusement or chagrin, depending on whether one was the target or a bystander.

Surg 6, it will be recalled, was also the service which was charged with the responsibility of taking care of the state prisoners. As a result of this juxtaposition the patient population on this service tended to be young and sometimes violent. In fact it was literally true that some individuals came onto Surg 6 as trauma patients (gunshot victims, for example) and later returned as prisoners (a fair number of the shots having been fired by police officers).

The trauma service at Grant Hospital was large, much larger than at "the U." This was the case for two reasons: 1) Grant successfully marketed and, in fact, structured itself as a trauma-first hospital, and 2) Grant was located in one of the worst neighborhoods in town. This was where the residents learned the management of "penetrating trauma," the "Knife and Gun Club" as we used to say. By contrast, most trauma cases at the University Hospital were blunt injuries: auto accidents, falls and so forth. At Grant, several trauma surgeons rotated as chiefs of the service, but being in private practice their focus was not really fixed on resident education. Despite this fact, the volume of trauma was so great that surgery residents from a number of different hospitals in the region rotated through Grant.

Trauma surgery was not a separate entity at Children's Hospital; any patients admitted for traumatic injuries came to the regular Pediatric Surgery service. Since none of the Pediatric Surgeons I met there seemed to have any special regard for trauma surgery (quite the opposite, in fact) their hand was clearly forced. Because there was no other children's hospital closer than Cincinnati, our institution had to become a Level 1 Center by default (it may, in fact, have been by law—I don't know). At any rate we got the cases.

At University Hospital, the Surg 6 trauma service was manned by two attendings and anywhere from four to six residents. The General Surgery attendings from the other services shared nighttime trauma call with the Surg 6 staff, so that the trauma docs would not be on call every other night (in return, the Surg 6 staff took some General Surgery call). The base surgery resident staff consisted of a Chief, a Senior, a second-year and an intern. This contingent was usually bolstered (or hampered, as the case might be) by rotating residents from the Departments of Emergency Medicine and Family Practice, whose faculty believed that they would benefit from some exposure to trauma. Since most of these "rotators" had, shall we say, a less well-developed work ethic, I can certainly confide that there were times when I would have enjoyed exposing a few of these individuals to considerable trauma. In any case, these were the personnel on board.

I get irritated by "reality" programs on television which purport to demonstrate what trauma care is like. Dramatic shows like ER are bad enough, with pulse-pounding music and wildly cavorting camera angles, but the supposedly-documentary cable programs, filmed at actual trauma centers, are even worse. It seems as if they actually make an effort to confuse the viewer, as if the events transpiring are too complex or happening too quickly for comprehension. In reality, there is an enforced order to the management of trauma patients, and very little improvisational barking of orders or outright panic arises.

So what actually happened when a trauma came in?

Well, if the injuries were thought by the emergency room attendings and the emergency medical technicians (the paramedics) to be so severe as to require immediate surgery, a "Level 1 Trauma" was called. If the injuries were somewhat less severe, but still considered to be serious enough to warrant immediate evaluation by the interdisciplinary "Trauma Team" (composed of surgeons, ER docs, pharmacists, nurse coordinators, radiology techs, the Surg 6 rotators, etc.), a "Level 2 Trauma" would be announced. These announcements would go out both by the paging system and by way of the hospital-wide loudspeakers. If you were anywhere in the complex, you knew when a Level 1 or a Level 2 was coming in. The actual delineation between theses two categories of Trauma alerts was defined by a set of specific criteria, which eliminated the guesswork. The details are somewhat involved and not worth re-counting. Practically speaking, everyone's sphincter tightened when-ever a trauma was called, but it ratcheted up a few extra notches when it was a Level 1.

The trauma cases were wheeled into a special bay in the emergency department that was designed to handle the resuscitation and evaluation of seriously injured patients. The team would arrive from the four corners of the medical center. In the absence of an attending, the senior-most surgery resident was in charge; he "ran the trauma."

Years ago, the American College of Surgeons decided that the best way to handle the initial management of patients with severe injury was essentially the same as the American Heart Association's best way to handle patients in cardiac arrest—STOP THINKING!

Protocols—recipes for the care of trauma patients—were devel-oped. Just like in the ACLS, flow charts and algorithms were drawn up and published. They, too, had to be memorized by surgery residents, who were required to take an analogous course called "ATLS"—Advanced Trauma Life Support.

There were some significant differences between the ACLS and the ATLS systems, though. Although the heart can fail in a variety of ways, ultimately the different manifestations of severe cardiac disturbance or arrest break down to just a few different categories. A handful of flow charts can be memorized which will cover the large majority of these circumstances. By contrast, the sheer number of possible scenarios of serious traumatic injury is so great that any set of algorithms would have to be impractically large to be complete. For this reason, a fair amount of generalization showed up in the ATLS algorithms. This allowed a measure of improvisation to creep in.

I should point out that the thrust of ATLS was the initial treatment of the trauma patient—essentially their rapid resuscitation and stabilization, along with the identification of life-threatening injuries. The actual operative treatment of specific injuries was too detailed and broad an issue to be covered in such a program.

Early in the fourth year, I had some trepidation about being the most senior surgery resident in the hospital when I was on call. I hadn't been on the trauma surgery service since my second year, and at that time I'd been so busy with the prisoners and doing the grunt work that the whole intellectual experience of trauma management had basically eluded me. Now I was expected to lead the trauma team through the whole ATLS process and make the decision about whether to operate or not. By policy, all Level 1 traumas had to be seen by the attending on call—I was off the hook when this happened; any decisions of importance were made by them. When the trauma was a Level 2, though, the staff surgeons were not required to come in (all the trauma surgeons took call from home). As a result, in these cases it was up to me to determine the proper course of action.

During the first dozen or so nights on senior trauma call I consulted my ATLS handbook rather liberally. In truth I never got a wink of sleep, because I was petrified of encountering a situation which I had no answer for. This method of learning—fear as motivator—is probably not very healthy, but it is certainly highly effective. In any case, it pervades surgery residency. After a few weeks I got comfortable enough to be able to sleep in between trauma alerts.

Oddly enough, when the alerts came, they usually were sounded over the hospital loudspeakers first. These were located in the hallways, not the patient rooms (they might go off all night, and the patients couldn't be subjected to that). Since all our call rooms were converted patient rooms (complete with 1960s-era TVs), it was sometimes hard to hear the announcements. The sounds of the hospital operators calmly alerting the trauma team with their monotone cadence would barely drift through the closed call room doors: "Trauma Alert, Category 2. Ten minutes. Trauma Alert, Category 2. Ten minutes."

A fair number of residents would sleep right through that repetitive drone, so the system was backed up by our omnipresent paging network. Approximately thirty seconds after the overhead announcement, a sequence of numbers would be beamed out from wherever the central paging point was to all members of the trauma team. This would either be a string of "7"s or of "2"s. The string of "2"s defined the severity of the situation as a Level 2 trauma. The series of sevens meant a Level 1, although why they didn't use "1"s is anybody's guess.

The sundry team members would then extricate themselves from whatever task they were laboring at (in my case, hopefully slumber) and board the ancient back elevators which were the only even-remotely-direct way to the Trauma Bay. After the rickety ride, we emerged from the dimly-lit lift into the bright, busy ER. The overhead operators were only vaguely accurate when it came to their call of the patients' ETAs, so it was generally a good idea to head to the ER as soon as the alert was given—the patient might even be there already. Usually the paramedics hadn't arrived yet, and over the next several minutes the group assembled. While waiting for the arrival of the trauma victim, we donned lead aprons (to protect ourselves from the multiple x-rays that would be taken) and protective gowns and gloves. Typically some small talk would ensue, along with a little nervous laughter.

Since the district of the university was relatively safe, the majority of our serious traumas arrived via "scoop-and-run" helicopters (by the way, these emergency evacuation chopper companies always have names that are dynamic-sounding amalgamations of aviation and medical terms: "SkyMed," "LifeFlight," etc.). The hospital helipad, marked by the brilliant, neon blue "H" that I had been told stood for "Hell," was located on the top of an adjacent building. Incredibly, after disembarking from the helicopter, the paramedics had to take an elevator to the basement of that building, then negotiate several hundred yards' worth of dank underground tunnels to make it to the ER. This trek might take ten minutes.

When the patient and his entourage finally did arrive, the gurney was brought alongside the hospital cart. One of the transport team was assigned the task of barking out the specifics of the case, and he would typically proceed to do this in his best TV-*ER* docudrama voice. This kind of media-driven crap always annoys me, and I was thankful for the unusual circumstances when someone sensible had the responsibility. All the information we needed to know was the patient's name and age, the specifics of the injury so far as they were known, and what the vital signs were. It takes about ten seconds to clearly state these facts, but most of the paramedics were so taken by the moment that they behaved as if they were stalking the stage at the Globe Theatre. They'd seen it done a certain way on television and thought that that must be the right way. In fact, it looks and sounds moronic on the small screen, and is even more so in person.

After the *status quo* soliloquy, the patient was moved, immobilized on a rigid backboard and with a cervical collar in place, over to the emergency department cart (the paramedics would need their gurney back, after all; there were more victims out in the night). Then we would begin to follow the ATLS protocols.

As if the need to separate the putative trauma surgeon from the whole thought process weren't in itself sufficiently insulting, the authors of the algorithms took it upon themselves to arrange the wording of the critical initial steps in trauma management in such a way as to sequentially represent the first five letters of the alphabet: A is for Airway, B is for Breathing, C is for Circulation, D is for Disability and E is for Exposure. This, of course, exonerates the physician from any responsibility for remembering anything he has learned since the age of three.

Of course, one did have to remember what the different actions were which were assigned to the alphabetical words.

A is for Airway: the first thing to do was establish or confirm the presence of a reliable conduit for the exchange of oxygen and carbon dioxide. If the victim were awake and alert, we could usually feel confident that he could protect his own airway. Unconscious or obtunded patients were much less trustworthy; usually it was safer to place an endotracheal breathing tube and put them on a ventilator. If they weren't awake enough to protect their airway, they might vomit and then aspirate, dying from asphyxiation in the way that Jimi Hendrix did when drugs rendered him incapable of even a gag reflex. The breathing tube minimized this risk. As I described earlier, in a patient with severe facial injuries—like Celeste Findlay—the nose and mouth might not be suitable as an airway, and a tracheotomy or cricothyroidotomy would then be required.

B is for Breathing: closely linked with identifying the presence of an adequate airway was an assessment of the trauma victim's breathing. Without an airway, of course, breathing efforts were fruitless, which was the reasoning behind the sequence of those considerations. Once an airway had been established, though, we had to make sure that there was effective gas exchange. In a sense, the patients were either breathing on their own or they weren't; if not, they needed to be put on a mechanical ventilator and the breathing done for them (in this case, the prognosis was usually bad). Some other thoughts came to mind while stuck on the letter "B," though. Breathing might be fatally impaired by a handful of intrathoracic injuries: tension pneumothorax (where air under pressure in the space between the lung and the chest wall causes collapse of that lung and impaired flow of venous blood to the heart), open pneumothorax (where a hole in the chest wall allows atmospheric pressure to crush the lung down into a functionless ball), massive hemothorax (where blood in the chest similarly collapses the lung, with the added insult of liters of the vital fluid drained from the circulation) and flail chest (where an entire segment of the ribcage had become disengaged from the chest wall). Only when an adequate airway had been established and the function of breathing confirmed—with the other injuries I've mentioned either excluded or treated—did we move on to the next letter in the alphabet.

C is for Circulation. This meant different things to different docs. In the ATLS, this is supposed to remind the surgeon to stop any bleeding; blood is what's circulating, get it? While it seems obvious that one should stop any external bleeding that's identified, the beauty of the protocols begins to shine at this point. The natural instinct is to put a hand on the bleeding to make it stop before doing anything else—but if the patient has lost his airway or has no spontaneous respiratory effort, he may well die or suffer permanent brain damage while you ignore these more important problems and concentrate on a minor superficial venous bleeder. ATLS is meant to save patient's lives, and the seemingly idiotic alphabet mnemonic is one fool-proof tool: if you follow ATLS, you ignore your instincts, hopefully to the benefit of the trauma victim.

"C" also reminded me to make sure that the patient had adequate intravenous access. In trauma, the surgeons like to use at least two large-bore IV lines, placed in the extremities. It is said that with the proper equipment, these types of IVs can administer fluids and medications even faster than big central venous catheters. I usually ignored this piece of information and placed central lines in patients with serious injuries: they're stitched in securely, and just seemed safer than precarious peripheral lines.

D is for Disability: this one was a mnemonic reach. The proper letter would be "N" for "Neurological." The idea was to remind the physician to perform neuro examinations on the trauma patients—both when they arrived and later during their evaluation—to assess their baseline and pinpoint any changes as early as possible. This was important because any change in a patient's level of consciousness was usually highly significant. Such a change could indicate an intracerebral hemorrhage or be a sign of significant injury elsewhere. Typically, there was a chart for grading out the level of awareness that a trauma patient displayed (nowhere in modern surgery is individual judgment held in less esteem). This derived from a standardization of consciousness in illness which had been developed in Scotland. It was known as the Glascow Coma Scale.

On the Glascow Scale, patients were assigned points in three categories (rather like contestants in the Miss America pageant, although "congeniality" was not awarded): movement of eyes (four possible points), verbal activity (five possible points) and motor function (six possible points). The maximum score, corresponding to a fully conversational, mobile human whose eyes engaged those of a questioner, was fifteen points. The lowest possible score, which could be obtained by a piece of furniture, was three points. A good trauma team leader would assess the Glascow score of the injured victim after the Big Three on the ATLS protocol (the ABCs) had been taken care of, then every ten minutes or so throughout the ER course of the case.

E is for Exposure. More straightforward than it might seem, this element of the code referred to the need to remove every stitch of every garment the trauma patient was wearing, then to examine him with the utmost care. We had all been taught about horrible, treatable fatal injuries that had been missed because examining physicians had succumbed to societal pressures of vanity and failed to examine a patient thoroughly. The trauma bay was no place for modesty, or for the consideration of such absurdities for the sake of a patient. Could there be anything worse than having a trauma victim bleed to death from a stab wound in the back, when no one had rolled him over to check out every possibility? Or having a patient die of a perforated colon because no one had done an adequate rectal exam? Having so much concern for a patient's dignity—or for our own discomfiture—that we failed to examine him thoroughly would be doing that patient a disservice and betraying our own code of ethics. So as to remove all traces of doubt, we had a credo on the Trauma Service: *A tube or a finger in every orifice.* In this way, there could be no question in the resident's mind about what to do.

All tolled, the "ABCDE"s of the ATLS constituted what was known as the "primary survey" of the trauma patient: the steps which constituted the initial resuscitation of the victim as well as the assessment which would largely guide the subsequent care. Intertwined amongst the steps I have described were the directed efforts of the members of the ancillary services who comprised the balance of the trauma team.

The radiology technicians dove in from time to time to take films of the chest, the pelvis and the cervical spine (the bones of the neck). These particular x-rays were obtained on virtually every trauma patient. Over the years, research into violent injury had shown that these films were useful in defining the more common and serious lesions that arose in the trauma victim, often when they were not suspected: fractures of the pelvis, injuries to the chest and lungs (such as those I've described above), and, especially, broken necks.

Very little motivated those taking care of the trauma patients with greater force than the fear of breaking a neck or, more spectacularly, inducing paralysis in one whose neck was already broken but who hadn't suffered any nerve injury. This was the incentive behind the fact that all trauma patients arrived in the ER in a cervical immobilization collar. Everyone was petrified of the possibility of moving a patient with an unstable neck fracture and severing his spinal cord. There was even a term for this: it was called "pithing" the patient. In truth very, very few individuals were injured in the neck in such a horrific way as to cause paralysis (a lá Christopher Reeve), at least without also suffering other grievous—and probably fatal—injuries. Still fewer sustained fractures of the neck which did not cause immediate neurologic injury but were unstable enough to predicate disaster with incautious motion. Nevertheless, this tiny fraction of patients was the motivation for the immobilization of countless necks. Still, in retrospect it was probably worth the inconvenience (which, in truth, was primarily to the patients). The minor discomfort of a neck brace was temporary—a "pithing" would be permanent.

After this "primary survey" was completed, if the patient were stable (that is, if they had normal or near-normal vital signs) another, more leisurely and more comprehensive examination would proceed. Reasonably enough, this was known as the "secondary survey." The object of this exercise was the discovery of any non-life-threatening injury which had been missed or glossed over in the initial exam. A key component of this was the ongoing neurological assessment: some brain injuries only manifest themselves after a period of lucidity and, in any case, unsuspected, ongoing internal bleeding might show up as loss of consciousness at any point. It was best to keep on your toes – trauma patients could go sour at the drop of a hat.

Anyone who had experienced any deviation from complete consciousness throughout the period of injury (or subsequently) got a head CT. This was pretty quick, and could rule out significant intracerebral bleeding—which was particularly useful if the patient were headed to the OR for another injury and would be under general anesthesia for a lengthy period. The possibility of fixing a broken leg while the patient slowly bled into their head to the point of brain death (unsuspected during the general anesthetic) was fearful, to say the least.

There were three ways to evaluate for intra-abdominal injury: ultrasound, CT scan and peritoneal lavage. The ultrasound device (which was right in the trauma bay and could be used very rapidly, even in unstable patients) was used to detect fluid in the belly. This was abnormal and suggested either hemorrhage or perforation of a hollow organ—either of which demanded surgical exploration. The CT scanner was excellent at giving detailed anatomy of injury to solid organs such as the spleen or liver, and also defined vascular structures well. It was a good choice in stable patients, although bowel injuries could be missed. Peritoneal lavage, which was the technique the jerk attending at Grant had tried on

Celeste Findlay as she was dying, entailed making a small hole in the belly and instilling a saline solution. After a few minutes this was recovered and the fluid examined; if there were considerable blood or fecal matter, the patient would need surgery. A refugee from the early 1960s, lavage was quick but imprecise—ultrasound was beginning to replace it in most trauma centers by the end of my residency.

In a disheartening number of cases (of blunt trauma, anyway) no operative intervention was required. Either our examinations demonstrated no injuries requiring surgery, or the injuries were so severe that the patients just died outright.

One night while I was trauma chief the redundant alert system blasted out the signal that two Level 1 traumas were imminent. In fact, the overhead operator announced: "Two Level 1 Traumas, STAT!" ("stat," the ubiquitous term from medical TV shows, is an abbreviation of the Latin word *statim*, which means "immediately").

I met Cathy Townes, the fourth-year resident on my Surg 6 team, at the elevator and we headed to the ER. By the time we got there, the two victims had already been moved to ER carts. There was blood everywhere.

It turned out that the two patients had been in, of all things, a knife fight. Although they had been fighting each other, both had lost.

It wasn't immediately obvious which one was more seriously injured, since they both were covered with blood and had deep, long lacerations almost anywhere one cared to look. One was screaming, but the other was silent and, apparently, unconscious. Cathy and I divided forces and began our ATLS protocols on each. I gave Cathy the one who was screaming, since I figured that the unconscious one was probably in a more life-threatening situation (this was just a guess, though).

I happened to be right. In fact, within a few seconds my patient lost his vital signs. After intubating him and putting him on a ventilator, I noticed several deep stab wounds in his chest and neck. I placed chest tubes in both sides (for those keeping score, we're at "B" on the protocol) and was rewarded by liters of blood from the left. With multiple large IVs in place, we pumped blood in. Unfortunately, it seemed to be coming right back out through the left chest tube. The victim clearly had a massive injury within his chest, probably to the heart itself. The only hope (a slight one, at that) was to perform a thoracotomy.

Dousing the left chest with Betadine, I made a long incision along the sixth rib. Plunging my hand between the fifth and sixth ribs, I placed a metal vise-like "rib-spreader" between them and cranked them apart.

The contents of the chest were now revealed to me. The lung had several tears in it, but these weren't the problem. The heart was actually uninjured, although it was empty since the man had virtually no blood left in his circulation, regardless of our efforts. In a few seconds, I found the problem. One of the neck lacerations had gone so deep that it had completely transected the left subclavian artery, the blood vessel that supplies the left arm. I got clamps across the two severed ends, which stopped the bleeding, but it was too late. The patient was dead.

Over in her room, Cathy was having better luck. It turned out that her patient had only one wound that wasn't superficial. This was a lucky stab that had gone between two ribs and left the lung exposed, although uninjured. We stapled the skin closed and, after ruling out other serious injury with our protocols, shipped the patient up to the OR for repair of his chest wall.

I was startled the next morning to see our survivor in an ordinary bed, without a police guard outside. We all knew that it had been his opponent in the knife fight who had died, weren't there any charges? As it turned out, the survivor had been mugged by the other guy outside a liquor store. Although he wasn't exactly a model citizen, he had just been defending himself in this instance, and no charges were filed. There were plenty of witnesses to exonerate him. Lucky for him, he'd been carrying a knife, too, and happened to be a little better at using it than his assailant.

Although the trauma surgery experience was an exhilarating one, it didn't really capture my imagination in the way say, vascular surgery had. I think this just stemmed from my innate dislike for major surprises, especially surgical ones. All specialties of surgery have their emergencies, of course (and not least of these, vascular), but in trauma surgery, *every* new case is a surprise. Some people like that life, constant unpredictability, but I'm not one of them.

20

Chief Resident

IN DR. NOLEN'S SPLENDID BOOK about surgery residency in the 1950s there is a climactic chapter entitled "Chief Resident at Last!" Such an exuberant title probably made more sense in that era. At that time most residencies were "pyramidal," meaning that a large number of interns were whittled down over the years to a small number of chief residents. A large, prestigious general surgery program might hire eight or ten interns, with the full realization that only one or two might make it through to become a chief. Some would be lost to attrition, finding that the surgical life-style really didn't fit their personality, but others would just be ruthlessly dismissed at some point. This obviously fostered deep resentments, unhealthy competition, lack of teamwork and other evils. Over time virtually every training program, even the hopelessly elitist, dumped the pyramid system. They didn't do this from a flash of selfless altruism, but simply because some of the best medical school graduates would avoid programs where they might get canned even if they were doing a fine job, just because the boss liked another guy better.

But in the context of this old system the achievement of chief residency was of real significance: it meant you were going to succeed, you were going to make it through residency and out into the world as a real, practicing surgeon (which in those days meant big-time money, too). Hence Nolen's exhilaration at being so selected.

There is another difference between surgical Chief Residency in the past and today, too. As I mentioned earlier, according to the original "Halstedian" scheme of residency the Chief Resident was meant to be essentially autonomous, with the skills (and responsibility) of an Attending. Although technically supervised by a fully-privileged staff member, he was allowed to function independently and make important decisions—as well as operate—without interference from above.

While this was still the case in Nolen's time, it certainly is not today. At no time during my Chief Resident year did I feel autonomous, and at no time did I feel that the watchful eye of Big Surgical Brother was not upon me. At the turn of the century there is no such thing as a Surgical Chief Resident as either Halsted or, for that matter, Bill Nolen would have understood the term.

Am I alone in thinking this? Not according to my fellow chiefs, both at Ohio State and, as I met them, from programs across the nation. Our experiences, and particularly the dilution of our experiences as students of medicine and surgery, appear to be universal.

What happened? Lawyers, mostly. And government. Put the two together and you have a formidable obstacle to clear thinking.

The lawyers are important because their suits have generated an environment in which self-protection outweighs the physician's mission to teach. An attending surgeon takes a chance any time he allows a resident to make any independent decision regarding patient care at all, from the amount of IV fluid to give to the proper dose of Advil. The potential liabilities of a surgeon (or his hospital) in permitting a resident to perform an operation without close supervision are monumental. This is different from the past, and not due to any egregious errors or botched resident surgeries. It is specifically due to the well-documented excessively litigious nature of our modern American society, and part of the stale by-product of this is a stout contribution to the absurdly high cost of health care in our country.

What about the government's well-intentioned role in interfering with resident education? The details are too boring and convoluted to relate in any comprehensive way, but essentially the federal government, through Medicare, has enforced a policy that any care from a health practitioner who is different from the biller should not be reimbursed. Further, if a practitioner bills for services which he did not perform, he is guilty of fraud. This all sounds good and seems to make perfect sense. But a doc can't be a provider until he's finished his training, so it means that no resident can perform an operation independently (at least without someone eating the cost, which ain't likely). "So what?" you say, "Who wants some snot-nosed resident doing their surgery anyway?" Well, on an individual basis probably no one with a functioning cerebral cortex; but on a nationwide basis, it's vitally important . . . if we want to have competent surgeons, that is. Surgeons learn by operating, and I can tell you that I learned more from the few minutes I spent alone in the OR as a resident than I did for hours assisting an attending. The snot-noses may be attendings doing your coronary bypass some day soon, and sleep will come more easily to you the night before that surgery if you are confident that they know how to operate without the boss looking over their shoulder.

As for me, the boss may not have been directly over my shoulder at all times, but he was close. And that's a decent compromise, I think. What I personally lost in experience as a Chief Resident I—and, I'm sure, the patients—made up for in peace of mind.

I started my Chief Year on the Surgery I service. Of course, this was the service with the largest census and the one which performed the most complex of the abdominal procedures. When I was an intern, Surg I had nearly gotten the best of me, with great floods of scut, mountains of paperwork and regularly 18-hour days (plus every third night call). In my third year the enormous time constraints of the service helped put the final nails in the coffin of my marriage. So it was with some trepidation that I took the reins of the Surg I juggernaut in late June, 1998. Dr. Atcheson himself used to say: "When you finish Surg 1 as a chief, you're done with residency."

The majority of the cases were straightforward: lap choles, hernias, etc. But a good 30% were real marquee-level general surgery cases: esophagectomies, liver resections, gastrectomies and examples of the mother of all abdominal surgeries: the Whipple.

The Whipple operation was initially devised by a surgeon of that name in New York in the 1930s. The goal of the Whipple is the complete resection of the head of the pancreas, almost always for cancer. Because the head of the pancreas is in a region where the blood supply of the abdominal viscera branches, several other local structures must also be removed or they will be deprived of blood and die. Specifically, these include the duodenum (the first part of the intestine beyond the stomach), the gall bladder and the bile ducts. After all these are removed, the stomach and bile ducts must be reattached to the intestine. Most surgeons would consider this operation to be the tour de force of abdominal general surgery. It is technically demanding, time-consuming and wrought with potential pitfalls. Since pancreatic cancer is resistant to every other known form of therapy, the Whipple is about the only hope for cure, which is why it is still performed, despite its shortcomings.

Amongst graduating chief residents around the country, a point of pride (or chagrin) is one's answer to the question, "How many Whipples have you done?" Honesty in the reply is, I assert, not the norm—rather like asking a drunk driver how many shots he's had, although the correction factor works in the opposite direction: if the answer is 15, it's probably more like 10, etc.

Surg I was where the Whipples were.

Drs. Chris Atcheson and Scott Marvin were the two attendings on Surg 1 when I was a chief. A third staff member, Bill Shuter, had been jettisoned to Surg 2—and there had never been a more substantive demonstration of the validity of the numerical designations of the services—prior to the new academic year. Shuter's shuffling was in preparation for his ultimate ejection from the faculty altogether, which happened shortly after my graduation. Practically speaking, Shuter's absence helped me out immensely. Not only was he an individual who had taken an irrational, abiding dislike to me (but the cowardly kind that only shows up in written evaluations, months later—he was another who played a large role in my third-year lynching), but the workload was lessened considerably by the slim vacuum his vacancy created. I would still be operating or seeing patients in the clinic all day, every day, but at least I would have a few hours a week to read and learn more about the procedures and diseases. This proved invaluable, and the three months I spent as Surg 1 Chief turned out to be the most intensive learning experience of my life, to that point.

Dr. Atcheson had a legacy to live up to. His father had trained under Dr. Zollinger and then gone on to become a famous chair of surgery at another university hospital. The younger Dr. Atcheson had himself risen upon his own merit to become Chief of General Surgery at Ohio State, and was clearly on a path to match the achievements of his father. He was in his late forties, with thinning red hair, a moderate paunch, wire-rim glasses and an engaging smile. He pronounced the sound of the letter "S" with a hint of a whistle, like you might expect from an old wag by the pickle barrel at the General Store. Usually upbeat and genuinely concerned about the welfare of his residents, Dr. Atcheson had built up an enormous practice through the great repute his name afforded as well as his considerable operative skill. In particular his gentle, caring demeanor toward his patients was both a great comfort to them and a tremendous example to his residents. His clinical practice and administrative duties combined to be a tremendous burden on his time, and I always thought of him as having too many irons in the fire (at times I suspect he thought precisely the same about me). Dr. Atcheson had a long fuse, but when he reached the end of it, watch out. As a surgeon he was very skillful but perhaps not technically brilliant; his chief asset was that he was scrupulously careful. Because of all of this there was much to be learned by the surgeon-in-training from Dr. Atcheson. He attracted tough cases from all over the Midwest and, as a result, each week we faced several challenging problems.

Scott Marvin was quite young, having been hired out of training by Atcheson who had supervised him in a gastrointestinal surgery fellowship at another hospital. Youthful exuberance may be a trite phrase and a bit of a cliché as well, but it accurately describes Marvin. He spoke at an astonishingly rapid pace (apparently thinking at that pace, too) and some part of him was in constant motion. At conferences it was a consistent source of amusement to watch him struggle to remain immobile after the fashion of polite society. Usually one leg would begin to agitate mildly, then increase its frequency of oscillation and finally bounce up and down frenetically. I half-expected him to involuntarily jerk into the Nazi salute, like Dr. Strangelove. But Marvin was no Nazi, subconsciously or not. He was just a very intense individual. Marvin stood about six feet, was slender and had aggressively thinning blonde hair. Sky blue eyes stared out of a pink face unblinkingly. The moderating adjective "fairly" seemed to find its way into nearly every sentence he uttered, as in "That seems fairly inappropriate" or "That was fairly stupid" (two actual examples, by the way).

On Monday mornings we had a case conference, where the attendings and residents would discuss the surgeries that were planned for the week. This was a good opportunity for Atcheson and Marvin to pimp me, and they did so with relish. I didn't mind, because I usually got the answers right by this point, plus it helped me consolidate my knowledge. Mainly I took notice of the big cases that were upcoming, especially the Whipples.

When I knew that a Whipple was planned, I would go down to the x-ray file room and dig up the patient's films. These were typically CT scans, but Atcheson also liked to get arteriograms from time to time, because these helped define the relationship of the pancreatic tumor to the blood vessels. Whatever the file consisted of, I would abscond with it and study the images for a few days, so as to be completely prepared for what we would find in the operating room.

When the day of surgery arrived, I liked to go and meet the patient in the preoperative holding room, where the anesthetists would put in IVs and so forth. Often I would run into Dr. Atcheson there, and it certainly didn't hurt to be seen by him being so involved in the care of the patient. Beyond this cynical reason, though, I found that the patients really did appreciate the personal attention. Even though I wasn't the attending, they put some faith and trust in me. Soon enough, I *would* be the final authority, and seeing the patients on the morning of surgery was a good habit to get into. It goes back to the issue of communication.

After the prepping and draping, we began the operation by placing a laparoscope into the belly to see if there was any obvious reason that the tumor couldn't be removed. If such were the case, it wasn't doing the patient any favor to subject them to a long, stem-to-stern midline incision. If we did that, they would spend two months out of their few left just healing up the big wound. If metastatic disease were identified, we just removed the scope and woke the patient up. Then they could leave the hospital the next day and spend the little time they had left with their families, not recovering from a big, useless belly incision.

Usually we didn't find anything to keep us from proceeding with the Whipple. Dr. Atcheson typically let me do the laparoscopy on my own, then he would telephone into the room to see if I had found any reason for the operation to be aborted. If I said no, he would come to the OR in a leisurely fashion, ordinarily showing up as I was placing the retractors which exposed the operative field.

Then we would proceed with the Whipple. After once more reassuring ourselves that their was no metastatic disease, or invasion of the tumor into major blood vessels, we would excise the head of the pancreas. This was a major undertaking, of course, and usually occupied a couple of hours. After the pancreatic head had been removed (along with the duodenum and the gall bladder), we would endeavor to reconstruct the anatomy by reconnecting the intestinal tract, as well as the bile and pancreatic ducts. If things went smoothly, this operation would take six to eight hours. If the patient had had previous surgery (which was common), the abdomen was invariably scarred in, and things would take much longer.

The post-op course of Whipple patients was often dicey. As a matter of course we usually placed stomach tubes to drain the secretions and any swallowed air. These served the same function as nasogastric tubes, but could stay in place much longer. The idea was to prevent any distention of the stomach from rupturing our fragile suture lines. Postoperative bile leaks were a frequent problem for which we had no such simple answer. The bile ducts were not particularly suited to being stitched into the intestinal wall, and this suture line broke down with depressing regularity. We kept drains in the abdomen near this site so as to at least be able to control the drainage if it should happen, but one theory held that these drains promoted leaks (by rubbing against the ducts) as much as they controlled them. The same thing could happen with leaks from the pancreatic duct suture line.

An almost universal complication of the Whipple was chronic nausea. The stomachs of these patients (what was left of them, that is) were flaccid and barely functional. If they survived any time at all after the surgery (and there was reasonably good evidence that this massive operation provided precious little extension of survival for patients with the dread diagnosis of pancreatic cancer), they usually lost a great deal of weight, like Rosanne Stoker.

On the whole, the Whipple is an appealing operation only from the standpoint of the surgeon who performs it. Although it takes tremendous patience and skill to do it right, the Whipple cures few and causes enormous grief to many. Hopefully, new, non-surgical therapies for pancreatic cancer will emerge in the not-too-distant future. In the meantime, though, it is an operation which provides plenty of ego reinforcement to general surgeons and residents nationwide.

After our up-and-down relationship of four years, I wondered how Dr. Atcheson would relate to my being his chief resident, performing all these Whipples (and other cases) with him. To my enormous relief he seemed to take my advancement in stride, although I'm sure there must have been an element of disbelief in the fact that so much time had passed so quickly. Hadn't I just arrived from San Francisco, fresh from the lab and waving a gaudy letter from Dr. Zollinger? Perhaps I'm just reflecting on my own feelings about the fact that I'd actually made it to Chief Residency alive, and in one (moderately damaged) piece. In any case, it never seemed as if Dr. Atcheson treated me any differently from the other chiefs, either those from my own class or from years past. This was a tremendous, but appropriately understated, boost to my confidence.

Although they provided a considerable amount of grist for our surgical mill, Whipples were not the only procedures we did on Surg 1. In addition to the relatively minor abdominal cases that I've already mentioned, we occasionally performed other interesting, major gas-trointestinal operations.

Pat Morris had had stomach and intestinal ulcers for years. She had been stricken with them during her youth in the 1970s, before the advent of all the new drugs. Pat was one of the few people who did not respond perfectly to the medications; later she was given antibiotics and the ulcers went away permanently—it had been discovered over the years that many such ulcers are caused by bacterial infection, not excess acid. In any case, Pat's ulcers were gone, but her troubles weren't. Ulcers near the pylorus—the point where the stomach joins the duodenum—are notorious for causing obstruction of the flow of food out of the stomach. Scarring from repeated ulcer formation and healing over the years had finally caught up with Pam, and she began having intractable vomiting. Virtually nothing she ate stayed down, except thin liquids like broth. At first we were all afraid that she had developed cancer of the stomach, certainly a possibility after the chronic ulcers. She underwent fiberoptic endoscopy, though, and the biopsies were negative for tumor. The problem was gastric outlet obstruction from benign ulcer disease. The only treatment was surgery: she needed to have that portion of her stomach removed.

Pat was a patient of Scott Marvin's. On the day we took her to surgery he happened to be on call for trauma. Sure enough, we had barely made the skin incision when a Level 1 was called. By policy Marvin had to leave to see what was up in the ER. On his way out, he told me to go ahead and get the exposure—that is, to finish opening up the belly and place the retractors and so forth in such a way as to provide access to the operative site—the pylorus.

I had a junior resident to help me and we carried on for the next several minutes. We divided the layers of the abdominal wall with the cautery, exposing the peritoneum, that sheet-like lining of the abdominal cavity. Grabbing this with a forceps, I carefully opened it with a scalpel. All the time I was imagining the sound of Marvin's hysterical cries if I should accidentally put a hole in the bowel while doing this. Such considerations helped me stay focused. With the peritoneum divided, we were now inside the abdomen proper.

I explored the belly, looking for any other abnormalities, as I had been taught. Sometimes you might run across a cancer or some other condition that hadn't been expected; in any case, even if no other disease were found, that in itself was valuable information. Finding nothing out of the ordinary, we set about exposing the stomach and duodenum. About this time Marvin reappeared, and my spirits sank. Damn, I thought, nearly there.

"Craig, the trauma's a gunshot to the belly," Marvin said.

"How bad is he?" I answered, barely concealing my glee—virtually all abdominal gunshot wounds require surgical exploration, and this would keep Marvin out of my hair.

"He's stable, but we're going to crack him. Do you want me to see if Atcheson's around to help you?"

"No, sir," I replied. "I think we've got it under control. We're going to resect the pylorus and do a 'B1' (this meant a Billroth Type 1 anastomosis, where the remaining end of the stomach is stitched to the duodenum)."

"You gonna do anything else?" Marvin asked, pointedly. I glanced at his sky blue eyes, peering over the surgical mask.

"We might get around to doing a vagotomy."

"Good. I'll be back as soon as I can. If you run into any trouble, we'll be in room 15."

"See you in recovery," I answered happily.

In reality, Marvin was faster than I thought. The gunshot victim turned out to be lucky; nothing of importance was injured. Marvin returned to our room just as I was finishing up the suture line connecting the stomach and intestine, and a happy little row of silk sutures stared up at him.

"Looks good," he said. "Do the vagotomy and get her out of here."

It did my surgical ego worlds of good to perform a major gastric operation in the absence of any significant supervision. I watched Pat like a hawk during her post-op period, but she did wonderfully and went home in less than a week.

On the same day that Pat Morris left the hospital a middle-aged man named Vince Jaffe was admitted. Like Pat, Vince had known ulcer disease. Unlike her, his was caused by the pain medications he had to take to control his terrible arthritis—these drugs eroded through his stomach lining no matter what antacid medication he took. Usually, the bleeding stopped on its own.

Vince had been admitted to the medicine service, and they decided to transfuse him, in an effort to wait it out. They were hoping that he would stop spontaneously, as before. This time, though, something was different. The bleeding didn't stop. They gave him two, then four, then eight units of blood, just to keep up with the loss. Vince had an NG tube in, and we could watch the blood pouring into the collection canister like someone had left a scarlet faucet on. They had tried to scope him, but hadn't been able to see anything because of all the blood.

After I saw Vince in consultation (once the internists had begun to panic), I tracked down Marvin, who was on call again.

"Dr. Marvin," I said, "we've got a bleeding duodenal ulcer. He takes NSAIDS (non-steroidal anti-inflammatory drugs) for arthritis and I'm sure that's the cause. The medicine team has transfused him eight units in the last six hours, but his hemoglobin keeps dropping. His coags are normal, but he's not gonna stop. I think we should pop the hood on him."

"Is he stable?"

"Yeah, but he might not be for long. I'll give him a couple of liters of fluid on the way to the OR."

"Sounds good. I'll see you down there."

It took about half an hour to get Vince into the operating room. In another ten minutes he was asleep and I went to scrub with the intern. Marvin had not appeared. After we scrubbed and got the patient prepped and draped, I asked the nurse to page Marvin. I didn't feel like we could wait much longer to get started—the blood was still bubbling up in the NG canister—and I didn't like to make an incision if the attending wasn't at least close by and aware. Who knew if Marvin was even in the building?

He was in the building, all right. He was three floors up, in his office, casually reading. He returned the page, and the message to me was a curt (but welcome): "get started."

The incision and exposure were exactly the same as for Pat Morris's operation. In a few seconds, I had the stomach exposed and the surrounding structures retracted so that we could perform the operation. Still no Marvin. I opened the stomach and duodenum longitudinally, and was immediately rewarded with the unmistakable view of a posterior penetrating duodenal ulcer. At the base of the lesion, a tiny artery—the gastroduodenal—merrily spurted blood into the air. There was no chance that it would have stopped on its own. With a quick "figure-of-eight" silk stitch, I eliminated the offending critter. I then performed a quick vagotomy (division of the nerves that stimulate acid secretion) and closed the incision in the gut. Marvin, as if clairvoyant, arrived at precisely that moment.

"What'd you find?"

"Gastroduodenal pumper. Oversewed it with a figure-of-eight. I closed the duodenum as a Heineke-Mickulicz pyloroplasty, and did a truncal vagotomy. We're ready to close. Think I'll keep him in the unit overnight."

Marvin put his hand on my shoulder.

"Not bad, Miller. When you dictate this, make sure you say what a great job I did."

Although Marvin demonstrated some trust in me during Pam Morris's case, when he had been forced to leave the OR, it was a very different story with Vince. That time he had been available, and had simply chosen not to scrub, so that I could do the whole operation on my own. Granted, the surgery was not the most complex in the world, but it was a great feeling to know that an attending felt I could perform a major abdominal emergency procedure without supervision. It was a big step in the making of this surgeon. It all comes down to confidence. At this stage of the game, I had it. Marvin had noticed it, too, and done exactly the right thing: he'd remembered his role as an educator and did the most nurturing thing he could: he'd left me alone.

21

Farewells

As THE LAST WEEKS OF RESIDENCY DREW CLOSE, I began to focus on a certain tradition that had been established amongst the residents over the years. In this ritual, at their last M&M conference, the graduating chief residents verbally roasted the attendings and, to a lesser extent, the incoming chiefs. Although I suspect that this had started as a kind of expression of reverence for the faculty, it had evolved into a real opportunity to unburden one's conscience with regard to the abuses that had been inflicted over the previous five years.

As the graduating chief with the most public speaking experience and, perhaps, the largest axe to grind, I was selected by the others to prepare the roast. The other guys made some minor contributions, but it was pretty clear that the brunt of the effort would be borne by me. In reality, of course, this afforded me the opportunity to do the most damage, so I relished the chance. I thought that I could conjure something which was both funny and made a point.

Realizing that visual-oriented multimedia humor would be more effective than standard Don Rickles-type verbal insults, I fashioned a plan which would rely on a slide-show presentation. I recalled a feature in *Spy* magazine in which photographs of different celebrities were juxtaposed in such a way as to suggest a resemblance between them that was not otherwise apparent. I think the feature was called "Separated at Birth," suggesting the possibility that the celebrities had been twins who somehow ended up in different families, but in any event it was usually hilarious. As soon as I remembered this, I decided that the central theme of my roast would be the idea that many of the faculty had been separated at birth from famous individuals. The opportunity to point out and emphasize certain unappealing characteristics among my victims can be appreciated.

The perfect tool already existed for constructing my *meisterwerk*: the internet.

The Department of Surgery had thoughtfully constructed a website which featured portraits of nearly all the attendings, readily available for downloading and storing on my hard drive. I established a comprehensive file containing the electronic images of all the staff. With this accomplished, I merely had to pick my brain to figure out which repulsive celebrity bore the greatest resemblance to the offending attending, then find an internet picture of this person and acquire it. Choosing the right celebrity was alternately easy and difficult, depending on the faculty member I was trying to insult. It took me a few weeks, but I eventually accumulated "twins" for about 2/3 of the attendings.

I decided that the others would have to be roasted in another manner, and soon remembered a series from *MAD* magazine called "Things we'd like to say (but never do)." As the title would imply, this consisted of a list of comments which would be terrific to make in response to everyday situations, but which we never do because we don't think of them right away or because they would basically be completely inappropriate. Things like telling a waiter, "My compliments to the chef—for having the nerve to pass this stuff off as food," or berating a tailor with "Does this come with two pairs of pants—the tie, I mean?" Anyway, I thought this stuff was funny, and I decided to generate a series of remarks which we residents would love to hear the attendings make, but which we knew they never would. This, of course, was a wonderful way of poking fun at their idiosyncrasies.

Before long, I had completed the roast as a PowerPoint slide-show presentation. I showed it to my fellow chiefs, who laughed hysterically at most of it and seemed frightened by other parts. I was delighted; this was exactly the type of response I had hoped for. I promised them that I would smooth off some of the sharper edges, but didn't change a thing.

Soon the day arrived. As it happened, this particular Thursday in late June was my final day of surgical residency. I would definitely go out with a bang.

The department began to gather a little before 7:30 AM. As at every other M&M, the residents and med students arrived first, gobbling up the dreadful coffee and doughnuts. Promptly at the appointed hour, the attendings began to appear. I waited until all the seats were taken. By the time Dr. Atcheson arrived, which was the unofficial signal to begin, the room was jam-packed and dozens of interns and students were standing or sitting along the walls. This was by far the biggest audience for an M&M that I'd ever seen: maybe some word had gotten out that this was a roast not to be missed.

Dr. Atcheson stood up as I made my way to the front of the room.

"There will be no usual M&M conference today," he said. "As most of you know, this is the last day for our graduating chief residents: Dr. Voss, Dr. Guy, Dr. Yankauer and Dr. Miller. There is a tradition in the Department of Surgery that, at their last M&M, the outgoing chiefs roast the faculty."

Atcheson looked at me with feigned suspicion.

"If I had known that Dr. Miller would be the master of these ceremonies this year, I would have considered suspending the tradition for this particular group. But here we are, so I guess we should let them proceed. Dr. Miller, the floor is yours...."

I glanced out at the audience. Nearly all the attendings were there. For a moment I hesitated, wondering at the last second if this was a good idea. What the hell, I thought. Damn the torpedoes, full speed ahead.

The first slide came up, a photo of Dr. Burns, the young blonde-haired hard-ass general surgeon who'd just finished his training at OSU and joined the faculty the year before. Under his picture I had placed as a caption a quote of his, a remark he had made to me early in the chief year. I pointed it out as a kind of recipe for living during residency: "I'll teach you what you need to know; I'll teach you *to hate....*"

There was a smattering of uneasy laughter. Then, with as serious an expression as I could muster I noted that, oddly enough, Dr. Burns had had a twin brother from whom he'd been separated at birth. With the click of a mouse, alongside the Burns picture a photo of the similarly-diminutive comedian David Spade appeared.

The room erupted with laughter, and I was off. For the next forty-five minutes I skewered the faculty with the accumulated ill will and grudging respect of five years. The laughter in the room became so loud that it interrupted a meeting of the OR nurses in an adjoining room. They broke up their conference and joined ours, filling in the few remaining spaces along the wall.

I was on a roll now, and the material couldn't miss. A special treat for me was displaying the loathsome visage of the detestable Dr. Daniels, then projecting as her twin one of the more unflattering Rosie O'Donnell portraits. In truth, this was more of an insult to O'Donnell. Daniels sat silently in her usual ringside seat, her Madame Dufarge-like vigil interrupted for the time being. The taste of victory was sweet indeed.

An affectionate slide drew the audience's attention to the under-stated wit of the colorectal surgeon, Dr. Arthur (he of the "dead babies" remark about Howard Baum). Two of Arthur's gems: "Thinking tends to inhibit action...." and "Old people only care about three things: can they eat? can they see? and can they take a crap?"

I got in a special dig at Dr. Shuter, whose back-stabbing had ruined my lab hiatus in the third year. His official on-line photo looked remark-ably like Alfred E. Newman, and it was easy enough to find an internet picture of that character to display as his long-lost twin (I definitely owed *MAD* magazine a debt of gratitude for their influence on my presenta-tion). As it turned out, he was on his way out in a few weeks anyway; I just happened to throw a little salt in the wound. As I let the images linger on the screen, milking them for all the comic effect I could, Shuter leaned against the wall in the back of the room, expressionless.

Dr. Neher, the surgical oncologist who taught very little in the OR but listened to a lot of show tunes, turned out to be a good candidate for a slide of "Things we'd like to hear (but never will)." I concocted a set of imaginary Neher quotes like, "Who put this John Denver on? If I don't hear some Metallica soon, I'm gonna hurl," and "Why don't you dictate this case? Hell, you did the whole thing yourself!" The senior residents howled with laughter as Neher turned crimson. The juniors all looked at each other with expressions of thinly-veiled concern.

The only faculty members of significance who escaped the on-slaught were Dr. Atcheson and Dr. Treves. The Division Chief had a genuine regard for me and the other residents, and he had written a glowing letter of recommendation on my behalf which went a long way toward securing for me the vascular surgery fellowship which I would be starting in a few days. I couldn't bring myself to slam him, even in a good-natured way. Similarly, Treves was just too much of a positive influence for me to roast him.

When the roast was over the room burst into applause. Dr. Atcheson remarked to the audience that a new standard had been set in the roasting of the attendings but that it should not be a goal of the next group to surpass my performance. He came over and shook my hand with a renewal of his customary wry grin.

"I suppose you know it's a good thing your leaving here today!" he laughed.

I thanked him and retrieved my disk from the department's laptop—it wouldn't do to have that sort of thing floating around, even though I would be gone.

The members of my Surg 6 team gathered around me as the room emptied. The medical students looked at me like I was some sort of mythical figure—after all, I had publicly insulted the attending surgeons for almost an hour, and they had not only laughed at it, they'd congratulated me for the effort! Cathy Townes, the fourth-year on the service, started to tell me about the patients. After a minute, she noticed the look on my face.

"Sorry, Craig. You probably don't care that much about these patients any more, do you?"

"Cathy, I care about them, but now you're the chief resident on the service. They're your responsibility from here, doctor."

She knew what to do. She didn't need me any more.

"When you're done with rounds, come down to my office. Let's get some coffee or something."

"OK, chief."

Cathy and the Surg 6 team left to finish rounds and take care of whatever scut arose. Although the chiefs were technically still working that day, three of us had new jobs out-of-state starting soon—I had by far the longest trip, to the west coast—and Dr. Atcheson had agreed to let us hit the road after M&M.

My mind was numb as I returned to my office and began to clean out my desk. I had literally dreamed of this day for five years and now here it was. All the incredible work, the terrible hours, the repeated humiliations were coming to a close. The stress of caring for patients would always be there, throughout my whole career, but I welcomed that—loved it, in fact. The 100-hour work weeks were another story. It was dread of this tremendous schedule, and the unreasonable judgment and petty power-plays of others that was vanishing as I took down my photographs and placed them in boxes. That dread was something anyone—everyone—could do without.

I ran across my notes from the mock oral boards and briefly reflected on the profound difference between the fearful youth who had failed this dress-rehearsal examination in his third year and the (comparatively) seasoned chief who'd aced it just two months before.

Among another stack of loose papers I found, incredibly, the rotation schedule from my internship year. This showed the whole 1994 house-staff pyramid, from the fourteen interns in my class at the bottom all the way up through the four chief residents at the top. I wondered what had become of those chiefs from my first year: Ron Rausch, the West Point cadet who was ramrod straight yet could fall asleep while listening to a patient's heart; Ramya Singh, the tiny woman who embodied sensibility but stole my med student labor from me; Katherine McCormick, the glib blonde who could get out of any mess with a straight-faced lie; Howard Baum, the HODAD who changed TPN rates one cc at a time....

It only took three boxes to pack all of my things from the office. Many mementos of the worst events found their way swiftly to the trash can. Why have keepsakes of misery? I thought. I gathered up my boxes and headed to the car. It was a stiflingly hot day, with the humidity that only a Midwestern summer can generate. I couldn't wait to change out of my coat and tie. After I had filled the trunk, I wandered back into the hospital for a last look around. Cathy was in my office; apparently Surg 6 rounds were over. She asked me if I was leaving for San Francisco right away.

"Hell, yes," I replied. "I've got to get out of here before those guys realize what a hatchet job I did on them this morning. Do you want to get a cup of coffee?"

Cathy smiled.

"I can't, Craig. Remember Mr. Simmons? It looks like his gall bladder's getting worse, not better. We're going to take it out as an emergency case this morning. In fact, the OR paged me just before you came in, so I gotta run. Keep in touch, though."

Naturally. No long good-byes in surgery residency. There was work to do. Cathy hugged me and hurried off to her unplanned gall bladder operation. I dutifully returned my keys to the residency office, then strolled slowly down the hallway that housed the Department of Surgery. On the walls hung portraits of all the residents who had graduated from the program, dating back half a century. These faces that I'd come to know by reputation or just by repetition stared back at me. I'd met some of these men and women over the years, listening with a calmly detached interest as they recalled the struggles of their years in residency. Soon my own photo would be among them, although that still didn't seem possible. I walked past the office that had been Dr. Zollinger's so many years before, and reflected on everything that I had gone through to get to this point: not just residency and medical school but college and even high school—how any number of different things had to align just right for it all to have worked out. There were a million chances to screw up, a million different things beyond my control. I wasn't sure yet that it had all worked out for the best, but it had all worked out.

I passed through the entrance for the last time and looked back up at the edifice of the main hospital. There, of course, was the glowing blue beacon that directed the LifeFlight helicopters to their landing pad. An indescribable feeling of pride and sorrow mixed in my mind, along with an understanding that would have been impossible—even obscene—a few months before.

Although it would always have its old meaning for me, the blue light now had a new one, too.

The H meant "home."

As I loaded my car to begin the long drive to the west coast, where I would start my year-long fellowship in vascular surgery, I looked back on the process of becoming a surgeon. Back in the frozen pre-dawn mornings of my internship year, this time had seemed so far off as to be nearly incomprehensible. At that early stage so much was yet to come, much of it painful, some triumphant: a thousand operations, seven hundred nights on call, countless petty humblings and victories; these all were still in the future then. Now, incredibly, they existed in my memory, not my apprehension.

In *Intruder in the Dust*, William Faulkner observed that time is an inconsequential, even artificial thing:

> *It's all* now *you see. Yesterday won't be over until tomorrow and tomorrow began ten thousand years ago....*

There were moments back on those dark internship mornings when I saw the portrait of the great, glowering Dr. Zollinger by the dim orange street light and couldn't shake the eerie feeling of being, myself, an old man, looking back on my efforts even as I was experiencing them for the first time. I never knew exactly what was going to happen, but this sense told me that I would survive it, whatever it was. I already had.

Now there were new experiences awaiting me, and that little black-and-white picture of Zollinger was packed away in a brown cardboard box. I had more than 2500 miles to drive to make it to California, and they were expecting me in San Francisco in four days. I took a deep breath, turned on the car radio, and headed down the interstate. In the rear view mirror I caught a last view of the University Hospital, the garish blue "H" glowing in the late-morning sunlight.

22

The Making
of a Surgeon

I HAD A PROFESSOR IN MEDICAL SCHOOL who was famous for having discovered a type of leukemia. She was quite old, probably in her seventies at the time I knew her, and spoke English with an accented precision. I think she hailed from South America originally. This professor made a remark to me which has always stuck, for reasons that I can't quite explain. In any event, out of the blue one day, while we were discussing some clinical cases one-on-one, she said, "Craig, medicine is not a job. Never look at it as a job. It is a way of life."

In the spirit of this wise observation, I would submit that a surgeon is not made—not any more than a person is made. The making of a surgeon—like the development of an individual—is an ongoing process. It continues, as we live and we learn.

But there is certainly a time when a surgical trainee sheds his all-encompassing fear and worry, a time when he begins to gradually, perhaps even imperceptibly, grasp both the subtleties of surgical diagnosis and the mastery of the technical art of surgery. At this point, the resident, the combined apprentice and journeyman, becomes a surgeon.

I can think of no better way of relating this nebulous transition than by recalling a certain point in time, in my chief year, when the pages in the middle of the night ceased to be causes of *concern*, and began to be causes of *annoyance*.

From the first time I began taking call from home, back in the days of the plastic surgery rotation in my second year, I had lived with a

233

phenomenon known as "beeper anxiety." This was the overwhelming worry that the pager either was about to go off, or it had already gone off and somehow I'd missed it. It was an electronic-age variant of obsessive-compulsive disorder, I'm sure, but I can tell you without speculation that it ruined many a night's sleep (in fact, to this day I still will wake up when on call—frequently several times a night—and check the pager to make sure it hasn't gone off without my knowledge or malfunctioned in some way). When the beeper did sound, whether I was in the hospital or at home, during the earlier years I would dread the message from the voice on the other end of the phone. That voice would inevitably ask me a question—a question requiring some sort of significant medical decision. Many times, having "made the call," I would then lie awake, staring at the ceiling and second-guessing myself.

Sometime toward the middle of the chief resident year my response to the nocturnal pages changed. I don't recall exactly when, and there may not have been a particular date. In any case, I stopped worrying about what the voice was going to ask me.

It wasn't as if I thought that I had all the answers: obviously I didn't; even the best surgeons in the world make mistakes. But I had a sense that whatever decision I made, it would—first of all—not harm the patient (the primary, overriding statement of the Hippocratic Oath—in Latin "primum non nocere"), and, I felt confident, it would be a reasonable approach to solving the problem. By this time, I had simply seen so many different things that anything I encountered would almost have to be some variation of a case I had already dealt with. That kind of experience breeds confidence, which is indispensable in surgery.

So when the pager went off, I no longer worried for the rest of the night; I simply made the decision that was required and cursed the idiot intern who had woken me up!

By the same token, the operating room had become a place of great comfort for me. Although I knew that I was fallible, as the chief year progressed, the number of on-table surgical situations which vexed me shrunk to a tiny fraction of the whole. By the spring of that year, the attendings were more of an annoyance in the OR than a resource! I felt that I could cope with nearly any operative scenario that I might reasonably be expected to encounter. Having the good sense to know when to ask for help was a big part of this newfound maturity, of course, but it was nice to feel that the need to do this was diminishing. It was equally gratifying to realize that the attendings felt the same way about me. The big gastric operations on Pam Morris and Vince Jaffe that Dr. Marvin allowed me to do on my own were good examples of the confidence that the staff now had in me. I'm sure there were times when they thought the task was hopeless, but somehow, by fits and starts, by cajoling and threatening, they had produced a surgeon.

Late in the year—in the spring, that is—I was covering trauma. It was to be one of my last nights of in-house call. A fellow had gotten into a bar fight, and been stabbed in the neck with a pocket knife. This was his only injury, since the assailant had apparently fled after delivering what he must have thought was a fatal blow. In fact it had all the makings of a serious injury: for sheer numbers of vital structures in a small space, few places in the body can top the neck between the chin and breastbone.

There is a fairly standard practice in trauma surgery that all penetrating injuries of this portion of the neck which extend deeper then the superficial muscle layer ought to be surgically explored. This guy certainly fit into this category and, after thoroughly examining him to rule out other injuries, I called the OR to book him as an emergency case.

The attending on trauma that night was the inimitable Dr. Arthur. I outlined my plan to him and he said he would join me in the operating room shortly.

After a quick elevator ride up to the fourth floor, the anesthesia resident and I rolled our stabbing victim into the OR. In a few minutes he was asleep. The third-year resident and I scrubbed, then prepped and draped the patient. Arthur wasn't there yet, but I knew what to do and made a four-inch incision along the front of the sternocleidomastoid, the long band of muscle that extends from the breastbone to just behind the ear. I retracted this muscle and opened the carotid sheath, a fibrous covering that encloses the carotid artery, the jugular vein and the important vagus nerve. It was clear that the knife had not hit any of these vital structures; it had passed just to one side. It also stopped short of reaching the esophagus. Our patient was lucky. After cleaning the wound out with a liter or so of sterile saline irrigation, I began to close the incision. At this point, Dr. Arthur came in to the room.

I heard his unmistakable New York voice ask me how things were going. I replied that the neck exploration was negative, and I was getting ready to close. He was over by the circulating nurse, signing some paperwork. In a few seconds he was finished with this, and was headed for the door; he hadn't bothered even to look at the wound. The circulator asked him if he wanted her to get a set of gloves and gown for him.

Dr. Arthur never stopped walking. As he passed through the door, he said, "No. Dr. Miller is a trained surgeon. I have complete faith in his findings."

I would have had to break scrub to do it, but if Arthur hadn't been out of the room already, I think I would have hugged him.

I received the certificate documenting my completion of residency about a week later. But no piece of paper could evoke the feeling of pride and accomplishment that Arthur's words did. As with Marvin's actions in allowing me to do the big cases by myself, they gave me great confidence to tackle the problems which I would face in the future.

These would no doubt be numerous, and daunting. But I would be okay; I was no longer a resident, I was a surgeon.

Epilogue

I HAVE STRANGELY AMBIVALENT FEELINGS about the surgical residency system as it currently exists. While the process and the individuals who administer it can be vicious and demeaning, it is a stunningly effective tool for producing excellence in surgery. These were the worst five years of my life, but I wouldn't trade them for anything. I also wouldn't repeat them under any circumstances.

It's my impression that, across the nation, surgical residency is marginally more humane today than it was in years past. The actual, intentional physical and emotional abuse that prevailed for years is long gone; it simply won't be tolerated in 21st century America. But the question of the hours spent on-duty remains a difficult one. Our society doesn't have the need for many surgeons, so the training programs remain small. On the other hand, the nature of surgical emergencies and patient care demand the on-site presence of physicians with surgical skills and knowledge, i.e., the residents, *in the hospitals.* This simple inequality between the number of surgeons needed by the community and the number necessary to man a hospital generates the atrocious schedules. The only way to ease the workload would be to dilute the house-staff workforce with trainees from other specialties. This is being done already at some institutions (such as with the off-service rotators on the University trauma service), and the results are almost universally unappealing. Suffice it to say that you don't want the decision whether you need an operation or not to come down to an intern who is preparing for a radiology career. Unfortunately, I think the manpower consider-ations will force on-call schedules to remain as they are: brutal.

The issue of the hours spent in-house must be addressed from another perspective, too. From the standpoint of surgical education, there is undeniable truth to the old saw that experience is the best teacher. An old joke among surgery residents says, "If you're only on call every other night, you miss half the good cases." The bitter humor in this is that it's accurate. Even if the resident spent an extra night off reading textbooks (highly unlikely, by the way), you can't learn how to take out an appendix by reading a book.

In any case, the old surgeons, a very conservative group by any standards (and the ones holding the reins of power), resist any changes in the residency system as it is now administered. Part of this resistance arises from the Neanderthal mentality of "Well, I survived residency, and look what a damn good surgeon I am." The rest comes from the arguments I've already given.

While it's true that the residency programs produce excellent surgeons, there still must be some alternative to a system that chews up individuals and crushes families with such ruthless efficiency. We must be able to train surgeons without destroying their lives.

The only way that change will be effected any time soon is by legislation, as was the case in New York a few years ago following a celebrated incident involving the death of a prominent lawyer's daughter. A careless and fatal mistake had been made by an exhausted resident, who was post-call. Aroused by this event, the lawmakers sought to render the work schedules of house-staff in their state more reasonable. Although the goal in this instance was noble, in general, legislative effort in the arena of medical training is probably not to be encouraged. Interference by politicians does not, of course, ordinarily yield improved results.

As this book goes to press, the governing body of American graduate medical education has mandated maximum 80-hour work weeks for residents. What impact this may have, or even if it can be enforced, remains to be seen. It seems like a step in the right direction

In the meantime, life at the university hospitals goes on. Interns still shuffle around, weary-eyed on post-call mornings, trying to track down X-rays and do H&Ps. Junior residents still practice tying knots on drawer handles and bedposts. Chief residents still lie awake at night, worrying about their decisions and wondering if they'll be ready to go out on their own come the next July.

It's all *now*, you see.

About the Author

CRAIG A. MILLER, M.D., was born in Columbus, Ohio. He attended college at Northwestern University in Evanston, Illinois, graduating with honors in Physics. Dr. Miller completed medical school and surgery residency at the Ohio State University Medical Center in Columbus, Ohio, and a fellowship in Vascular Surgery at the University of California, San Francisco. He is a Board Certified surgeon in private practice in Indiana. A recipient of numerous regional and national awards for his investigations into the causes and treatments of surgical disease, Dr. Miller has authored many articles and book chapters.